QUINN HARDING

WOOD PELLET SMOKER AND GRILL COOKBOOK

Flavorful Grilling and Smoking Recipes for
Your Wood Pellet Smoker
(2024 Guide for Beginners)

Copyright © 2023 by Quinn Harding

All rights reserved. No part of this publication may be reproduced, stored or transmitted in any form or by any means, electronic, mechanical, photocopying, recording, scanning, or otherwise without written permission from the publisher. It is illegal to copy this book, post it to a website, or distribute it by any other means without permission.

First edition

This book was professionally typeset on Reedsy.
Find out more at reedsy.com

Contents

1	The Fire broil and Flame broil Book	1
2	Presentation	3
3	Wood Pellet Smoker-Grill- An Overview	5
4	Mixed Recipes, Appetizers, and Sides	9
	1. Buffalo turds that are atomized	9
	2. A casserole with mashed potatoes	11
	3. Wrapped asparagus in bacon	12
	4. baked beans with brisket	13
	5. Wedges of garlic and parmesan	15
	6. Vegetables roasted	16
	7. Pasta Baked Two Times	17
	8. Cheddar with applewood smoke	18
	9. Moink ball skewers with hickory smoke	19
	10. Homemade pepperoni pizza baked by artisans	20
	11. No-Knead Garlic Bread with a Crunch	21
	12. Rolls made with pizza dough	22
	13. Traditional apple pie	23
	14. Cobbler with peach and blueberry	24
	15. An easy chicken brine	25
	16. Brined pork	25
	17. brine of salmon and trout	26
	18. Rubbing with Cajun spices	27
	19. The initial marinade made by Jan	27
	20. Spice sauce for poultry	28
	21. Marinade for shellfish	29
	22. Pork and beans on a smoker-grill	30

23. Dumplings of herb and smoked chicken stew	31
24. Tuscan bistecca with an over-the-coals view	33
25. Corn chowder with salmon	34
26. Ham and alder-smoked sea salt in split pea soup	35
28. Panini with cheese, prosciutto, and romesco sauce with a hint of smoke	36
28. Smoky fish paella	37
29. Soft-shell steamed mussels	39
30. Crab with Burnt Ends	40
31. BBQ oysters with a smoke flavor	41
32. Pie in a Dutch oven without kneading	42
33. Nonsense chocolate cake from mom	44
34. The hobo cake that Dad loved.	45

5 Poultry — 47

1. Shish kabob in Cajun style	47
2. Quail quarters grilled	48
3. Tuscan-style roasted thighs	49
4. Drumsticks with Teriyaki and smoke	50
4. Turkey breast with the bone in, smoked	52
5. Turkey suckling in hickory smoke	53
6. Cordon bleu de bacon	54
7. Lemon filled with crab Hens from Cornwall.	55
8. Pickled drumsticks of turkey	57
9. Smoked a young turkey while tailgating	58
10. I 'orange roasted duck	59

6 Red Meat — 61

1. Steaks cooked to perfection	61
2. Tri-tip roast with smoke	63
3. Ribs with meaty chuck.	63
4. New York strip roast hickory	64
5. Brisket flat in the Texas manner	65
6. Beef Wellington (Pet-za)	66
7. Peppers with packed traffic light	68

8. Lamb rack wrapped in applewood walnuts	69
9. Lamb leg roast	71
7 Pork	73
1. A roast pork loin	73
2. Roast pork Hickory smoked fashion	74
3. Ham that has been double smoked	75
4. BBQ Ribs Hickory smoked fashion	75
5. Juicy, tender pork chops that are grilled.	76
6. Pork loin with rib eyes, Florence	77
7. Ribeye roast with buttermilk pig	79
8. Tenderloins made of smoked pig	80
9. Pork butts pulled from hickory smoke	81
10. 3 different ways to cook pork sirloin tips	82
8 Preparing Authentic Artisan Breads and Flatbreads	84
1. Fundamental pizza crust and dough	85
2. Fresh mozzarella, radicchio, and mushrooms on a forno pizza	86
3. Toast topped with ricotta salata, basil oil, and oven-roasted tomatoes	87
4. Essential oil of basil	89
6. Mount Taylor Sourdough Bread with Five Seeds	91
7. Sourdough initiator	93
8. Moroccan flatbread with cumin, onion, and parsley inside	94
9. Crusty old-fashioned baguettes	96
10. Pita bread	99
11. Spicy flatbread with meat filling, Turkish style	100
12. Spanish coca with smoky romesco and potatoes	102
9 Seafood	105
1. Quenelles	105
2. Angle drop soup	107
3. Bluefish smoked over fennel	108
4. Rosemary-smoked herring	109
5. Smoked bonito with green sauce	109

6. Smoked salmon pâté	111
7. Smoked salmon spread	112
8. Curried trout timbales	113
9. Tickled pink shellfish	114
10. Smoked shad roe–potato balls	115
11. Smoked whitefish	116
12. Smoked salmon pizza with blended wild mushrooms	117
13. Non-rising pizza batter	118
14. Gravad and smoked salmon with cilantro-mint rub	119
15. Smoked gravlax with an orange-dill rub	120
16. Smoked sable	121
17. Catfish wrapped in collard greens	122
18. Sunnies dijon	123
19. Barbecued butterflied trout	124
21. Flame broiled freshwater roost with blood orange serving of mixed greens	126
22. Smoked lake trout with olive-mustard sauce	127
23. Barbecued smallmouth bass wrapped in cornhusks	128
24. Barbecued walleye with grapes and shaggy mane mushrooms	129
25. Smoked walleye with a dried mushroom–pumpkin seed rub	130
26. Smoked burbot with wild mushroom, plum & mint sauce	131
27. Smoked walleye with ruddy pepper sauce	132
28. Mixed eggs with smoked shad milt	132
29. Walleye hash browns	133
30. Smoked butterflied largemouth bass	134
31. Smoked apache trout	135
32. Smoked rainbow trout	136
33. Smoked pike with dried cherry and pear sauce	136
34. Smoked yellow roost in grapefruit marinade	137
35. Maple syrup salmon steaks	138
36. Columbia stream chinook with cherry balsamic sauce	139
37. Hoisin-grilled coho	140

38. Salmon and boletus kebabs	141
39. Flame broiled wild lord salmon with smoked lobster–tarragon	142
40. Flame broiled halibut in coconut drain and soy sauce	144
41. Lemon sorbet–glazed mahi-mahi	145
42. Fish kebabs	146
43. Dark cod with stamped orange sorbet sauce	147
44. Tilapia and coffeehouse stuffing	148
45. Fish steaks and blood oranges in thwart	149
46. Barbecued fish burgers	150
47. Curried barbecued pompano	151
48. Striped bass with cattail shoots and morels	152
49. Striped bass with curried shrimp sauce	153
50. Bluefish with tomato and basil	154
51. Heated new wild sockeye salmon	155
52. Pacific rockfish	156
53. Shrimp-stuffed tilapia	156
54. Cold-hot smoked salmon	158
55. Hot-smoked teriyaki fish	159
56. Smoked salmon & Dungeness crab chowder	160
57. Birch wood–smoked boned trout	161
10 Cooking with Clay Pots and Cast Iron Smokers and Grills	163
1. Tiella of sheep with fennel, pecorino, and potatoes	164
2. Soufflé casserole of chard, goat cheese, and new herbs	166
3. Crab gratin with potatoes, leeks, and spinach	167
4. Three-cheese prepared penne with pancetta	169
5. Eggplant, ruddy pepper, and goat cheese gratin	171
6. Moroccan tagine of halibut, potatoes, and artichokes	173
7. Prepared risotto with asparagus and Swiss chard	174
8. White Tuscan beans with frankfurter	176
9. Bouillabaisse	177
10. Two-bean pozole with cumin crème fraiche	178
11. Cumin crème Fraiche	180
12. Smoky French onion soup	181

13. Curried lentil and vegetable cassoulet	182
14. Fava bean, potato, and escarole soup	183
15. Broiled garlic bread garnishes	185

11 Baking and BBQ with Wood Pellet Grill — 186

1. Shiitake and Simmered Garlic Tart	186
2. Fresh potato, artichoke, leek, and gruyere tart	188
3. Tuscan torta with spinach, chard, and raisins	190
4. Wild mushroom, fennel, chard, and gruyère tart	192
5. Puff baked good pissaladière	195
6. Milanese risotto, leek, and asparagus tart	196
7. Provincial Corn, Tomato, and Basil Tart	197
8. Spinach, mushroom, and feta pie	199
9. Juicy smoked salmon	202
10. Olive oil–poached fish with fennel, orange, and olive serving of mixed greens	203
11. Wine-Poached Shrimp with Smoky Tomato Sauce	205
12. Smoky tomato sauce	206
13. Beer-Braised Brief Ribs	207
14. Solitary Star Grilled Brisket	208
15. Slow-roasted part turkey with citrus-chili coat	210
16. Milk-braised pork with mushroom-artichoke ragù	212
17. Sheep Braised in Yogurt with Onions and Tomatoes	214
18. Provençal Chicken	216
19. Clambake in a Box	217
20. Overnight meat chili Colorado	218
21. Wood-smoked cheese fondue	220
22. Braised Cauliflower, Potato, and Onion Curry	221

12 Wood Pellet Barbecue Desserts and Sweets — 223

1. Apple-Prune Galette	224
2. Apricot Tart with Lavender Crème Anglaise	225
3. Lavender crème anglaise	227
4. Breakfast Focaccia with Grapes and Figs	228
5. Candied orange peel	229

13	Wood Pellet Barbecuing and Simmering	231
	1. Flame broiled cilantro-mint naan	231
	2. Tuscan barbecued pizza with escarole	233
	3. Joanne weir's pizza batter	234
	4. Flame broiled flank steak with ruddy peppers and fontina cheese	235
	5. Flame broiled pork loin stuffed with chard, fennel, and olives	237
	6. Toasted walnut sauce	239
	7. Mediterranean sheep kebabs with pomegranate coat	239
	8. Flame broiled duck breasts with lavender-herb rub	241
	9. Tandoori chicken	242
	10. Plank-roasted pacific salmon	244
	11. Fennel-rubbed halibut with fava bean ragout	245
	12. Barbecued shrimp with herb vinaigrette	247
	13. Herb vinaigrette	248
	14. Barbecued Panzanella with treasure tomatoes	249
	15. Salade niçoise with spring vegetables	251
	16. Spanish-style potato serving of mixed greens with saffron-aioli dressing	253
	17. Saffron-aioli dressing	253
	18. Spit-roasted leg of sheep with tzatziki	254
	19. Mustard and lemon chicken	256
	20. Mushroom-rubbed plank-roasted steak	257
	21. Wood-roasted antipasti platter	259
	22. Mushroom-artichoke ragout	260
	23. Wood-roasted artichokes	261
	24. Best-ever brussels grows	262
	25. Salt-roasted potatoes	263
	26. Simmered tomatoes provençal	264
14	Conclusion	266
15	Outdoor Gas Griddle	267
16	Presentation	268

17	Grilling: A Synopsis	270
18	Ideas for Grilled Fish	275
	1. Barbecued Angle Steaks	276
	2. Straightforward Prepared Flame broiled Angle	277
	3. Barbecued Lemon with Flame broiled Angle	278
	4. Flame broiled Angle in Garlic Butter Sauce Formula	279
	5. Spicy Grilled Angle	280
	6. Flame broiled Tilapia	282
	7. Barbecued Branzino	283
	8. Barbecued Halibut	284
	9. Maple Coated Salmon Steaks	285
	10. Salmon with Flame broiled Lemons and Yogurt Sauce	287
	11. Simple Cedar Board Salmon Serving of mixed greens	289
	12. Garlic Butter Salmon	290
19	Grilled Chicken Recipes	292
	1. The Most excellent Flame broiled Chicken	293
	2. The Finest Delicious Barbecued Chicken	294
	3. Filipino BarbecuedChicken	296
	4. Kentucky Flame broiled Chicken	297
	5. Barbecued Chicken Breast with Avocado Salsa	298
	6. Lexington Fashion Barbecued Chicken Formula	300
	7. Barbecued Chicken Breasts with Lemon and Thyme	301
	8. Barbecued Chicken Shawarma	302
	9. Bratwurst and Chicken Kabobs	303
	10. Chicken Breasts with Romesco Sauce	305
	11. California Flame broiled Chicken	307
	12. Barbecued Butterflied Chicken with Lemongrass Sauce	308
20	Cookbooks for Grilled Meat	311
	1. Flame broiled Meat Steaks	312
	2. Argentinean Barbecued Meat Platter (Parilla)	313
	3. Barbecued Steak and Vegetables	314
	4. Flame broiled Balsamic Flank Steak for Wraps and Servings of mixed greens	316

5. Flame broiled Marinated Steak Kebabs	317
6. Sweet Tea Marinated Ribeyes	318
7. Porterhouse with Summer Au Poivre Sauce	320
8. Hasselback Brief Rib Bulgogi	321
9. Flame broiled Steak Tacos	323
10. Brisket	325
11. Santa Maria Broil Meat	326
12. California Burger Wraps	327
21 Recipes for Grilled Lamb	329
1. Racks of Sheep with Roasted-Shallot Vinaigrette	330
2. Flame broiled Sheep Chops	331
3. Rosemary Sheep Chops	332
4. Child Sheep Chops	334
5. Sheep Chops Barbecued in Rosemary Smoke	335
6. Make-Ahead Moment Pot Barbecued Ribs	336
7. 3-Ingredient Barbecued Pineapple, Steak and Avocado Serving of mixed greens	338
8. Flame broiled Herb Crusted Rack of Lamb	339
9. Tandoori Sheep Ribs	340
10. Barbecued Leg of Sheep (Boneless or Bone-in)	342
11. Barbecued Sheep Chops American Fashion	343
12. Sheep Leg Broiled	344
13. Rosemary and Garlic smoked grill sheep loin	345
22 Vegetable Recipes for Grilling	347
1. Barbecued Eggplant Serving of mixed greens with Freekeh and Yogurt Dressing	348
2. Mexican-Style Corn on the Cob	350
3. Simmered Root Vegetables with Garlic and Rosemary	351
4. Zesty Barbecued Broccoli	352
5. Flame broiled Carrots	353
6. Barbecued Pattypans	355
7. Barbecued Potato Serving of mixed greens with Chiles and Basil	356

8. Barbecued Artichokes	357
9. Flame broiled Veggie Pizza	359
10. Portobello Burgers	360
11. Simple Barbecued Squash	361
12. Brown Sugar Flame broiled Peaches	362
13. Warm Artichoke Plunge	363
14. Flame broiled Vegetable Platter	365
15. Corn with Lemon-Pepper Butter	366
16. Baba Ghanoush	367
23 Conclusion	369

2

Presentation

In a wood pellet smoker-grill, compressed hardwood sawdust made of apple, cherry, hickory, maple, mesquite, and other species of wood is utilized to smoke, flame broil, cook, and arrange nourishment. The terms "pellet flame broil," "pellet smoker," and "pellet smoker-grill" are persistently utilized to portray a wood pellet smoker and barbecue. We'll intimate to it as a "wood pellet smoker-grill" all through this book. This book's proposed approaches, conditions, and centers of see shouldn't be treated as gospel. As you're cautious, everybody has specific culinary inclines. The data in this book can be related completely as composed, something else you will be able examine and have fun. Fire broil is the primitive cooking procedure in closeness. In our point of view, barbecuing is the "coordinate and moo" utilize of circuitous warm to smoke and cook nourishment. The comes around of barbecuing with flavors, circuitous warm rubs, smoke and the meats' standard juices are astonishing. Fire broiling and barbecuing have noteworthy contrasts, be that because it may different individuals are not cautious of them and utilize the terms inaccurately. We fight that orchestrating ground sirloin sandwiches, hot mutts, or fowl over smoky cinders or a gas grill isn't the same as "barbecuing." Do not get us off-base; you may be able grill astonishing nourishment and dinners utilizing underhanded warm and charcoal or gas. We won't go into all of the debate and concepts put forward by unmistakable experts over what constitutes

BBQ. We'll let them make that choice. BBQ is best done on fire broils that burn wood pellets.

3

Wood Pellet Smoker-Grill- An Overview

FUEL AND HEAT FLOW

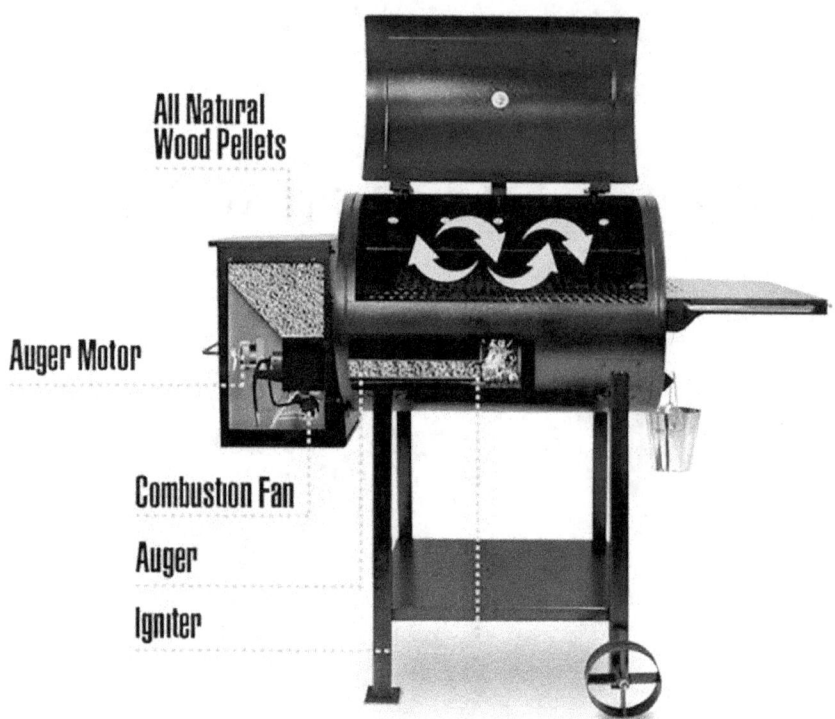

Since it were cooking with hardwood can pass on the flavor profiles and dampness that the wood pellet smoker fire broil offers. Fire broil temperatures might modify depending on the sort and creator. Fire broil temperatures may run from 150°F to well over 600°F on a few sorts, depending on the brand and outline. The days of utilizing a wood pellet smoker fire broil for both barbecuing and burning are long gone. Unmatched by charcoal or gas fire broils, wood pellet smoker grills offer succulence, ease, and security. Compared to other smokers you will be commonplace with, the smoke profile is gentler. They make the versatility and centers of charmed of a convection wood pellet smoker flame broil due to their organize. Smoker barbecues made of wood pellets are secure and fundamental to utilize.

Temperature Regulation

The word "control" is crucial. "Set it, and forget it." The controller adjusts the fan speed and pellet flow rate, as we previously mentioned, to keep the temperature at the desired level. A controller is typically chosen by manufacturers from outside sources or designed in-house. All controllers are not created equal, of course. There are a few options that are better than others for wood pellet smoker grills, and they merit careful consideration. A controller with accurate heat control is what you should aim for. PID, analog, and digital are the three primary types of controllers.

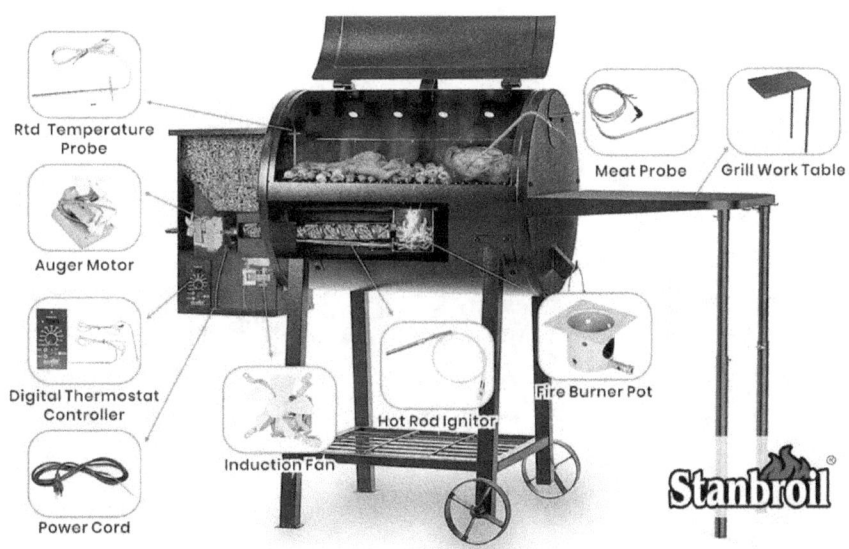

Cooking rules

Depending on the length and temperature, cooking procedures like smoking and barbecuing can give particularly differentiating comes almost. Keep track of everything you cooked, at what temperature, for how long, and the comes almost for idealize comes nearly. For the another period, alter it to your getting a charge out of. Hone makes idealize. The culinary methodology of hot smoking calls for longer cooking periods but produces meat with more of a characteristic wood taste (as well as the required smoke ring). Shorter cooking times at higher cooking temperatures result in less smoke flavor being held. TIP: After cooking, allow meats time to rest for idealize comes around. This comes around in a much wealthier, more delightful cut by allowing the common liquids emigrate back into the meat fiber. Depending on the aggregate of the protein, resting periods might increase from 3 to 60 minutes.

4

Mixed Recipes, Appetizers, and Sides

1. Buffalo turds that are atomized

15 to 45 minutes for preparation; 10 per serving; 72.2 kcal for calories
  Ingredients

- A ten-piece medium jalapeño pepper
- A quarter of an ounce of room temperature normal cream cheese
- a quarter cup of Monterey shredded Blended cheese of Jack and Cheddar, optional
- A single tsp of paprika smoked
- One teaspoon powdered garlic.
- 1/4 teaspoon of cayenne
- Half a teaspoon of red chili flakes
- Twenty sausages from Little Smokies.
- Half a dozen thinly sliced bacon strips

Instructive

1. Put on your nourishment advantage gloves inside the event merely just have got them. Jalapeno peppers need to be washed and cut the long way. Carefully clear and organize of the seeds and veins with a spoon or paring cut. On a barbecuing plate for vegetables, organize the jalapenos and take off them there.
2. Cream cheese, demolished cheese, paprika, garlic powder, cayenne pepper, and ruddy pepper chips, inside the event that utilized, need to be all be completely combined in a small bowl.
3. The cream cheese blend have to be be set interior the hollowed-out jalapeno pepper parts.
4. Each filled jalapeno pepper half got to be have a little aggregate of Smokies sausage on best of it.
5. Each jalapeno pepper half have to be be wrapped by a half-slice of slant bacon.
6. To put through the bacon to the wiener, utilize a toothpick, being cautious not to enter the pepper. The ABTs ought to be put on a fire broiling holder or plate.
7. Utilizing hickory pellets or a combination, set up your wood pellet smoker fire broil for circuitous cooking and warm it to 250°F.
8. To form the bacon cooked and firm, smoke the jalapeno peppers for

around one and a half to 2 hours at 250 °F.
9. The ABTs ought to be be taken from the flame broil and given five minutes to rest a couple of time as of late being served as an hors d'oeuvre.

2. A casserole with mashed potatoes

Take thirty to forty-five minutes to prepare; serve eight people; 357.9 kcal

Ingredients

- Eight to ten pieces of bacon
- ½ cup, or ½ stick bacon fat or salted butter
- Thinly slice one small red onion
- Every three cups of mashed potatoes, one yellow, green, and red bell pepper
- 1/4 cup of sour cream.
- 1/4 tspn Texas Barbecue Spice
- Divide 4 cups of frozen hash brown potatoes among 3 cups of finely shred strong cheddar cheese.

Lighting up

- Generally 5 minutes on each side, cook the bacon in a wide skillet over medium warm on a wood pellet smoker-grill until unused. Isolated the bacon.
- The rendered bacon fat ought to be be exchanged to a glass holder.
- The ruddy onion and chime peppers got to be be sautéed until al dente in butter or bacon oil that has been warmed over medium warm on a wood pellet smoker-grill. Put aside.
- Spread the beat potatoes interior the foot of a 9 x 11-inch casserole dish and coat with nonstick cooking sprinkle.
- Join Texas Fire broil Rub to the cruel cream some time as of late topping the beat potatoes.

- Keeping the butter or bacon oil interior the skillet, organize the sautéed vegetables on best of the potatoes.
- The cemented hash brown potatoes are set on beat, taken after by one and a half glasses of the sharp cheddar cheese.
- Best the hash browns with crumbled bacon and the riches butter or bacon oil from the sautéed vegetables.
- The remaining one and a half glasses of sharp cheddar cheese have to be sprinkled on beat many time as of late the casserole dish is secured with a beat or aluminum thwart.
- Utilize your favored pellets to warm your wood pellet smoker/grill to 350°F and set it up for circuitous cooking.
- Until the cheese is bubbling, warm the beat potato casserole for 45 to 60 minutes.
- A couple of time as of late serving, permit it to rest for ten minutes.

3. Wrapped asparagus in bacon

Take 25 to 30 minutes to prepare; serve 6; and count 160 calories.

Ingredients

- 15–20 thick spears of fresh asparagus, weighing 1 pound
- virgin olive oil extra
- Five pieces of bacon, thinly cut
- One teaspoon. Pete's Country Store Apply salt and pepper.

Directions

1. Snap off the asparagus woody and trim it to a length that is almost equal.
2. Drizzle with oil after arranging the asparagus spears in bundles of three.
3. Before seasoning each bundle with salt and pepper to taste, wrap one piece of bacon around it.

MIXED RECIPES, APPETIZERS, AND SIDES

4. To avoid the asparagus adhering to the grill grates, place Teflon-coated fiberglass mats over the grates while setting up your wood pellet smoker grill for indirect cooking. To preheat to 400°F, use any kind of pellets. One might preheat the grill while the asparagus is cooking.
5. The asparagus wrapped in bacon should be grilled for 25 to 30 minutes, or until it becomes crisp and tender.

4. baked beans with brisket

Prep time: 20 mins | Serve: 12 | Calories: 200kcal
Fixings

- Two tbsps. extra-virgin olive oil
- 1 huge yellow onion, diced
- 1 medium green chime pepper, diced
- 1 medium ruddy chime pepper, diced

- 2 to 6 jalapeño peppers, diced
- 3 mugs chopped Texas-Style Brisket Level
- 1 (28-ounce) can of prepared beans, like Bush's Nation Fashion Heated Beans
- 1 (28-ounce) can of pork and beans
- 1 (14-ounce) can of ruddy kidney beans, washed and depleted
- 1 glass grill sauce, like Sweet Infant Ray's Grill Sauce
- Half container stuffed brown sugar
- 3 garlic cloves, chopped
- Two tsps. ground mustard
- Half tsp. legitimate salt
- Half tsp. dark pepper

Informational

1. The diced onion, peppers, and jalapenos are included once the olive oil has warmed up in a skillet over medium warm on a wood pellet smoker barbecue. Cook, sometimes mixing, for 8 to 10 minutes or until the onions are straightforward.
2. Prepared beans, pork and beans, kidney beans, sauteed onion and peppers, chopped brisket, grill sauce, brown sugar, garlic, ground mustard, salt, and dark pepper ought to all be combined in a 4-quart casserole dish.
3. Set your wood pellet smoker/grill up for circuitous cooking and warm it up to 325°F along with your favored pellets. Heated beans made with brisket ought to be cooked revealed for 1 1/2 to 2 hours or until they are thick and bubbling. 15 minutes ought to pass some time recently serving.

5. Wedges of garlic and parmesan

Half an hour for preparation; three servings; 384 kcal of calories; ingredients

- Three large russet potatoes and ¼ cup extra virgin olive oil.
- 1/4 teaspoon of salt
- Half a teaspoon of ground black pepper
- Two teaspoons of garlic powder.
- Grated Parmesan cheese, one-fourth cup.
- Two tablespoons freshly chopped flat-leaf parsley or cilantro, if desired.
- For dipping, each serving has a half-cup of ranch or blue cheese dressing (optional).

Informational

1. Utilize a vegetable brush to delicately scour the potatoes in cold water, at that point let them discuss dry.
2. Cut the potatoes in thirds after cutting them in half longwise.
3. To totally evacuate the fluid that's discharged once you chop the potatoes, utilize a paper towel. The wedges are kept from getting to be fresh by dampness.
4. In a expansive bowl, combine the potato wedges, olive oil, salt, pepper, and garlic powder. Tenderly hurl the fixings together with your hands to combine.
5. Put the wedges on a nonstick flame broiling plate, dish, or wicker container that measures roughly 15 by 12 inches.
6. Any kind of wood pellet ought to be utilized to warm your wood pellet smoker or flame broil to 425°F and set up for backhanded cooking.
7. The potato wedges ought to be broiled for 15 minutes in your preheated smoker barbecue some time recently turning. Fork-tender on the interior and firm brilliant brown on the exterior; broil the potato wedges for an extra 15 to 20 minutes.

8. In the event that wanted, embellish the potato wedges with cilantro or parsley and a few Parmesan cheese. In case wanted, serve with blue cheese or farm.

6. Vegetables roasted

Serves four; prep time: sixty minutes. Ingredients: Calories: 151kcal

- Half a cup of cauliflower florets
- One cup of halved tiny mushrooms
- Slit and cut in half a medium zucchini
- Slicing and halving a medium yellow squash
- One medium-sized pepper
- One little red onion
- Half a pound of tiny baby carrots
- Cut six asparagus spears with medium stems into 1-inch sections.
- 1 cup of grape or cherry tomatoes
- 1/2 cup extra virgin olive oil infused with roasted garlic
- 2 tablespoons of balsamic vinegar
- t three minced garlic cloves
- One tablespoon dried thyme
- Tsp of dried oregano
- Garlic salt, one teaspoon
- 1/4 tsp black pepper

Directions

1. A big bowl should have the following ingredients: tomatoes, carrots, asparagus, zucchini, yellow squash, red bell pepper, red onion, and cauliflower florets.
2. Black pepper, garlic salt, oregano, garlic, thyme, and olive oil should be used to prepare the veggies.
3. Once the veggies are well coated in olive oil, herbs, and spices, gently

MIXED RECIPES, APPETIZERS, AND SIDES

toss them by hand.
4. After seasoning the vegetables, distribute them evenly on a nonstick grilling tray, pan, or basket that measures roughly 15 by 12.
5. Heat your wood pellet grill or smoker to 425°F and prepare it for indirect cooking using any form of wood pellet.
6. The vegetables should be roasted for 20 to 40 minutes, or until they are crisp-tender, on the grilling tray placed over the prepared smoker-grill. Quickly serve.

7. Pasta Baked Two Times

1.5 hours for preparation; 4 servings; 214 calories

Ingredients

- one spaghetti squash, medium
- Tbsp. extra virgin olive oil
- One teaspoon salt
- Half a teaspoon of pepper
- divided half a cup of shredded mozzarella cheese
- Partially shredded half a cup of Parmesan cheese,

Enlightening

1. Utilize a huge, sharp cut to carefully chop the squash in half longwise. Utilize a spoon to scoop out the seeds and mash from each half.
2. Sprinkle salt and pepper on the interior of the squash parts and sprinkle with olive oil.
3. Utilize any kind of wood pellets to warm your wood pellet smoker-grill to 375°F and set it up for circuitous cooking.
4. Squash parts ought to be put face-up on hot barbecue grates.
5. The squash ought to be heated for 45 minutes or until it comes to 170°F interior. When wrapped up, the spaghetti squash will be delicate and fork friendly.

6. After moving the squash to a cutting board, grant it 10 minutes to cool.
7. Warm the smoker-grill utilizing wood pellets to 425°F.
8. Utilize a fork to rake back and forward over the squash to evacuate the tissue in strands, being cautious to keep the shells intaglio. Take note of how the stands take after spaghetti.
9. Put the threads into a big bowl. Add half of the Parmesan and mozzarella cheeses and stir to mix.
10. After adding more mixture to the squash shells, sprinkle the remaining Parmesan and mozzarella cheeses on top.
11. Bake for a further fifteen minutes, or until the cheese starts to brown, on the spaghetti squash halves at 425°F.

8. Cheddar with applewood smoke

1 hour 15 minutes for preparation; many servings 120 kcal in calories

Ingredients

- Pelletized animals: Apple
- Suggested cheeses: 1 to 2½-pound block of the following: Extremely sharp Gouda cheese aged for three years
- Monterrey Jack of pepper The Swiss Jack

Directions

1. Depending on how they are shaped, cut the cheese blocks into portions that are manageable—roughly 4 by 4 inches—to enhance smoke penetration.
2. Cover the cheese and let it on the counter for one hour to form a very thin crust or shell that keeps heat out while allowing smoke to enter through.
3. To prepare for cold smoking, install a cold-smoke box and put your wood pellet smoker grill on indirect heat. A fully open smoker box

louver vent will allow moisture to leave the box.
4. Set the temperature of your wood pellet smoker-grill to 180°F, or the smoke setting if you have one, and use apple pellets for a milder tasting smoke.
5. Spread the cheese and cold smoke for two hours on nonstick fiberglass grill mats covered with Teflon.
6. Once taken out of the oven, allow the smoked cheese to cool on the counter for an hour using a cooling rack.
7. Your smoked cheeses should be vacuum-sealed and labeled before being kept in the refrigerator for at least two weeks to allow the smoke to permeate and the flavor to develop.

9. Moink ball skewers with hickory smoke

One and fifty minutes for preparation; nine for serving Calories (148 kcal)
Ingredients

- Eighty percent lean ground beef, ½ pound
- Grounded pork sausage, ½ pound
- one big egg
- Cup and a half of Italian bread crumbs
- Finely chopped red onions, half a cup
- Parmesan cheese, half a cup, grated
- Dicing sugar, about ¼ cup
- ¼ cup of whole milk
- one or two minced garlic cloves 1 tsp of crushed garlic
- One tsp of oregano
- A half-tsp kosher salt
- 1/4 tsp black pepper
- 1 pound of thinly sliced, split in half bacon; ¼ cup barbecue sauce, such as Sweet Baby Ray's;

Directions

1. In one large bowl, combine the ground beef, ground pork sausage, egg, bread crumbs, onion, parsley, milk, garlic, salt, and pepper. Prevent overtaxing your body.
2. Roll the meat into 1-1/2-ounce balls about 1 1/2 inches in diameter, and place on a Teflon-coated fiberglass mat.
3. Half-slices of thin bacon enclose each meatball. Skewer six skewers and top each with three moink balls.
4. Adjust the indirect heat setting on your wood pellet smoker or grill.
5. Your wood pellet smoker/grill should be heated to 225°F using hickory pellets.
6. The moink ball skewers should be smoked for thirty minutes.
7. Moink balls should be brushed with your favorite barbecue sauce during the last five minutes of cooking.
8. When the moink ball skewers are still heated, serve them.

10. Homemade pepperoni pizza baked by artisans

10-15 minutes for preparation; 4 servings; 102 kcal per calories

Ingredients

- Take-and-bake pie, like the Kirkland Signature variety from Costco Take and Bake Handmade Pepperoni Pizza with Your Choice of Toppings

Directions

- Heat your wood pellet smoker or grill to 400°F using any kind of pellet and prepare it for indirect cooking.
- 30 minutes before baking, remove the refrigerated pizza from the refrigerator.
- Preheat the traditional grill grates and bake the pizza directly on them for 10 to 15 minutes, or until the dough is golden brown and the cheese is bubbling, for a crispier crust.

- Pizza should be carefully lifted from the grill using a pizza paddle, then allowed to stand for five minutes before slicing and serving.

11. No-Knead Garlic Bread with a Crunch

45 to 60 minutes for preparation; 4–6 servings; 110 kcal for calories

Ingredients

- 3.25 cups all-purpose or bread flour
- A tsp and a half of kosher salt
- Quick-rise or half-tsp. instant yeast
- A quarter of a cup of water at room temperature

Informational

1. Combine the flour, salt, and yeast in a huge bowl.
2. When the batter contains a sticky, shaggy consistency, include the water and mix with a wooden spoon. Wrap the bowl with plastic wrap and take off it at room temperature for 12 to 18 hours.
3. The mixture will have risen, dotted with bubbles, and sticky to the touch after 12 or more hours.
4. Design your wood pellet smoker-grill for roundabout cooking and preheat to 450°F utilizing any pellets.
5. With floured hands, carefully evacuate the batter from the bowl and put it on a softly floured, clean, and dry surface. Tenderly frame the batter into a ball and freely cover it with plastic wrap.
6. Preheat a 5 or 6-quart enameled Dutch broiler for 30 minutes at 450°F whereas the batter is resting.
7. Expel the hot Dutch broiler carefully from the flame broil and put the mixture within the center. Cover and prepare for 30 minutes.
8. Evacuate the cover and heat revealed for an extra 15 to 30 minutes.
9. Permit the bread to rest on a cooling rack for 15 minutes some time recently serving.

12. Rolls made with pizza dough

Take 45–60 minutes to prepare; serve 4–6. 240 kcal in calories

Ingredients

- a half-cup of all-purpose or bread flour
- One teaspoon quick-rise or grow yeast
- A tsp of kosher salt
- One teaspoon sugar
- Warm water in one cup
- Tbsp. extra virgin olive oil

Enlightening

1. Combine the flour, yeast, salt, and sugar in a sizable bowl.
2. Utilize a wooden spoon to blend within the water and olive oil until the mixture is sticky and shaggy.
3. Pizza batter ought to be delicately worked for 3 to 4 minutes with floured hands some time recently being secured with a flour pillage towel.
4. For one hour, at room temperature, let sit secured. The batter should to extend by two times.
5. Pizza mixture ought to be separated into 8 break even with areas and put on a clean, dry surface that has been delicately floured. Make rolls out of each portion utilizing floured hands.
6. Rolls ought to be set on material paper that has been set over a heating sheet or pizza dish. Rolls ought to be secured with a flour pillage towel.
7. Re-rising the rolls ought to take 30 to 60 minutes or until they have multiplied in measure.
8. Set your wood pellet smoker/grill up for roundabout warm and warm any pellets to 400°F.
9. Each roll of pizza batter ought to have an "X" cut out of it employing

a match of scissors.
10. When the rolls are brilliant brown, put the parchment-covered sheet or skillet specifically on the barbecue grates and prepare for 15 to 20 minutes.

13. Traditional apple pie

45–60 minutes for preparation; 8 servings. 40 kcal in calories

Ingredients

- Six cups of peeled Granny Smith apples, finely sliced (five large)
- 3/4 cup of sugar
- Two tablespoons all-purpose flour.
- 1/4 tsp lemon juice
- One-half teaspoon ground cinnamon 1/8 teaspoon of salt
- 1 tsp ground nutmeg
- Two rounds of pie dough, either homemade or from a box

Informational

1. In a sizable bowl, combine the apple cuts, sugar, flour, lemon juice, cinnamon, salt, and nutmeg.
2. Solidly press one-half of the pie batter onto the foot and side of a 10-inch pie plate that has not been oiled.
3. Fill the pie plate with the crusted foot with the apple blend.
4. With the moment pie shell encasing the filling. The edges of the two outsides ought to be pleated together to seal utilizing both hands.
5. Make crosshatch cuts within the pie's beat with a sharp cut.
6. Utilize any pellets to preheat your wood pellet smoker/grill to 425°F with an circuitous cooking setup.
7. The pie needs 15 minutes of heating. To halt the crust's edge from burning after 15 minutes, wrap it in a long strip of thwart.
8. Bake the outside within the broiler for a add up to of 45 to 60 minutes

or until brilliant brown.
9. Cool on a cooling rack for at slightest an hour some time recently serving.

14. Cobbler with peach and blueberry

45–60 minutes for preparation; 8 servings. 3.5 kilocalories

Ingredients

- Half a cup of ripe peaches, peeled and sliced
- One cup of fresh blueberries
- Half a cup of white sugar, separated
- One half cup of melted salted butter
- A single cup of all-purpose flour
- A couple of tsp baking powder One cup full milk and one half teaspoon salt
- A half-tsp of pure vanilla essence

Informational

1. Combine the peaches, blueberries, and Three-fourth glass of sugar in a medium bowl, tenderly mixing until the natural product is completely coated, and set aside.
2. Dissolve the butter and set aside.
3. In a huge bowl, whisk the flour, heating powder, salt, and Half the remaining container of sugar.
4. Include the drain, vanilla extricate, and liquefied butter, and blend until fair combined. Don't overstir the player; many knots are Alright.
5. Pour the hitter into a 2-quart ungreased heating dish.
6. Evenly pour the blueberries and peaches onto the hitter (don't mix the cobbler).
7. Utilize any pellets to warm your wood pellet smoker-grill to 375°F and set it up for backhanded cooking.

8. Prepare the cobbler for 45 to 70 minutes, or until it is firm and brilliant brown.
9. Some time recently serving hot, rest for five minutes.

15. An easy chicken brine

45–60 minutes for preparation; 8 servings. 40 kcal in calories

Ingredients

- A single gallon of filtered water and half a cup of white sugar
- Half a cup pickling salt or kosher
- cut, quartered, sliced, or grated zest of a fresh lemon
- 1/2 cup olive oil and 2 bay leaves
- 1/4 cup of soy sauce
- 1/4 cup of vinaigrette for salads four to five garlic cloves, as well as dried or fresh seasonings and herbs (such as cloves, sage, oregano, parsley, thyme, and rosemary).

Directions

1. Fill a bringing container with all of the ingredients.
2. Combine all ingredients, then blend well and simmer on a smoker grill for a few minutes.
3. Check that the meat is well covered with brine.
4. Refrigerate to preserve.

16. Brined pork

45–60 minutes for preparation; 8 servings. 40 kcal in calories

Ingredients

- One-gallon filtered water
- 1/4 cup of brown sugar

- 1/4 cup of kosher salt
- 1 cup of pure apple juice
- 1/4 tsp mustard powder
- two broken garlic cloves
- Twists of rosemary or thyme, two
- One-half teaspoon black peppercorns.
- 1/2 tsp red pepper flakes

Directions

1. Fill a bringing container with all of the ingredients.
2. Combine all ingredients, then blend well and simmer on a smoker grill for a few minutes.
3. Check that the meat is well covered with brine.
4. Refrigerate to preserve.

17. brine of salmon and trout

Take 45–60 minutes to prepare; serve 8 people; 40kcal per serving.

Ingredients

- One cup soy sauce or teriyaki sauce
- Half a cup kosher salt, or for pickling
- A half-cup of brown sugar
- TWO TABLE SPOONS garlic powder
- Two tablespoons onion powder
- A single teaspoon of cayenne

Directions

1. Fill a bringing container with all of the ingredients.
2. Combine and cook on a smoker grill for one to two minutes.
3. Refrigerate to preserve.

MIXED RECIPES, APPETIZERS, AND SIDES

18. Rubbing with Cajun spices

45–60 minutes for preparation; 8 servings. 40 kcal in calories

Ingredients

- Two teaspoons of garlic powder.
- A tsp of onion powder
- Half a teaspoon of paprika
- One tsp of oregano
- A single teaspoon of thyme
- 1/4 teaspoon of cayenne
- Half a teaspoon of red chili flakes

When adding to chicken, add:

- Half a teaspoon of rosemary
- one-half teaspoon of sage
- One-half cup of water

Directions

1. Whisk all the ingredients together in a small bowl to ensure they are well combined.
2. Combine and cook on a smoker grill for one to two minutes.
3. Store in a cool, dark area in an airtight container or a plastic bag that can be closed.

19. The initial marinade made by Jan

45–60 minutes for preparation; 8 servings. 40 kcal in calories

Ingredients

- one-fourth cup seasoned Lawry's salt

- 1/4 cup of garlic salt and 1/4 cup plus 1/4 teaspoon of celery salt
- ¼ cup salt with onions
- 1/4 cup paprika
- Two tablespoons of chili powder
- Two tsp of black pepper
- One teaspoon of lemon pepper
- Two teaspoons of celery seed
- Half a teaspoon of dry powdered sage
- Dried mustard, one teaspoon
- Dried ground thyme, half a teaspoon
- 1/4 teaspoon of cayenne
- One-half cup of water

Directions

1. Place all the ingredients in a medium-sized bowl and mix until well combined.
2. In a smoker grill, after combining, simmer for a few minutes.
3. Store in a cool, dark area in an airtight container or a plastic bag that can be closed.

20. Spice sauce for poultry

45–60 minutes for preparation; 8 servings. 40 kcal in calories

Ingredients

- One teaspoon of dried thyme.
- One tablespoon ground marjoram
- A single tsp of rosemary leaves
- Celery salt, one tsp
- 1 tsp paprika smoked
- Oven powder, half a teaspoon
- A half-tsp of ground nutsauce

- Half a teaspoon of black pepper
- One-half cup of water

Directions

1. Whisk all the ingredients together in a small bowl to ensure they are well combined.
2. In a smoker grill, after combining, simmer for a few minutes.
3. Store in a cool, dark area in an airtight container or a plastic bag that can be closed.

21. Marinade for shellfish

45–60 minutes for preparation; 8 servings. 40 kcal in calories

Ingredients

- 2 tablespoons of dried mustard
- Two tablespoons onion powder
- Celery salt, one tablespoon.
- Smoky paprika, one tablespoon
- One teaspoon of black pepper
- A single teaspoon of cayenne
- A half-tsp of ground cloves
- Allspice powder, half a teaspoon
- 1/2 tsp ground ginger
- Half a teaspoon of crushed cinnamon
- One-half cup of water

Directions

1. Whisk all the ingredients together in a small bowl to ensure they are well combined.
2. In a smoker grill, after combining, simmer for a few minutes.

3. Store in a cool, dark area in an airtight container or a plastic bag that can be closed.

22. Pork and beans on a smoker-grill

Takes 1 hour and 50 minutes to prepare; serves 10; has 238 calories.

Ingredients

- Dried pinto or navy beans, two cups
- One-third cup canola oil
- a single spoonful of cumin seeds
- Quarter of a cup finely chopped onion
- One cup of finely chopped bacon or pork
- Six shattered juniper berries
- One teaspoon of powdered chipotle chilies
- Thinly slice four garlic cloves.
- One-tspn dried oregano
- Two and a half quarts of water, or more if necessary
- Tomato paste, two tablespoons
- Two tsp of brown sugar
- One tsp kosher salt

Enlightening

1. Plan a medium-hot flame broil fire (450°F) or a medium-hot smoker-grill (a 3-second fire).
2. Put the dried beans in a Dutch stove or huge pot after depleting. Cover the zone with 3 inches of water; depending on the freshness of the beans, put on the grind set over a campfire and stew at a moo bubble until fair cooked, approximately an hour. For the ultimate 30 minutes of cooking, cover.
3. Warm the cumin and oil in a Dutch broiler. Include the onion and salt pork after a fast, fragrant sear. Cook for 5 to 10 minutes, or until

delicately browned. Get freed of any fat. Drain the beans and after that include them, along with the juniper berries, chipotle powder, garlic, and oregano, to the Dutch stove with fair sufficient water to cover. Bring to a stew, cover, and cook the meat and beans for roughly one and a half hours or until they are delicate. Include the legitimate salt, brown sugar, and tomato glue by blending. When the sauce has marginally decreased, reveal it and cook. To taste and season as vital.

23. Dumplings of herb and smoked chicken stew

50 minutes for prep; 8 servings; 924 calories

Ingredients

- Eight glasses of chicken stock
- Cut into ½-inch-thick slices and washed, 8 bacon slices and 1 pound of chopped leeks (white half only)
- Cut 3 celery stalks into ½-inch pieces.
- 0.5-inch-thick slices of two unpeeled carrots
- One pound of red potatoes, without peeling and chopped into 1-inch chunks
- Peel, roughly grate, or chop 1 celery root into ½-inch pieces.
- Spiral-fried 12-oz smoked chicken
- one tsp kosher salt
- A quarter-teaspoon of dried tarragon
- Two tsp of fresh thyme herb
- ¼ cup finely chopped fresh flat-leaf parsley
- 1 cup of thick cream
- a little pinch of newly ground black pepper

Puddings

- Two cups of white flour (all purpose)
- Two tsp powdered baking powder

- one tsp kosher salt
- Herbes de Provence, two tablespoons
- Half a cup of milk, served cold
- 1/4 cup of melted butter
- Two big beaten eggs
- A tsp of finely grated Parmesan cheese

Directions

1. To cook with indirect heat, build up a bonfire or wood-fired grill.
2. The stock should be simmered in a large stockpot. Cozy up by the fireplace. Cook the bacon in a Dutch oven until it's slightly crispy. Trim the bacon and fat by one-third. Once added, sauté the leeks for five minutes.
3. The vegetables should be sautéed for five minutes after they are added. When the potatoes, celery root, and warm stock are added, bring to a boil. Let it cook for ten minutes before adding the smoked chicken, salt, tarragon, and thyme. Bringing everything back to a simmer After covering and simmering the potatoes for around 20 minutes, they should become tender. Then stir in the cream, bacon, and parsley. Adjust the seasoning with a tiny bit of salt and white pepper.
4. The flour and baking powder for the dumplings should be combined in a bowl. Stir in the herbs and salt after adding. Whisk together the butter, eggs, and milk in a bowl. Add the dry ingredients to them and mix to incorporate. Incorporate the cheese and blend thoroughly.
5. Top the stew with the dumplings. If the dumplings are firm yet plump, simmer them for 10 to 12 minutes while covered. Open the lid for the last five minutes of cooking if you like your food to taste more like smoke.
6. For each dish, use a bowl to hold one or two dumplings.

MIXED RECIPES, APPETIZERS, AND SIDES

24. Tuscan bistecca with an over-the-coals view

25 minutes for preparation; 4 servings; 1035 calories.

Ingredients

- One 2-pound steak, 2 inches thick, either the porterhouse or T-bone kind
- In kosher Pepper and salt to taste
- One teaspoon of thyme, dried
- 2 and a half cups of arugula
- 1 minced garlic clove, 2 tablespoons olive oil, plus additional for drizzling (optional)
- One lemon's juice. Sea salt that is coarse or smoked, or citrus-flavored salt for garnish (see Wood-roasted, flavored, and smoked sea salts).
- Crème Fraîches de Parmigiano

Directions

1. Light a wood-fired smoker-grill or grill, and let the coals burn for 6 to 7 seconds, or until they are reduced to hot ember bits.
2. Directly over the hot embers is how you sear a steak. After flipping, generously season the meat with salt and pepper. Remove the steak from the fire easily after 5 to 6 minutes, or until it is browned on one side. To taste, add more salt, pepper, and thyme after flipping the casserole over. Add another 5 to 6 minutes of cooking time for the second side if medium-rare. There will be a slight increase in cooking time for each side of the meat because it is cooked on a grill instead of over embers. Give it a five-minute rest after removing the heat source.
3. The arugula should be mixed with garlic, two tablespoons olive oil, lemon juice, and salt to taste.
4. Quarter an inch thick slices of beef should be cut diagonally. Serve immediately with arugula salad, shavings of Parmesan cheese, and

coarse sea salt or smoked salt for decoration. It's not necessary to add more olive oil.

25. Corn chowder with salmon

35 minutes of prep; 6 servings 291kcal of calories

Ingredients

- three tsp olive oil Half an inch thick slices cut from two celery stalks
- Cut into 1-inch cubes, 8 ounces of tiny red potatoes that have not been peeled
- one tsp kosher salt
- One-half tsp freshly ground white pepper
- One bunch of coarsely chopped green onions that includes half of the greens
- one-quarter cup (about two ears) corn kernels
- Four cups stock, either fish or chicken.
- 1 cup of thick cream
- Two pounds of skinned and pinboned salmon fillets, divided into 2-inch portions
- one lemon, finely grated and juiced
- ¼ cup finely chopped fresh dill

Directions

1. To cook with indirect heat, build up a bonfire or wood-fired grill.
2. After sautéing the celery for three minutes, place a large, heavy skillet or Dutch oven over medium heat with the olive oil. Simmer for 5 minutes, stirring often, after adding the potatoes, salt, and pepper. Next add the green onions and corn, and stir in 2 cups of the stock. The potatoes should be virtually tender after 15 minutes of simmering, covered, and lowering the heat after bringing to a boil.
3. Stir in the cream and cook, covered, for an additional five to seven

minutes. After adding the fish and the zest of the lemon, boil the mixture for 3 to 4 minutes, or until the salmon is fully cooked. Pour in more stock as needed, and taste and add more lemon juice. according to taste and seasoning. Pour into plates and garnish with dill.

26. Ham and alder-smoked sea salt in split pea soup

Serve after 8 minutes of preparation and 190 kcal of calories.

Ingredients

- 1 to 2 pounds of cracked ham shank or 1 ham bone
- If using canned stock, use 3 quarts of low-sodium water or chicken or veggie stock.
- One pound, or roughly 3½ cups. two large leeks (only the white and light green bits), cut, cleaned, and dried green split peas
- Three carrots, peeled and thinly sliced, plus one large chopped yellow onion
- One cut stalk of celery
- One teaspoon of dried thyme or six thyme sprigs
- Crushed garlic cloves three or more, according to flavor
- A single bay leaf
- Add extra for seasoning and use one teaspoon of alder-smoked sea salt.
- Add more black pepper for flavor, add ½ teaspoon freshly ground

Directions

1. Start a hot fire (a 2-second fire) in a woodfired oven, fire pit, or smoker-grill.
2. Put the ham shank and stock into a 6-quart cast-iron or clay saucepan. Before lowering the heat to a simmer, raise the heat to a boil. Remove any white froth that rises to the surface while the stock warms. Simmer until there's no more visible froth on the surface, around 10 minutes. Add the other ingredients, stirring from time to time, and heat until

boiling. Split peas and vegetables should be cooked until they are tender by covering the pan and lowering the heat to a simmer. Transfer the shank of ham to a dish and set it aside once it's cold enough to handle.
3. Pour soup into a new 6-quart pot and grind it with a food mill. Prior to adding the food mill to the soup pot, make careful to scrape the bottom. Alternatively, remove the bay leaf and discard the thyme sprigs before blending or processing the soup in batches.
4. After removing the skin and fat from the ham shank, cut the meat into 1-inch pieces. Place the meat into the soup.
5. If necessary, warm up the soup again in a medium-heat oven. as needed, to taste and season.

Smoked sea salt from alder

This salt adds a wonderful smokey flavor to the soup. It also gives barbecue sauce a wonderful natural smoky flavor, so you may use it there as well. The salt is smoked over the red alder tree for a full twenty-four hours in order to properly infuse it with the rich, full aroma.

28. Panini with cheese, prosciutto, and romesco sauce with a hint of smoke

30 minutes for preparation, 6 for serving, and 560 calories.

Ingredients

- two tsp olive oil
- six cups of spinach leaves
- minced and blanched three large cloves of garlic
- kosher salt
- Cut into ½-inch-thick slices, two one-pound loaves of artisan multi-grain bread
- Six tsp room-temperature unsalted butter
- ¾ cup Romesco sauce with smoke.

MIXED RECIPES, APPETIZERS, AND SIDES

- 6 ounces of prosciutto slices, cut lengthwise, and 14 ounces of thinly sliced Gruyère cheese

Directions

1. In a pan with olive oil, sauté the spinach over medium-high heat until it begins to wither. Toss in the garlic and a tiny pinch of salt. After allowing the mixture to cool slightly, use the back of a large spoon to press it through a sieve to extract moisture.
2. Place the bread pieces with their oiled side facing down on a chopping board after buttering one side of each one. A thin coating of romesco sauce ought to be applied to every slice. After the cheese pieces, scatter the wilted spinach and prosciutto on top of them. Once one side of the sandwich has a couple more cheese slices, close it.
3. Build a hot fire (two seconds or less) for the smoker grill.
4. Lightly heat a grill pan or cast-iron skillet. Before the cheese begins to melt and the bread is softly browned, grilling the sandwich over low heat takes about 7 minutes. Press the sandwich flat after placing a heavy skillet on top and turning it over. Grease the other side until it turns golden. Do the same with the remaining sandwiches.
5. With any leftover Romesco sauce on the side for dipping, divide each sandwich in half and serve.

28. Smoky fish paella

Prep time: 40mins | Serve: 8 | Calories: 376kcal

Fixings

- 1 pound cleaned calamari
- 1 teaspoon saffron strings
- 1 glass bubbling water
- 2 teaspoons blended dried thyme, rosemary, and sage
- ¼ container extra-virgin olive oil

- 2 yellow onions, chopped
- 4 cloves garlic, minced
- 2 huge ruddy chime peppers, seeded and cut into ¼-inch-wide strips
- 3½ glasses Spanish short-grain or arborio rice
- 8 to 1 Two glasses chicken broth ½ pound serrano ham or prosciutto
- 1 pound Spanish chorizo wiener, cut into 1-inch pieces
- 1 pound firm white angle filets, cut into 1-inch pieces
- 4 huge ready tomatoes
- Two mugs of green peas
- One and a half pounds of mussels, scoured
- One and a half pounds of clams, scoured
- 1 pound medium shrimp within the shell
- 1 teaspoon minced new thyme
- 1 teaspoon minced new oregano

Directions

1. A medium-hot fire, lasting three seconds, should be prepared for a smoker-grill or woodfired grill.
2. Trim the calamari bodies of their tentacles, then cut them into 12-inch-wide rings. In a separate dish, mix the saffron threads with the boiling water and set aside until required.
3. Put a 12-inch paella container or comparable wide, shallow skillet on a barbecue grind over the fire. To toast the dried herbs, diffuse them in and mix briefly. When the onions are straightforward, include the garlic, onions, and olive oil and stir-fry for almost 3 minutes. When the chime peppers are included, sauté them for a assist three minutes or until they mellow. Include the rice and warm it whereas blending until it gleams and marginally changes color. Bring to a bubble the saffron water, 6 mugs of broth, and other fixings. Cook for 5 minutes after including the calamari, ham, chorizo, angle, and tomatoes. Incorporate the green peas. Cook until the larger part of the fluid has been retained, but not all of it. In case the fluid dissipates as

well quickly from the warm and the rice begins to stay, include more broth from time to time. Up until the rice is cooked, keep blending the rice and including broth as essential.

4. Spread the clams, mussels, and shrimp over the rice and gently press them into it. Simmer the mussels, clams, and shrimp until they open and turn pink, without stirring. This should take around ten minutes. Remove the pan of paella from the stove. Scatter the fresh herbs on top, cover loosely with a towel or foil, and let for five minutes to allow the flavors to combine. Should any clams or mussels remain closed, they ought to be discarded. Warm food is served.

29. Soft-shell steamed mussels

25 minutes for preparation; 4 servings 160kcal of calories

Ingredients

- Two tsp olive oil
- 4–6 huge garlic cloves, cut into pieces
- Half a cup of vermouth or dry white wine
- Two glasses of water or stock made with shellfish.
- Two bay leaves.
- 1 tsp dry thyme or 1 tsp dried herbs de Provence
- Red pepper flakes with a pinch
- Three and a half pounds of tiny Manila clams washed in kosher or fine sea salt.
- Unsalted butter, four teaspoons
- 1/2 cup finely chopped fresh flat-leaf parsley
- Three tsp Pernod Lemon Juice

Directions

1. For a two-second fire, start a hot fire in a smoker-grill or grill using wood.

2. Warm the olive oil over high heat in a clay pot or Dutch oven. Simmer the garlic for two minutes after adding it and turning the heat down to indirect.
3. Include the wine, water, and bay leaves and return to the direct heat. Warm up to a simmer. Add the optional pepper flakes and thyme to the liquid, then place the clams in. The clams should be cooked until they open, roughly ten minutes over indirect heat.
4. Sprinkle with salt to taste. With the lid off, heat for ten minutes after adding the butter, parsley, and Pernod. Add a squeeze of lemon juice to taste and serve hot with crusty bread.

30. Crab with Burnt Ends

40 minutes for preparation; 4 servings; 98 kcal for calorie count

Ingredients

- 2 crabs (4 to 4½ pounds total) Cooked and cleaned Dungeness crabs with olive oil to pour
- Eight wedges cut from two lemons and four thinly sliced garlic cloves
- Half a cup of dry white wine
- 1/2 tsp red pepper flakes
- Sea salt.

Directions

1. Start a medium heat fire (a 4- to 5-second fire) in a grill, oven, or other appliance that runs on wood or a smoker grill.
2. Cut the bodies and legs of the crabs apart. They should be drenched in olive oil and set in a large cast-iron skillet or clay oven. Place wedges of lemon in between the crab chunks and slices of garlic underneath. A little coating with aluminum foil should be followed by the addition of wine. Place the cover back on and continue roasting for a further 10 minutes, or until the shells are toasted, after the initial 10 minutes

of indirect cooking. After adding to taste, add salt and pepper. Serve immediately, with warm crusty bread.

Crab reserves

Don't discard the roasted crab shells; keep cooking them in the clay oven until they take on a beautiful color. Place a stockpot lid-on and simmer for 30 minutes; cool and drain. Cover and refrigerate to keep fresh for up to 3 days or up to 3 months frozen.

31. BBQ oysters with a smoke flavor

25 minutes for preparation; 4 servings Calories (76 kcal)

Ingredients

Cleaned and encased in 24 oyster shells

BBQ sauce with a smoky masala flavor.

- Three tsp olive oil
- Finely slice one small onion.
- Two minced cloves of garlic
- Quarter of a cup pure white vinegar
- A half-cup of tomato sauce
- Adequacy of the grilled oyster liquid
- One-fourth of a cup dense brown sugar
- Half a teaspoon of garam masala and one teaspoon of sweet pimentón (smoky Spanish paprika).
- One-half teaspoon of ground and toasted cumin seeds.
- A tiny bit of Worcestershire sauce.
- Finely crushed pepper and kosher salt

Directions

1. For a two-second fire, start a hot fire in a smoker-grill or grill using wood.

2. Sear the oysters for 6 to 7 minutes, or until they open, with the deep-shell side down on the grill or smoker-grill grate. Maybe they want very little to be open. Allow them to continue burning for one more minute, but no longer. Juice ought to be remaining inside the shell when the heat source is removed. Reserve the oyster liquor for usage in the sauce.
3. For the barbecue sauce, heat the oil in a medium skillet over medium heat and sauté the onion for 5 minutes, or until it is tender. Five minutes more are added after the garlic is added. Add vinegar and stir until fully combined. Before bringing the mixture slowly to a boil, add the oyster liquor and tomato sauce. Stir in brown sugar until dissolved. You should add pimentón, garam masala, cumin seeds, and Worcestershire sauce. Remove pan from heat and allow to cool after cooking for 5 minutes. Add water to thin, if required. Add salt and pepper according to taste. Store in the refrigerator for up to a week, or use immediately.
4. While wearing a heat-resistant glove, break off the top shell and serve in the deep shell. On a platter covered with rock salt, serve hot with a dollop of barbecue sauce.

32. Pie in a Dutch oven without kneading

Prepare in 3 hours and 15 minutes, serve in 4 portions, and consume 67kcal of calories.

Ingredients

- a half-cup of all-purpose flour + additional for dusting
- 1/4 cup whole-wheat flour
- A tsp of instant yeast
- two kosher salt tspn
- A pint of room temperature (about 70°F) water. Fine sea salt cornmeal

Directions

1. In a large bowl, mix the flour, salt, and yeast. Stir to incorporate the water after adding it. It will seem rough and feel a little sticky at first. Let it sit at room temperature for a duration of 12 to 18 hours, sealed inside a container. The dough is ready when bubbles begin to appear on the top.
2. Gently turn the dough out onto a lightly floured surface, then fold it over on itself twice using a bowl or bench scraper. Set aside, covered with a kitchen towel, for fifteen minutes.
3. The dough should rise to a large enough basin, which should be lined with a flour sack or linen kitchen towel. Load the towel's bowl section with a thick coating of all-purpose flour, or a flour-cornmeal mixture.
4. The dough should be shaped into a ball. Immediately place the ball, seam side down, in the prepared bowl after dusting your hands and the work surface with flour if needed. After covering with the ends of the towel, the dough should rest for about two hours, or until doubled in size.
5. Light a hot fire (a 2-second fire) in a smoker-grill, wood-fired oven, cooker, or grill. Preheat an empty 4-quart baking dish made of clay, ceramic, or cast iron in a hot oven or on the grill for half an hour before baking.
6. Gently place the dough, seam side up, in the pot and slip it out of the oven using one hand beneath the cloth. You can accept any jagged edges. They will become crunchy and crispy during the baking process. Grind in a little sea salt.
7. When using a Dutch oven over coals, place a piece of aluminum foil over the ridge and fasten the lid. After setting the legs over ten or so hot coals that are positioned over the top of the lid, return the oven to the fire. Bake 20 minutes. After removing the lid, continue baking the loaf for a minimum of 15 minutes, or until it has a deep golden hue. Slide the pan out to cool on a wire rack. Give yourself one hour to rest before serving.

Variations

You can adjust the flour quantity to include ground nuts or flaxseed, or you can just use all-purpose flour. For additional layers of flavor, stir in some finely chopped herbs, fire-roasted garlic, or citrus zest right before folding the dough.

33. Nonsense chocolate cake from mom

1.10 hours for preparation; 4 servings Calories (424 kcal)

Ingredients

- a quarter cup all-purpose flour
- Five tsp of chocolate powder without sweetness
- one cup sucrose
- one tsp baking soda
- One teaspoon distilled white vinegar and one-half teaspoon kosher salt
- Measure out one teaspoon of vanilla extract.
- One cup water and five tablespoons of canola oil

Candy Frosting

- 1 cup powdered sugar
- Two tablespoons of cocoa powder without sweetness
- Two tsp room-temperature unsalted butter
- Half a teaspoon of vanilla extract
- 1 tablespoon of milk, or more if required

Directions

1. Set up a wood-fired oven or cooker with a smoker-grill grill for indirect cooking, or use a medium heat fire (four seconds).
2. Combine flour, baking soda, sugar, cocoa powder, and salt in a sieve and transfer to an 8-inch square cake pan. Prepare three wells in the

dry ingredients. After the vinegar and vanilla are added to the first two containers, pour the oil into the third one. Blend everything until smooth after adding the water. Once the surface has been leveled, cover it with foil. 35 minutes of baking should result in a toothpick inserted into the center of the cake coming out clean. Assign to cooling.
3. For the frosting, put the powdered sugar and cocoa powder in a bowl. Mix vanilla into butter until well blended. To make the frosting spreadable and soft, just the right amount of milk needs to be added. Before slicing and serving, allow the cake to sit for half an hour after the spreading.

34. The hobo cake that Dad loved.

1.10 hours for preparation; 6 servings; 410 calories

Ingredients

- A single spoonful of butter without salt
- A half-cup of all-purpose flour + additional for dusting
- at one cup of sugar powder
- Half a cup of dense brown sugar
- One teaspoon of nutmeg, ground
- 1/4 teaspoon of kosher salt
- One-fourth cup canola oil
- Two tsp powdered cinnamon
- Half a cup of walnuts, chopped finely
- One tsp baking soda
- One tsp baking powder
- One big egg, whisked
- One cup buttermilk

Directions

1. Set up a wood-fired oven or stove with a medium heat fire (four seconds) or a smoker grill with a grate for cooking over indirect heat.
2. Once a cast-iron skillet has been coated with butter, dust it with flour. Combine the flour, oil, salt, sugars, and nutmeg in a bowl. Stir to mix. To 12 cups of this mixture in a another bowl, add the walnuts and cinnamon. Preserve for use as the garnish.
3. When adding the egg and buttermilk, the flour mixture should be thoroughly combined with the baking powder and baking soda. Stir to mix. Top the mixture with the garnish after pouring it onto the pan that has been prepared. 20 minutes of baking should result in a clean toothpick or knife placed into the center.

5

Poultry

1. Shish kabob in Cajun style

3 hours 30 minutes of preparation; 4 servings; 270 kcal of calories.
   Ingredients

- From four to six tablespoons. virgin olive oil extra
- About four tablespoons. Cajun Flavour Rubin
- Hickory, Blend, and Pecan
- Young chicken weighing four to five pounds

Directions

1. With the chicken breast-side down, set it on a cutting board.
2. Apply kitchen or poultry shears along both sides of the backbone to cut it out.
3. Turn the chicken breast over and press down hard to make it flatten. The skin of the breast, thigh, and drumstick should be carefully peeled back.
4. Apply olive oil on your skin and the rest of your body. Season the chicken from head to toe, even the meat that is not visible.
5. Put the chicken in the fridge for three hours, covered with plastic wrap, to enable the flavors to mingle.
6. Use hickory, pecan, or a combination of the two to heat your wood pellet smoker-grill to 225°F for indirect cooking.
7. If your appliance—such as an MAK Grills 2 Star—supports temperature meat probe inputs, place the probe in the thickest part of the breast.
8. Smoke the chicken for 1.5 hours.
9. Cover the chicken loosely with foil and let it rest for 15 minutes before slicing.

2. Quail quarters grilled

3.30 hours of preparation; 4 servings; 478 kcal of calories

Ingredients

- Four pieces of chicken.
- About four tablespoons. Jan's Customized Dry Rub

- From four to six tablespoons. Extra virgin olive oil

Directions

1. Cut the chicken quarters to remove any excess skin and fat. Peel back each chicken quarter gently, then rub the olive oil on and under the skin.
2. Sprinkle the skin underneath and on the backs of the chicken quarters with Jan's Original Dry Rub.
3. After seasoning the chicken halves, cover them with plastic wrap and refrigerate for two to four hours to enable the flavors to combine.
4. Lightly cook indirect food by adding any pellets to your wood pellet smoker-grill. Put it on to 325°F after that. The chicken quarters should be grilled for one hour at 325°F.
5. To finish the chicken quarters and crisp the skins, raise the pit temperature to 400°F after an hour.
6. Allow chicken portions to rest in a tent made of loose foil for 15 minutes before serving.

3. Tuscan-style roasted thighs

Three hours for preparation; four hours for serving; 110.8 kcal of calories

Ingredients

- Eight thighs with skin on chickens
- Olive oil.
- A trio of teaspoons. Topaz Flavoring
- Three tablespoons roasted garlic

Directions

1. Eliminate any excess skin from the chicken thighs, but allow a 14-inch margin to allow for shrinkage.

2. Peel the skin down, being cautious, to remove any noticeable fat deposits on the back of the thigh and underneath.
3. The backs of the thighs and the area beneath their skin should be lightly massaged with olive oil. The skins and backs of the thighs should be seasoned with Tuscan spice, under and around.
4. Place the chicken thighs in the refrigerator for one to two hours before roasting to allow the flavors to mingle. You may also wrap them in plastic wrap.
5. Set up your wood pellet smoker-grill for indirect cooking by heating it to 375°F using any kind of pellet material.
6. In order to get the internal temperature of the chicken thighs to 180°F at their thickest point, roast them for 40 to 60 minutes, depending on the size of your wood pellet smoker-grill. Roasted Tuscan thighs should lie under a loose foil tent for 15 minutes before serving.

4. Drumsticks with Teriyaki and smoke

2.20 hours of preparation; 4 servings; 200 calories

Ingredients

- One teaspoon powdered garlic.
- Marinade and sauce made of teriyaki, three cups
- Ten drumsticks of chicken.
- A trio of teaspoons.

Directions for Glazing Poultry

- Toss together the marinade, cooking sauce, poultry seasoning, and garlic powder in a medium bowl.
- Peel back the skin of the drumsticks to allow the marinade to seep into them.
- Fill a one-gallon plastic bag with airtight closure or marinate the drumsticks in a skillet. Let it cool for the night.
- Drumsticks of chicken should be rotated in the morning.
- A wood pellet stove can be used to set up indirect heat for your BBQ.
- Place the drumsticks back inside their skin and let them drain on a baking sheet in your kitchen while you preheat the grill. Paper towels can be used to gently dab the drumsticks to dry them if you don't have a rack for chicken legs and wings.
- For optimal results, heat your wood pellet smoker grill to 180°F using hickory or maple pellets.
- Marinate chicken drumsticks for one hour and smoke them.
- After one hour, continue cooking the drumsticks for an additional 30 to 45 minutes at 350°F, or until the interior temperature of the thickest part of the drumsticks reaches 180°F.
- The chicken drumsticks should be allowed to rest in a loose foil tent for 15 minutes before serving.

4. Turkey breast with the bone in, smoked

About 3 hours and 50 minutes to prepare; 8 servings; 400 calories
Ingredients

- A single bone-in turkey breast
- Six teaspoons. Exceptionally pure olive oil
- A five-tsp. A Poultry Seasoning or Jan's Original Dry Rub

Directions

1. Trim the turkey breast of any excess fat and skin.
2. As you carefully separate the skin from the breast, do not cut it. External application, subcutaneous application, and internal usage of olive oil are recommended.
3. Massacre the skin, the area beneath the skin, and the breast cavity with the rub or seasoning.
4. On the grill grates or in a V-rack, place the turkey breast breast-side up for easier handling.
5. Set the turkey breast aside to come to room temperature on the kitchen tabletop while your wood pellet smoker grill heats up.
6. Bring your wood pellet smoker-grill up to 225°F using hickory or pecan pellets, then prepare it for indirect cooking."
7. Smoke the bone-in turkey breast at 225°F for two hours on the V-rack or directly on the grill grates.
8. Raise the temperature in the pit to 325°F after burning the hickory for two hours.
9. Once the thickest part of the breast achieves an internal temperature of 170°F, and the juices run clear, roast the turkey.
10. The hickory-smoked turkey breast should rest under a loose foil tent for 20 minutes before carving against the grain.

5. Turkey suckling in hickory smoke

3 hours and 50 minutes for preparation; 10 servings; 48.2 kcal for calories.

Ingredients

- Scoop of olive oil and one young turkey
- Six teaspoons. Dressing for Poultry
- 1/4 cup of roasted garlic

Directions

1. Make a cut on both sides of the backbone of the turkey using a poultry shear or a large butcher's knife.
2. Flatten the turkey after it has been patchcocked by pressing on the breast bone.
3. Eliminate the breast's excess skin and fat.
4. As you carefully separate the skin from the breast, do not cut it. Applied topically, under the skin, and into the breast cavity, olive oil is recommended.
5. To season the breast cavity, under the skin, and on the skin, use the seasoning or dry rub.
6. Hickory pellets should be used to heat your wood pellet smoker/grill to 225°F for indirect cooking. 2. Place the spatchcocked turkey, skin-side down, on a nonstick fiberglass grill mat.
7. The turkey is cooked at 225 degrees for 2 hours.
8. Once two hours had passed, raise the pit temperature to 350°F.
9. Once the thickest part of the breast achieves an internal temperature of 170°F, and the juices run clear, roast the turkey.
10. The hickory-smoked, roasted turkey should rest beneath a loose foil canopy for 20 minutes before carving.

6. Cordon bleu de bacon

6 people served; prep time: 2 hours, 30 minutes; calories: 620 kcal

Ingredients

- 24 pieces of bacon.
- Three big chicken breasts, deboned and without skin
- Three tablespoons of extra virgin olive oil with a roasted garlic taste
- Thumbs up three times. Dressing for Poultry
- Black forest ham cut into twelve pieces.
- A total of twelve provolone cheese slices

Enlightening

1. Four cuts of bacon ought to be firmly wood pellet smoker-grill at, the side extra room cleared out at the closes. The chicken cordon bleu is wrapped in a bacon weave, which interlocks distinctive pieces of bacon.
2. Olive oil ought to be connected to both sides of two lean chicken breast filets.
3. The flavoring ought to be connected to the chicken breast filets on both sides.
4. On best of one prepared chicken filet, put one cut of ham and one cut of provolone cheese.
5. With a moment chicken filet, ham, and cheese, rehash the method.
6. Overlay in half the cheese, ham, and chicken.
7. To completely cover the chicken cordon blue, cross the bacon strips from the restricting corners.
8. To hold the bacon strips in put, utilize butcher's string, silicone cooking groups, or toothpicks. 8. Rehash the method with the remaining fixings and chicken breasts.
9. Set your wood pellet smoker-grill up for circuitous cooking and warm it to a smoking temperature (180 to 200 degrees Fahrenheit) with apple

or cherry pellets.
10. For one hour, smoke the bacon cordon bleu.
11. After an hour of smoking, raise the pit's temperature to 350°F.
12. Some time recently serving, rest for 15 minutes beneath a unstable thwart tent.

7. Lemon filled with crab Hens from Cornwall.

3.30 hours to prepare; 4 servings; 520 calories

Ingredients

- Two hens from Cornwall
- One lemon cut in half
- About four tablespoons. Chicken rub
- Two cups Stuffing Made With Crabmeat

Directions

1. After properly cleaning the hens on the inside and outside, pat them dry.
2. Skin from the breasts and legs should be gently removed. All over the skin, under the skin, and inside the cavities, rub the lemon. Incorporate Pete's Western Give the flesh on the legs, breasts, and underneath them a gentle rub. With caution, return the skin to its original position.
3. Put the Cornish hens in the fridge for two to three hours after wrapping them in plastic wrap to let the flavors mingle.
4. When preparing the crabmeat stuffing, follow the recipe's directions. Be sure the meal has cooled completely before stuffing the birds.
5. Stuff each hen cavity with a small amount of crab stuffing.
6. The legs of the Cornish fowl should be joined using butcher's twine to keep the filling inside.
7. Before you begin cooking, preheat any pellets to 375°F in your wood

pellet smoker or grill.

8. Position the filled hens inside a baking dish on a rack. One alternative is to place the birds directly into the baking dish if you don't have a rack big enough.
9. Verify that the stuffing made of crabmeat has reached 165°F by taking its temperature.
10. Allow the roasted birds to rest in a loose foil tent for 15 minutes before serving.
11. After properly cleaning the hens on the inside and outside, pat them dry.
12. Skin from the breasts and legs should be gently removed. All over the skin, under the skin, and inside the cavities, rub the lemon. Incorporate Pete's Western Give the flesh on the legs, breasts, and underneath them a gentle rub. With caution, return the skin to its original position.
13. Put the Cornish hens in the fridge for two to three hours after wrapping them in plastic wrap to let the flavors mingle.
14. When preparing the crabmeat stuffing, follow the recipe's directions.
15. Be sure the meal has cooled completely before stuffing the birds.
16. Stuff each hen cavity with a small amount of crab stuffing.
17. The legs of the Cornish fowl should be joined using butcher's twine to keep the filling inside.
18. Before you begin cooking, preheat any pellets to 375°F in your wood pellet smoker or grill.
19. Position the filled hens inside a baking dish on a rack. One alternative is to place the birds directly into the baking dish if you don't have a rack big enough.
20. Verify that the stuffing made of crabmeat has reached 165°F by taking its temperature.
21. Allow the roasted birds to rest in a loose foil tent for 15 minutes before serving.

8. Pickled drumsticks of turkey

3 hours and 15 minutes for preparation; 3 servings; 190 kcal for calorie count

Ingredients

- Three huge drumsticks of turkey
- 3 tablespoons extra virgin olive oil

Brine components

- Quarts of filtered water
- Pink curing salt, one-eighth teaspoon
- Quarter of a cup brown sugar
- A single teaspoon of poultry Flavoring
- 1/4 cup of kosher sea salt
- Half a teaspoon of red chili flakes
- One teaspoon powdered garlic.

Directions

1. Blend the ingredients for the brine together in a 1-gallon sealable bag. Following a 12-hour period of refrigeration, the brine should be put to the bird's drumsticks.
2. After soaking in the brine for 12 hours, remove the drumsticks, rinse with cool water, and pat dry with paper towels.
3. Remove the drumsticks from the refrigerator and allow them air dry for two hours.
4. Remove the drumsticks from the refrigerator, and then give each one a skin and underside massage with one tablespoon of extra virgin olive oil.
5. When your wood pellet smoker-grill reaches 250°F, use hickory or maple pellets to prepare it for indirect cooking.

6. Before smoking the drumsticks for two hours at 250°F, set them on the grill grates.
7. After two hours, turn the grill up to 325°F.
8. Turkey drumsticks should be cooked at 325°F until the thickest part of each drumstick reads 180°F on an instant-read digital thermometer.
9. Allow the turkey drumsticks to rest in a foil tent for 15 minutes before serving.

9. Smoked a young turkey while tailgating

4 hours, 40 minutes for preparation; 10 for serving; 190 kcal.

Ingredients

- Apple
- one juvenile turkey
- Six teaspoons. roasted shallot
- A teaspoon of olive oil
- Six teaspoons. Dressing for Poultry

Directions

1. Pinch off any excess skin and fat from the breast and cavity of the turkey.
2. When removing the skin from the turkey breast and leg quarters, take care to keep it intact.
3. Use of olive oil on the skin, under the skin, and within the breast cavity is advised.
4. Massacre the skin, the area beneath the skin, and the breast cavity with the rub or seasoning.
5. Indirect smoking and grilling is the ideal way to use your tailgate wood pellet grill and smoker. Heat the oven to 225°F using apple or cherry pellets.
6. Position the turkey breast-side up on the grill.

7. The turkey breast should be smoked for 4 to 412 hours at 225°F, or until the thickest part reaches an internal temperature of 170°F and the juices run clear.
8. Give the turkey 20 minutes to rest beneath a loose foil tent before slicing.

10. I 'orange roasted duck

4. Serve after 2 hours and 40 minutes of preparation. 455 calories.

Ingredients

- Just one duck.
- Three stalks of celery.
- Thumbs up three times. Dressing for Poultry
- One-half of a little red onion
- A single, substantial orange

With regard to the orange sauce:

- Orange juice in two cups.
- A pair of tablespoons of honey
- Soy sauce, two tablespoons
- Fresh ginger, grated, three teaspoons
- Two tablespoons. candied oranges

Directions

1. Once removed from the duck's neck and cavities, any giblets should be disposed of or stored for later use. After washing, use paper towels to dry the duck.
2. The cavity, neck, and tail should all have any excess fat removed. Using the point of a sharp paring knife, pierce the duck skin all over, being cautious not to cut through to the duck meat, to aid in melting the fat

layer beneath the skin.
3. Inside the cavity, season with 1 tbsp of the rub or spice.
4. Rub or spice the outside of the duck with the remaining mixture.
5. Inside the hollow, arrange the onion, celery, and orange slices. Tie butcher's twine between the duck legs to help hold the stuffing in place. With the duck breast side up, arrange it on a small rack in a shallow roasting pan.
6. When the sauce thickens and turns syrupy, add all of the ingredients and simmer over low heat. Set apart and allow to cool.
7. Lightly cook indirect food by adding any pellets to your wood pellet smoker-grill. After that, preheat it to 350°.
8. Place the duck in the oven at 350°F for two hours.
9. Coat the duck generously with the orange sauce after two hours.
10. Give the duck 20 minutes to rest under a loose foil tent before serving.
11. Don't save the orange wedges, celery, or onion. Once the duck is quartered, serve it using poultry shears.

6

Red Meat

1. Steaks cooked to perfection

1.15 hours for preparation; 2 hours for serving; 179 kcal
Ingredients

- USDA Choice or Prime, second New York strip steaks, around 12 to 14 ounces each, with a thickness of 1¼ to 1½ inches
- Virgin olive oil extra
- Pete's Western with 4 tsp Mix together the salt and pepper, dividing them.

Directions

1. To bring the steaks to room temperature, remove them from the refrigerator 45 minutes before cooking and cover them loosely with plastic wrap.
2. When the steaks are cool enough to handle, lightly coat both sides with olive oil.
3. To prepare the steaks for grilling, season both sides with one teaspoon of the rub or salt and pepper and allow to stand at room temperature for at least five minutes.
4. Heat your wood pellet smoker-grill to a minimum of 450°F for direct cooking, using searing grates, a high temperature setting, and any available pellets.
5. Before the steaks start to brown, grill them for two to three minutes on each side.
6. Cook the steaks for an extra two to three minutes after flipping them 90 degrees to achieve cross grill marks.
7. Once the appropriate level of doneness has been achieved, flip the steaks.
8. Assuming an internal temperature of 135°F, medium-rare cooking takes three to five minutes.
9. It takes 6 to 7 minutes for medium (an interior temperature of 140°F).
10. For a medium-well (150°F internal temperature), 8 to 10 minutes
11. Steaks should be rested for five minutes on a tray under loose foil tenting before serving.

2. Tri-tip roast with smoke

2 hours and 30 minutes for preparation; 6 servings Energy: 270 kcal
Ingredients

- One 2.5–3 pound entire peeled tri-tip roast
- Two tsp roasted garlic extra virgin olive oil
- Two tablespoons. Your preferred Santa Maria-style rub or Pete's Western Rub

Directions

1. After rubbing Pete's Western Rub or similar rub onto the tri-whole tip's surface, apply olive oil.
2. Once the tri-tip roast has been double wrapped in plastic wrap, refrigerate it overnight.
3. Preheat your wood pellet smoker-grill to 180°F using hickory pellets or a combination of them.
4. When smoking the tri-tip roast for an hour, insert the meat probe into the thickest part of the roast, if your device has one.
5. After 60 minutes, increase the pit's temperature to 325°F. The meal should be cooked through, with an internal temperature of 140 to 145 degrees Fahrenheit.
6. The smoked tri-tip should be allowed to rest in a loose foil tent for 15 minutes before serving.
7. Trim the roast against the grain, using the below figure as a guide.

3. Ribs with meaty chuck.

4 servings, 3 hours, 30 minutes of preparation, and 430 calories.
Ingredients

- English-style cut 4 slabs of short ribs, beef chuck,

- Three or four tablespoons of extra virgin olive oil or yellow mustard.
- Three to five tablespoons Pete's Rub from the West

Directions

1. With 14 inches of fat remaining on the ribs, remove any silver skin and trim the fat cap.
2. You may correctly season the meat by separating the membrane from the bones by running the handle of a spoon beneath the membrane and lifting a piece. Using a paper towel, grasp the membrane and take it away from the bones.
3. Mix the mustard or olive oil all over the surface of the short rib slab.
4. Cover all sides with a generous amount of rub.
5. Put your wood pellet smoker/grill on indirect heat and use mesquite or hickory pellets to heat it to 225 degrees.
6. Positioning your wood pellet smoker-grill or remote meat probe on the thickest section of the slab of ribs is smart. Check throughout cooking by using an instant-read digital thermometer.
7. Smould the short ribs for five hours at 225°F on a grill with the bone side down.
8. Should the internal temperature of the ribs remain below 195°F after five hours of cooking, increase the temperature in the pit to 250°F and cook the ribs until they achieve an internal temperature between 195° and 205°F.
9. After 15 minutes of resting under a loose foil tent, serve the smoked short ribs.

4. New York strip roast hickory

Make: 8 servings in 3 hours and 40 minutes; Calorie: 430kcal
Ingredients

- USDA Choice or Prime 6-pound beef New York strip roast

- One-third cup extra virgin olive oil infused with roasted garlic
- 1/2 cup of Texas Barbecue Rub or your preferred seasoning for prime rib

Directions

1. Once the fat cap has been removed off the roast, use a sharp boning knife to trim away any remaining excess fat and silver skin.
2. Roast should be well seasoned or rub after a liberal amount of olive oil has been spread on all sides.
3. The roast should be covered with plastic wrap twice and refrigerated for the entire night.
4. Remove from the refrigerator 45 minutes before cooking to allow the roast to come to room temperature.
5. Utilizing hickory pellets, preheat your wood pellet smoker/grill to 240°F for indirect cooking.
6. Insert your meat thermometer or wood pellet smoker-grill meat probe into the thickest portion of the roast. Two to three hours should pass while the New York strip roast is smoked at 240°F.
7. Give the roast 20 minutes to rest beneath a loose foil tent before serving.
8. Slice against the grain to get the right thickness from the roast.

5. Brisket flat in the Texas manner

5 hours, 40 minutes for preparation; 10 minutes for serving; 590 kcal.
Ingredients

- Mesquite Oak
- Sixteen-oz flat beef brisket
- ½ cup extra virgin olive oil infused with roasted garlic
- Or use your preferred brisket rub in a half cup, Texas-style.

Directions

1. Remove any silver skin from the brisket and trim off the fat cap.
2. Coat the trimmed meat with olive oil, leaving it well covered.
3. Apply the rub to both sides of the brisket to ensure it covers the entire surface.
4. Place the brisket in the refrigerator overnight, double-wrapped, to allow the rub to seep into the meat. Cook the brisket immediately if you'd like.
5. When the brisket is still cold, insert a remote meat probe or your wood pellet smoker grill into the thickest part of the beef.
6. Check if your grill has a meat probe or if you have a remote meat probe by using an instant-read digital thermometer during the cooking process.
7. A wood pellet smoker-grill can be used for indirect cooking by heating it to 250°F using mesquite or oak pellets.
8. It will take around 4 hours to smoke the brisket at 250 degrees Fahrenheit.
9. Reinstall the smoker grill after removing the brisket from it and wrapping it twice with heavy aluminum foil, making sure to retain the meat probe in place.
10. The brisket should be cooked for a further two hours after the pit temperature is raised to 325°F.
11. Once the brisket is removed from its foil, wrap it in a towel and store it in the refrigerator. Let stand for two to four hours in the refrigerator, then slice against the grain and serve.

6. Beef Wellington (Pet-za)

3 hours, 40 minutes for preparation; 8 servings 2851 kcal in calories

Meatloaf ingredients include:

- One pound of 90% lean ground beef.

- One-pound pork sausage, similar to Jimmy Dean's
- two huge eggs
- 1 cup of bread crumbs from Italy
- Serve with ½ cup extra pizza sauce on top of the half cup.
- A half-tsp of garlic salt
- One-half teaspoon seasoned salt
- Ground pepper, half a teaspoon
- Grated garlic, half a teaspoon

Concerning the pizza filling:

- Twist-up extra virgin olive oil twice
- Six small portobello mushrooms, cut into one cup
- Slicing one small onion into ⅔ cup of red onion
- Slicing one medium green pepper into ⅔ cup
- One little red pepper and a half cup of chopped red bell pepper
- A dash of black pepper and salt
- Crumbled mozzarella cheese into two cups.
- Duplicate two cups of Jack or cheddar cheese
- Slabbed three ounces of pepperoni sausage

Directions

1. In a big basin, using your hands, thoroughly combine all of the meatloaf ingredients for best results.
2. The mushrooms, red onion, green bell pepper, and red bell pepper should be sautéed for about two minutes, or until the vegetables are al dente, over a wood pellet smoker-grill over medium-high heat.
3. Dust the vegetables with a little salt and black pepper. Put away.
4. Line a parchment paper with the meatloaf and flatten it into a rectangle about 3/8 inch thick. Distribute the sautéed vegetables equally over the meat. Arrange the vegetables first, then the mozzarella and finally the jack or cheddar. On top of the cheese, place the pepperoni.

5. Securing any ends and seams, roll up the meatloaf in the parchment paper.
6. 225°F can be reached by using oak pellets or a mix of pellets in your wood pellet grill set up for indirect cooking.
7. Pizza filling meatloaf should be smoked for one hour.
8. When the meatloaf reaches an internal temperature of 170°F, increase the pit temperature to 350°F after an hour.
9. Tent the meatloaf loosely with foil and let it rest for fifteen minutes before serving. Cover with half of the remaining cup of pizza sauce.

7. Peppers with packed traffic light

6 servings, 2 hours and 20 minutes of preparation, and 458 calories.

Ingredients

- Higgins Apple
- 6-7 sizable bell peppers (yellow, red, and green).
- one little red onion
- 3 stalks of celery
- Twist-up extra virgin olive oil twice
- One pound of 90% lean ground beef. Tomato sauce from one (28-ounce) can
- Two cups of prepared white rice.
- A teaspoon of seasoned salt
- 1/4 tsp black pepper
- two minced cloves of garlic
- 1 tsp of crushed garlic

Directions

1. Remove the tops of the bell peppers and set them aside for filling. Remove the seeds from the peppers and core them.
2. Finely chop celery, onion, and bell pepper tips.

3. When you are ready to sauté the vegetables for 3 to 4 minutes, or until they are tender-crisp, heat the olive oil in a 10-inch skillet over medium heat on a wood pellet smoker barbecue. After removing from the pan, set aside the vegetables.
4. Over medium heat on a wood pellet smoker-grill, cook the ground beef in the same skillet, stirring frequently, for 8 to 10 minutes, or until it becomes brown. Cut out the fat.
5. Preserve a half cup of tomato sauce to drizzle over the filled peppers.
6. Combine the cooked rice, leftover tomato sauce, and browned ground beef in a large bowl. Salt, pepper, and garlic should be added for seasoning.
7. Finally, pour the remaining tomato sauce over the top of the loosely filled bell peppers.
8. Once your wood pellet smoker-grill reaches 180°F, you can set it up for indirect cooking by using apple or hickory pellets.
9. It takes forty-five minutes for the peppers to smoke.
10. After you get the pit temperature up to 350°F, cook for an additional 45 minutes.
11. The peppers should be rested for 10 minutes before serving, after removing the foil tent.

8. Lamb rack wrapped in applewood walnuts

2 hours, 20 minutes for preparation; 4 servings; 1320 calories.
Ingredients: Apple

- Two tablespoons of Dijon mustard
- one or two minced garlic cloves One tablespoon of crushed garlic
- Garlic powder, half a teaspoon
- A half-tsp kosher salt
- 1/4 tsp black pepper
- Half a teaspoon of rosemary
- One one and a half to two pound rack of Frenched lamb

- One cup of chopped walnuts

Directions

1. Garlic powder, mustard, salt, pepper, and rosemary should all be combined in a little bowl.
2. After applying the spice mixture equally on all sides of the lamb, sprinkle chopped walnuts on top. Use your palm to gently push the walnuts into the meat to bind them.
3. To allow the flavors in the walnut crust to seep into the meat, refrigerate the rack of lamb for at least a whole night.
4. Remove from the refrigerator and let the lamb rack with the walnut crust sit at room temperature for half an hour.
5. Assume indirect cooking mode and preheat your wood pellet smoker/grill to 225°F using apple pellets.
6. Right side down, place the lamb rack directly onto the grill.
7. Utilizing a digital instant-read thermometer, ascertain the necessary internal temperature of the rack of lamb by smoking it at 225°F until the thickest portion exceeds the designated time intervals on the chart.
8. Allow the lamb to rest beneath a loosely covering of foil for five minutes before serving.

9. Lamb leg roast

RED MEAT

2 hours and 40 minutes for prep; 8 servings. 219kcal of calories

Ingredients

- One 4-oz leg of lamb without any bones
- Half cup extra virgin olive oil infused with roasted garlic
- One-fourth cup of dehydrated parsley
- t three minced garlic cloves
- Two tablespoons. lemon juice straight out of the squeezing Zest from one medium lemon, one tablespoon
- Two tablespoons of dried oregano
- 1/4 tsp dried rosemary
- 1/4 tsp black pepper

Informational

1. Kill any netting from the sheep leg. Trim any considerable chunks of fat, silver skin, or cartilage.

2. Olive oil, parsley, garlic, lemon juice or pizzazz, oregano, rosemary, and pepper ought to all be combined in a little bowl.
3. On both the interior and exterior of the boneless leg of sheep, knead the zest blend.
4. To affix the boneless leg of sheep, utilize butcher's twine or silicone cooking groups of the most elevated quality. To form and protect the lamb's essential shape, utilize groups or twine.
5. To let the flavors enter the sheep, cover it freely in plastic wrap and put it within the fridge overnight.
6. Sheep ought to be taken out of the ice chest and given an hour to come to room temperature.
7. Utilize your favored pellets to warm your wood pellet smoker/grill to 400°F and set it up for roundabout cooking.
8. Take off the lamb's plastic wrap.
9. The thickest segment of the sheep ought to be where you embed your inaccessible meat test or wood pellet smoker-grill meat test. Utilize an instant-read advanced thermometer amid the cook to check in the event that your grill does not have meat test capabilities otherwise you do not have a farther meat test. The lamb ought to be broiled at 400°F until the thickest portion comes to the specified doneness.
10. Some time recently carving and serving, let the sheep rest for 10 minutes beneath a free thwart tent.

7

Pork

1. A roast pork loin

6 hours of preparation; 12 hours of serving; 30 kcal of calories
Ingredients

- One roast of tip of pork sirloin
- BBQ Marinade

Directions

1. The pork should be marinated for the entire night with the pork marinade.
2. Simmer on low heat for two hours while using a wood pellet smoker grill.
3. After that, give it four hours of steam on the grill by setting a sieve over hot water.

2. Roast pork Hickory smoked fashion

60kcal of preparation time, 12 servings, and 80kcal of calories

Ingredients

- One roast of tip of pork sirloin
- Two tablespoons of extra virgin olive oil with a roasted garlic taste.
- Take five teaspoons of Pork Dry.

Enlightening

1. With a paper towel, dry the broil.
2. Olive oil ought to be connected to the complete broil. Apply the rub to the broil.
3. To guarantee that the broil keeps its shape whereas cooking, truss it utilizing two to three silicone cooking groups made for nourishment or butcher's twine.
4. The tip cook ought to be secured in plastic wrap and chilled overnight.
5. Whereas the barbecue is warming up, expel the sirloin tip cook from the fridge and let it stay there.
6. Set your wood pellet smoker/grill up for circuitous cooking, at that

point utilize hickory pellets to warm to 130°C.
7. Take off the plastic from the broil utilized to wrap it, at that point penetrate the thickest area of it with a inaccessible meat test or a wood pellet smoker-grill meat test.
8. Put the broil on the flame broil grates, and smoke it for three hours.
9. For 15 minutes, put a free thwart tent over the cook to rest.
10. Carve the cook against the grain after expelling any cooking groups or twine.

3. Ham that has been double smoked

Six hours for preparation; twelve hours for serving Calories (132 kcal)
Ingredients

- A ten-pound apple wood-smoked ham that is fully cooked, boneless, and ready to eat, or a smoked ham with the bone in

Directions

1. After the ham is removed from its packaging, it should sit at room temperature for thirty minutes.
2. Set the temperature of your wood pellet grill to 180 degrees Fahrenheit. The ham should smoke for an hour after it has been placed on the grill's grates.
3. Preheat the oven to 350°F an hour later.

4. BBQ Ribs Hickory smoked fashion

Six hours of preparation; twelve hours of serving; sixty thousand calories
Ingredients

- Approximately six ribs on one pork rack
- Just one tablespoon. Rub Dry Pork

- Fourteenth cup grilled garlic
- A couple of tablespoons. Olive oil.

Directions

1. Remove the pork rack's silver skin and fatty crown. Similar to how a slab of ribs is covered in membrane, a rack of pork has the same. Grasping the bone membrane with a paper towel, you can lift it off the bones by working the spoon handle beneath it.
2. Apply enough of olive oil to the meat's surface. Make sure all areas of the meat are rubbed with the seasoning. The seasoned pork rack should be double wrapped in plastic wrap and refrigerated for two to four hours or overnight.
3. The seasoned rack of pork should be left at room temperature for half an hour before cooking.
4. Hickory pellets should be used to heat your wood pellet smoker/grill to 225°F for indirect cooking.
5. Your remote meat probe or wood pellet smoker-grill meat probe should be inserted into the thickest part of the pork rack. In the event that your grill lacks meat probe capabilities or a remote meat probe, use an instant-read digital thermometer to check the internal temperature of the meat while it is cooking.
6. Arrange the rack with the ribs facing up directly on the BBQ grates.
7. The meat should lie under a loose foil tent for fifteen minutes after being taken out of the smoker before being sliced.

5. Juicy, tender pork chops that are grilled.

Takes 6 hours to prepare; serves 12; and has 40kcal of calories.

Ingredients

- 6 center-cut, boneless loin chops that are 1 to 1½ inches thick
- Two quarts of Boursino

- Two tablespoons of extra virgin olive oil with a roasted garlic taste.
- One teaspoon of black pepper

Enlightening

1. Trim the pork chops' additional fat and silver skin. Refrigerate the pork chops and brine for at slightest 12 hours or overnight in a 1-gallon sealable pack.
2. The pork chops ought to be taken out of the brine and dried with paper towels.
3. Both sides of each pork chop ought to be rubbed with olive oil and pepper. Some time recently barbecuing, do not salt the brined pork chops since the brine as of now contains the basic salt.
4. Whereas the wood pellet smoker-grill is warming up, let the pork chops rest.
5. To set up your wood pellet smoker barbecue for coordinate cooking, utilize burning grates. Apply cooking shower to the grates' surface.
6. Utilizing any pellets, turn the flame broil on tall and warm it to at slightest 450°F.
7. For three minutes on one side, burn the pork chops.
8. To get those stylishly wonderful cross flame broil markings, turn the pork chops 90 degrees.
9. For an extra 3 minutes, barbecue the chops.
10. Pork chops in a brine cook more rapidly than chops that aren't, so be careful of inner temperature readings. Some time recently serving, let the pork chops rest for five minutes in a thwart tent.

6. Pork loin with rib eyes, Florence

Six hours for preparation; twelve hours for serving 145kcal of calories

Ingredients

- Roast pork loin, one boneless rib eye

- Four tsp olive oil
- Shredded mozzarella cheese, one-fourth cup
- Two tablespoons. Rub Dry Pork
- Six bowls of raw spinach
- Garlic cloves six
- Quarter of a bacon slice
- One tiny, finely chopped red onion

Enlightening

1. Evacuate any additional fat and maturing skin. Ask that your butcher butterfly the pork loin for you. There are a ton of incredible recordings online that give in-depth enlightening on the numerous strategies for butterflying a loin cook.
2. The butterflied broil ought to be prepared on both sides and after that rubbed with Two tbsps of olive oil.
3. In a enormous skillet over medium warm, cook the bacon. Disintegrate, at that point put aside. Put the bacon fat aside.
4. Two tbsps. The spared bacon oil ought to be warmed in a sizable skillet over medium-high warm in arrange to shrink the spinach some time recently expelling it.
5. 2 more tablespoons of bacon fat ought to be warmed within the same expansive skillet over medium-high warm some time recently the onion is cooked for almost 8 minutes or until it turns translucent.
6. Within the center of the butterflied pork loin, organize the shriveled spinach, garlic fragments, destroyed mozzarella, disintegrated bacon, and onion.
7. Butterflied pork loin solidly rolled. At 2-inch interims, secure the stuffed rib-eye pork loin with butcher's twine.
8. Utilize any pellets to warm your wood pellet smoker-grill to 375°F and set it up for circuitous cooking.
9. The thickest area of the pork loin ought to be where you embed your inaccessible meat test or wood pellet smoker-grill meat test. Utilize

an instant-read advanced thermometer amid the cook to check in case your barbecue does not have meat test capabilities otherwise you do not have a inaccessible meat test.
10. Cook the pork loin on the flame broil for 60 to 75 minutes, or until it comes to an inside temperature of 140°F at its thickest point.
11. Some time recently cutting against the grain, let the pork loin rest for 15 minutes beneath a free thwart tent.

7. Ribeye roast with buttermilk pig

Take 6 hours to prepare; 12 hours to serve; 32.7 kcal per calorie

Ingredients

- A single roast pork sirloin
- A single quirked buttermilk barley

Directions

1. Remove any visible fat and silver skin from the roast pork.
2. Put the roast and the buttermilk brine into a 1-gallon sealed plastic bag or suitable brining container.
3. Turn the roast occasionally if you can, and keep it refrigerated over night.
4. Once soaked in brine, the pork sirloin roast needs to be removed and patted dry with paper towels.
5. Push a meat probe into the thickest part of the roast.
6. Your wood pellet smoker/grill should be heated to 225°F using apple or cherry pellets, then adjusted for indirect cooking.
7. Remove the roast from the loose foil tent and cut the meat against the grain after 15 minutes of resting it.

8. Tenderloins made of smoked pig

3.20 hours of preparation; 6 servings; 219 kcal of calories

Ingredients

- Hickory Fruit
- Dozens of pork tenderloins
- 1/4 cup of olive oil-grilled garlic
- Pork Dry Rub, 1/4 cup

Enlightening

1. Trim the meat of any additional fat and silver skin. Olive oil ought to be connected to the tenderloins' entirety surface some time recently being cleaned with rub.
2. Refrigerate the prepared tenderloins for two to four hours after wrapping them in plastic wrap.
3. Utilize hickory or apple pellets to warm your wood pellet smoker-grill to 230°F and set it up for circuitous cooking.
4. Evacuate the plastic wrap from the meat and put a inaccessible meat test or a wood pellet smoker barbecue test into the center of each tenderloin. Utilize an instant-read advanced thermometer amid the cook to check in case your barbecue does not have meat test capabilities otherwise you do not have a farther meat test.
5. Straightforwardly on the flame broil, smoke the tenderloins for 45 minutes at 230°F.
6. The tenderloins ought to proceed to cook for almost 45 minutes more.
7. Some time recently serving, let the pork tenderloins rest for 10 minutes beneath a free thwart tent.

9. Pork butts pulled from hickory smoke

Ingredients: 6 hours, 20 minutes for preparation; 20 minutes for serving; 229 kcal

- Two pig butts without any bone
- Grilled garlic with olive oil in a single cup
- 1/4 cup of Pork Dry Rub
- Dry Rub by Jan

Informational

1. Trim each pig butt as essential, counting the fat cap and any promptly available noteworthy areas of additional fat. Since a few pitmasters hold the supposition that softening fat bastes the butts as they cook, a few favor to diminish the fat cap to 14 inches or take off the total fat cap on. This procedure anticipates the development of bark in greasy zones.
2. In this manner, in arrange to maximize the sum of prized bark, I prompt expelling the fat cap. By dividing each pork butt. To keep the meat together whereas taking care of and cooking, utilize butcher's twine or silicone food-grade cooking groups.
3. Oil ought to be connected to each pork butt's entirety surface. Spread the rub well over each pig butt some time recently giving it a hand pat-down.
4. Refrigerate the prepared boneless pork butts overnight after double wrapping each one solidly in plastic wrap.
5. Set your wood pellet smoker/grill up for roundabout cooking and warm it with hickory pellets to 225°F.
6. Whereas your wood pellet smoker-grill is warming up, evacuate the pork butts from the fridge and dispose of the plastic wrap. The pork butts do not have to be reach room temperature totally. The thickest zone of one or more pork butts ought to be examined along with your

inaccessible meat test or wood pellet smoker-grill meat tests. On the off chance that your flame broil isn't prepared with a meat test include otherwise you do not have a farther meat test, you ought to utilize an instant-read advanced thermometer to check the insides temperature of the meat whereas it's cooking.

7. For three hours, smoke the pork butts. Co. Pork butts ought to be taken from the grill and double-wrapped in tough aluminum thwart. As you double-wrap the meat, lookout to keep the meat tests within the butts.
8. To the 350°F pellet smoker-grill, include the wrapped pork butts once more.
9. Cook the foil-wrapped pork butts for a advance 20 to 25 minutes or until they reach an inner temperature of 200 to 205°F.
10. Some time recently pulling and serving, evacuate the pig butts for three to four hours.
11. Your favored pulling procedure ought to be used to shred the smoked pig butt into modest, tasty pieces. When wearing heat-resistant gloves, I like to utilize my hands.
12. On the off chance that there are any remaining juices, you'll be able combine the pulled pork butts with them.
13. On the other hand, serve the pulled pork with garnishes like lettuce, tomato, ruddy onion, mayo, cheese, and horseradish. Serve the pulled pork with grill sauce on a crisply prepared roll topped with coleslaw.

10. 3 different ways to cook pork sirloin tips

3.20 hours of preparation; 6 servings; 398 kcal of calories

Ingredients

- Apple-Injected Roasted Pork Sirloin Tip Roast with Hickory and Apple
- One roast of tip of pork sirloin
- A quarter-cup of pure apple juice
- Two tablespoons. grilled garlic in a little oil

- A commercial rub like Plowboys BBQ Bovine Bold or five teaspoons of pork dry rub

Informational

1. With a paper towel, dry the cook. Utilize a flavor/marinade injector to equitably convey apple juice all through the tip cook. After altogether applying the rub, knead the olive oil all over the broil.
2. To truss the cook, utilize two silicone cooking groups made for nourishment or butcher's twine.
3. The tip broil ought to be secured in plastic wrap and chilled overnight.
4. Whereas the pit is warming up, expel the cook from the fridge and set it aside on the counter.
5. Set your wood pellet smoker/grill up for backhanded cooking and warm it with apple pellets to 350°F.
6. Evacuate the plastic wrap from the broil, at that point puncture the thickest segment of it with a farther meat test or a wood pellet smoker-grill meat test. Utilize an instant-read computerized thermometer amid the cook to check in the event that your flame broil does not have meat test capabilities otherwise you do not have a inaccessible meat test.
7. It takes generally hours to broil the meat to an inner temperature of 145°F.
8. For 15 minutes, put a free thwart tent over the cook to rest.
9. Carve the cook against the grain after expelling any cooking groups or twine.

8

Preparing Authentic Artisan Breads and Flatbreads

PREPARING AUTHENTIC ARTISAN BREADS AND FLATBREADS

1. Fundamental pizza crust and dough

72 kcal of prep time, 20 minutes of cooking, and 4 servings.

Ingredients

- Active dry yeast, two teaspoons
- Four cups whole-wheat flour without bleaching
- One teaspoon of kosher salt
- 1.5 cups water, or additional as necessary When brushing, use olive oil.

Enlightening

1. Blend the yeast, flour, and salt in a stand blender with a batter snare connection for two minutes on moo speed some time recently including one and a half glasses of water slowly. To start making gluten, increment the speed up to medium for five minutes, at that point turn it back down to moo for two more minutes. To make a batter that pulls absent from the blender bowl's dividers and feels to some degree shabby to the touch, include up to 12 mugs of additional water as essential. (The sum of water required will depend on the encompassing stickiness.)
2. Shape the batter into a ball and put it on a softly tidied surface. Put in an oil-coated bowl, turning the batter to equally disperse the oil. The mixture ought to rise for around 2 hours in a warm area, secured with a sodden cloth or plastic wrap.
3. Put the mixture in a secured holder and refrigerate it overnight to include more flavor. Earlier to beating down and shaping it into a ball, permit the mixture to sit at room temperature for around an hour. After punching it down, dump the mixture onto a gently tidied board, roll it into a ball, and after that separate it into four rise to pieces.
4. Each piece ought to be carefully extended, rolled, and the foot of the mixture tucked beneath. (Dough punchers call this the "stomach button" of the bread.)

5. Put each ball on a preparing sheet that has been liberally cleaned with flour, and delicately brush each ball with olive oil.
6. Wrap freely in a towel or piece of plastic. Permit rising for at slightest an hour, or until multiplied. In the event that using later, store it within the fridge.
7. On the other hand, you may put each batter ball in an oiled self-sealing plastic pack and store it within the cooler for up to 3 days or within the cooler for up to a month.
8. Some time recently utilizing, let the chilled batter rest at room temperature for one hour. When the batter is warm and has nearly multiplied in measure, it is prepared to be utilized. Defrost solidified mixture within the pack at room temperature.
9. Preheat the wood pellet flame broil to 180 degrees Celsius, and after straightening the mixture in pizza container, put it on the flame broil. Cook for 5 minutes, and the hull will be prepared.

2. Fresh mozzarella, radicchio, and mushrooms on a forno pizza

25 minutes for preparation; 4 servings 480 kilocalories

Ingredients

- Extra olive oil for brushing and drizzling in addition to the two tablespoons
- One pound of finely sliced white or cremini mushrooms
- One head of red radicchio, cored and chopped into 1-inch wedges, along with three thinly sliced cloves of garlic
- Balsamic vinegar, or Saba, two tablespoons simple pizza dough Sea salt, coarse enough to sprinkle
- Two tablespoons freshly plucked thyme
- Dried 12-oz blue cheese (Gorgonzola or similar)

Enlightening

1. In a wood pellet smoker-grill or cooker, get ready an awfully hot fire (650 to 700 degrees Fahrenheit). The Two tbsps. Olive oil ought to be warmed to medium warm some time recently the mushrooms and garlic are sautéed for a advance 5 minutes in a cast-iron skillet or heat-resistant preparing dish.
2. Turn off the warm and permit it to cool. Hurl the radicchio with the balsamic vinegar in a medium bowl. Each mixture ball ought to be shaped into a 10-inch circular on a preparing sheet that has been floured.
3. Olive oil ought to be brushed on, being cautious not to urge any on the peel.
4. Include a little sum of ocean salt. Beat with the mushrooms, taken after by the radicchio, thyme, and Gorgonzola, taking off a 12-inch outside border.
5. Sprinkle once more with ocean salt after sprinkling olive oil (counting the edges) on the nourishment. Pizzas are slid off the peel and set specifically on the wood pellet smoker-grill floor. Heat for 7 to 10 minutes, turning the skillet once, or until the cheese is liquefied and the sides are brown.
6. Permit cooling for five minutes some time recently serving wedge-shaped.

3. Toast topped with ricotta salata, basil oil, and oven-roasted tomatoes

3 hours and 25 minutes for preparation; | Serve: 590 kcal in calories

Ingredients

- dough
- fifteen milligrams of active dry yeast
- two mugs of hot water

- 1/4 cup olive oil plus more to drizzle
- Two tablespoons of warm water with one tablespoon of soaked fennel seeds
- Four cups whole-wheat flour without bleaching
- One teaspoon of kosher salt Sea salt, coarse enough to sprinkle

Finishings

- To drizzle with basil oil Sweet potatoes roasted on a wood pellet grill
- 1.5 cups of fresh herbs, finely chopped: any combination of summer savory, basil, mint, chives, oregano
- Half a pound of crumbled or sliced ricotta salata cheese

Informational

1. Pour the yeast over the warm water in a bowl and whisk to break up it to deliver the batter. Permit standing for 10 minutes or until foamy. Include the fennel seeds and their juice to a container of olive oil. In a sizable bowl or the bowl of a stand blender, combine the flour and salt. Blend until completely combined after slowly consolidating the yeast blend into the dry fixings. Utilize a low-speed mixture snare on the off chance that utilizing a stand blender. Blend fair until the mixture starts to drag absent from the bowl's sides.
2. For making this flatbread, no manipulating is required. Put the mixture in a sizable, delicately oiled bowl and turn it to coat it with oil. Put the bowl in a warm area, cover it with a wet towel or plastic wrap, and permit it to rise until it has multiplied in estimate, 1 to one and a half hours.
3. The batter ought to be collapsed twice employing a mixture scrubber and secured to rise for an hour or until it has multiplied in measure once more. The batter can be secured and chilled overnight for extra flavor.
4. Some time recently forming, evacuate from the fridge and permit to

come to room temperature. In a wood pellet smoker-grill or barbecue, get a hot fire prepared (450° to 475°F).

5. In the event that employing a wood pellet smoker flame broil, maintain a little fire (one little log) within the wood pellet smoker grill's cleared out back. This will improve the flavor of the focaccia and help in protecting the suitable temperature. Gently oil a preparing sheet with a rim that measures 12 by 17 inches.
6. Line with a bit of material paper and liberally oil the pan's sides with extra virgin olive oil. Extend the batter to cover as much of the arranged skillet as you'll be able after putting it there. Extend the batter more by making dimples on the beat together with your fingertips.
7. Indeed whereas not all of the dimple markings will adhere to this greatly damp mixture, it's affirm. There will still be a few dimples, and these will capture the sleek spill. 15 minutes ought to be cleared out aside for unwinding, secured with a dry towel. Sprinkle one-fourth glass of the olive oil over the mixture.
8. Sprinkle coarse ocean salt on beat of the mixture after a moment dimpling.
9. Put 8 inches or so absent from the small fire within the center of the wood pellet smoker flame broil.
10. Prepare for 20 to 25 minutes, turning the container once or twice, until brilliant brown. After taking it out of the wood pellet smoker-grill, sprinkle it with basil oil. Put on a wire rack for ten minutes of cooling. Include cheese, tomatoes, and herbs as embellish. Cut into rectangles or squares that are fitting for serving.

4. Essential oil of basil

2.5 hours for preparation; 240 kcal each serving.
Ingredients

- Approximately one bunch or two cups of tightly packed fresh basil

leaves
- 1 cup extra virgin olive oil

Directions

1. Blanch the basil for five seconds on a wood pellet grill in a large saucepan of boiling, salted water. Once the herbs are empty, they are placed in a bowl of icy water. Once you have completely drained the liquid, squeeze it out.
2. Blend the olive oil till smooth. Keep covered for the night. Put everything through a fine double-mesh sieve. While it is optimal when used within a week, it can be kept in the refrigerator for up to one month after being poured into a clean glass container or plastic squeeze bottle, sealed, and kept cool.

5. Fontina, spinach, sausage, and pine nuts in a calzone

One hour of preparation, eight servings, and 1,200 calories.

Ingredients

- An additional tablespoon of olive oil for brushing
- Thinly slice two red onions.
- Scoop out and crumble 12 ounces of sweet Italian sausage from its casings.
- Peel and cut into eight large cloves.
- A pair of cups with tightly packed spinach leaves and a tsp red pepper flakes

A basic pizza crust

- Fresh mint, roughly chopped, two tablespoons
- Crumbled Italian fontina cheese into two glasses.
- Toast one cup of pine nuts in olive oil.
- Finely ground sea salt

Informational

1. Get ready a wood pellet smoker-grill or cooker with an awfully hot fire (650°F). Put the Two tbsps of olive oil in a cast-iron skillet or terra cotta heating dish that can withstand tall warm.
2. Include the sausage, onions, and garlic. Put within the center of the wood pellet smoker-grill and cook for 15 minutes, or until the onions and garlic are pleasantly caramelized, and the frankfurter is gently crisped. After taking it out of the wood pellet smoker-grill, blend within the spinach and red pepper pieces. Put aside to cool delicately.
3. When the batter is prepared to be shaped, flour a heating peel and roll out each batter ball onto an 8-inch circle. Olive oil ought to as it were be softly brushed onto the batter; dodge getting oil on the peel. On one half of the mixture, disperse the filling, taking off one fourth-inch border.
4. Sprinkle the cheese and pine nuts over the best after including the mint. Salt it delicately. After adjusting the borders, overlay the mixture over the filling. To encourage seal the edges, crease them over and utilize a fork to crease them closed. Sprinkle a small ocean salt on beat and light olive oil on the surface.
5. Allow to unwind for ten minutes. The calzones ought to be set on the floor of the wood pellet smoker flame broil, 8 to 10 inches absent from the warm source. Heat them for 10 to 15 minutes, flipping them sometimes for indeed color until they are puffy and brilliant.
6. After five minutes of cooling, cut in half and serve.

6. Mount Taylor Sourdough Bread with Five Seeds

3 hours, 40 minutes for preparation; 6 servings; 160 kcal for cooking.

- Contents: 28 ounces, or roughly 3½ cups Dough initiator
- 1/2 cup of buttermilk
- One-quarter cup rye flour and one-quarter cup whole-wheat flour

- Five cups high-protein flour
- The fourth cup plus
- Scoop out a half cup of seeds (flax, sesame, pumpkin, sunflower, poppy).
- A tsp kosher salt
- A quarter cup of hot (82°F) water

Enlightening

1. Starter and buttermilk ought to be mixed at a moo speed in a stand blender. In a sizable blending bowl, combine the flour and one-fourth container of the seed blend. One-fourth of the dry fixings ought to be included to the starting blend whereas the blender is set at moderate speed.
2. Rehash with the other 3 clumps, at that point mix for 6 minutes to consolidate all the flour. Salt included; blend for a encourage two minutes. The mixture ought to be exchanged to a sizable, straightforward plastic holder, secured, and sealed at room temperature for approximately 2 hours or until it has multiplied in estimate.
3. In a wood pellet smoker-grill, get ready a really hot fire (575 to 600°F), ideally with oak. Keep up a small fire in a corner. Bread can be heated at a temperature as moo as 475°F.
4. Four to six 9-inch circular or oval bushel can be lined with floured material, a flour pillage, or flour. After the mixture has extended to twice its unique measure, liberally flour the counter with approximately 12 mugs of flour some time recently exchanging the batter there with care. To avoid the metal baked good scrubber from following to the batter, hose it with chilled water some time recently cutting it into 1- to one-and-a-half-pound pieces. To avoid the batter from staying, clean your hands with flour some time recently shaping each piece into a round and putting it within the arranged bushel.
5. Keep firmly secured within the fridge for afterward utilize, or demonstrate the rounds once more at room temperature for one and a half hours or until they have multiplied in estimate. Roll the tops of

each lounge within the remaining seed blend, which has been spread out on a heating sheet.
6. Put the rounds specifically on the wood pellet smoker flame broils floor and prepare for 15 to 20 minutes, turning the container once or twice, until the rolls are toasted, well-browned, and empty at the foot when tapped. Put on a wire rack after being taken off the warm. Some time recently cutting, permit it cool for an hour.

7. Sourdough initiator

Ingredients; 5 hours of preparation; 6 hours of serving; 432 kcal of calories.

- thirty-five milligrams of rye or whole-wheat flour
- one-third cup of room temperature (about 70°F) unsweetened pineapple juice or filtered spring water

Enlightening

1. In a little bowl, combine the flour and juice with a spoon or whisk to deliver a glue five days some time recently preparing the bread. It got to take after hotcake player. Make beyond any doubt to whisk the blend until all the flour has been hydrated. For generally 48 hours, cover freely with plastic wrap and take off at room temperature. Circulate air through by mixing for 1 diminutive with a damp spoon or whisk two or three times each day.
2. Nourish one-fourth container of your unique starter with 1 container water (at around 75°F), 1 container unbleached flour, and one-fourth container whole wheat flour three days some time recently preparing (dispose of any unused unique starter).
3. Nourish with Two glasses of water (around 75°F), Two glasses of unbleached flour, and a Half container of whole-wheat flour after 4 hours. Nourish with 4 glasses of water (at generally 75°F), 4 glasses of unbleached flour, and 1 container of whole-wheat flour after another

4 to 6 hours. Wrap firmly in plastic wrap and take off to confirmation for 8 to 16 hours at room temperature.
4. Rehash feedings as some time recently two days before heating, disposing of half of the starter within the prepare.
5. Rehash feedings as some time recently, disposing of half of the starter the day some time recently heating.
6. Degree out the starter you'll require on preparing day and spare a few starters absent for afterward utilize. Provide beginning remains to individual pastry specialists or dispose of them. Saved starter ought to be secured and refrigerated for up to two weeks or solidified for six months. Some time recently utilization, bring it to room temperature.

8. Moroccan flatbread with cumin, onion, and parsley inside

25 minutes for preparation; 8 for serving; 206 kcal for calories

Ingredients

- Active dry yeast, half a teaspoon
- ¼ cup of warm water (between 105 and 115 degrees Fahrenheit)
- Extra flour for kneading, plus two cups of unbleached all-purpose flour
- One tablespoon of kosher salt and more for seasoning
- One yellow onion, very finely diced
- Roughly chop half a cup of fresh parsley, flat leaf
- 2 tablespoons room temperature unsalted butter
- One teaspoon of golden Hungarian paprika
- Half a teaspoon crushed cumin
- Five ounces of optionally brined cheese, like feta made from sheep's milk

Enlightening

1. In a flame broil or wood pellet smoker-grill with a wood fire, plan a

hot (475°F) fire. In a little bowl, include the yeast and warm water; blend to combine the fixings. Permit standing for five minutes or until foamy. In a bowl, combine the Two glasses of flour and One tsp. of salt. As you slowly consolidate everything along with your hands to form a somewhat sticky mixture, include the yeast blend. Without further ado work on a softly tidied surface, including flour as essential. After that, cover with an upside down bowl and let rest for 15 minutes.

2. The bowl will produce a warm climate that will permit a little rise within the batter. In a bowl, combine the cheese, butter, onion, parsley, flavors, and salt to taste. Some time recently combining it with the other fixings for the filling, brown the chopped onion on the griddle or within the wood pellet smoker barbecue for more flavor.

3. Partition the batter into 8 break even with segments, moisten your work region and hands with olive oil, and do so. Make a ball out of each. Make a really lean square by straightening 1 ball at a time. Permit the batter to rest for a short whereas some time recently endeavoring once more on the off chance that it is flexible and needs to bounce back. You ought to make the square as lean as you'll be able without having it tear. Over the dough, spread a few of the fillings. Comparable to a letter, fold it in thirds. Overlay the foot third toward the center, at that point the beat third underneath the center accordion-style to make a small square, beginning with the brief side that's closest to you. With the remaining mixture, rehash.

4. Extend and pat each small square into a 5-inch square utilizing oiled hands. In the event that you'd like, you'll do this with a rolling stick. You ought to make the square as lean as you'll without tearing the mixture.

5. A cast-iron griddle ought to be warmed to a medium-high temperature in the barbecue or the wood pellet smoker flame broil. Softly oil it with oil.

6. Half of the smoothed mixture squares ought to be put on the griddle and cooked for 2 minutes on each side or until brilliant brown. Cook

the remaining bread as some time recently, at that point exchange to a wire rack. Serve hot.

9. Crusty old-fashioned baguettes

6 servings, 3 hours, 25 minutes of preparation, and 253 calories.

Ingredients

- Sixteen quarters cup unbleached bread flour plus more for dusting
- 1/2 tsp Kosher salt
- a quarter-tsp quick yeast
- To make 3 cups of ice-cold (40°F) water, add 2¼ cups + 2 tablespoons.
- Dust with cornmeal or semolina flour.

Enlightening

1. Within the bowl of an electric blender fitted with a paddle, combine 6 mugs of the flour, salt, yeast, and 2¼ mugs furthermore Two tbsps of water. Blend on moo speed for 2 minutes. On medium speed, alter to the batter snare and proceed blending for 5 to 6 minutes. The batter ought to discharge from the bowl's sides but stay sticky on the foot of the bowl. On the off chance that not, include a small flour and blend until it does (or spill in water on the off chance that the batter appears as well solid and clears the foot as well as the sides of the bowl). Utilize a bowl scrubber or spatula plunged in water to rapidly exchange the batter into the delicately oiled huge bowl. Shower a few oil on the dough's best, at that point put plastic wrap over the bowl.
2. The bowl should be put within the fridge right absent and cleared out there overnight. Check to see in the event that the batter has risen within the fridge the taking after day. It is likely to rise to some degree but not twofold in measure (the sum of rising will depend on how cold the fridge is and how regularly the entryway is opened). To let the batter wake up, lose its chill, and proceed aging, take off the bowl

of mixture out at room temperature for two to three hours (or longer, in case required).

3. Bread flour (roughly 12 mugs) ought to be generously sprinkled on the counter once the mixture has multiplied from its starting prerefrigerated measure. Utilize a plastic batter scrubber that has been doused in cold water to gently transfer the batter to the floured counter. Plunge your hands within the water as well to avoid the batter from staying to them. When exchanging the mixture, attempt to do it as small as conceivable. In case the batter is truly damp, include more flour underneath as well as on beat of it. Dry your hands well some time recently digging them in flour. While carefully rolling the batter within the flour, extend it into an oval shape that's almost 8 inches long and 6 inches wide. Flour ought to still be sprinkled on it indeed in the event that it gets to be as well sticky to handle. To cut the mixture in half widthwise, drop a metal cake scrubber into cool water to anticipate it from staying to the batter. Press the scraper through the dough until it separate it, at that point plunge it back into the water and repeat the prepare until you've got cut down the whole length of the dough. Use this edge as a pincer rather than a saw, cutting the batter cleanly after each cut. Grant the mixture five minutes to unwind.
4. In a wood pellet smoker-grill, get ready a really hot fire (500°F; 550°F in case your wood pellet smoker-grill goes this tall). Two 17 by 12-inch sheetcontainer ought to have the backs secured with preparing material and tidied with cornmeal or semolina flour.
5. Rehash the cutting movement with the cake scrubber on 1 of the batter pieces, but this time cut off 3 equal-length pieces. After that, rehash the method with the other half. You ought to get 6 lengths as a result.
6. To exchange one of the mixture strips to the parchment-lined container, softly drag it to the length of the container or to the length of the heating stone whereas flouring your hands. Permit it to rest for five minutes on the off chance that it
7. springs back, at that point carefully draw it out once more. Rehash

8. Permit to verification for one to two hours at room temperature.
9. Bring one skillet to the preheated wood pellet smoker-grill, and carefully slide the dough, parchment, and all, onto the heating stone (you will select to slide the dough and material off the side of the sheet dish instead of the conclusion, depending on the heading of the stone), or heat specifically on the sheet pan. Confirm that none of the pieces are in contact with one another (you'll be able reach in and fix the material or the batter strips in case require be). Near the entryway after including one container of hot water to the steam skillet. Splash water on the wood pellet smokergrill dividers after 30 seconds, at that point closed the entryway. Whereas holding up, sprinkle flour over the remaining dish of strips, spritz them with oil, and put them in a food-grade plastic pack, a cloth, or plastic wrap.
10. Refrigerate the dish and prepare the strips afterward or the taking after day on the off chance that you do not need to prepare them within the another hour.
11. Inside 8 to 9 minutes, the bread should start to turn brilliant brown. Rotate the pieces 180 degrees in case they are as of now heating unevenly.
12. Heat the bread for a assist 10 to 15 minutes, or until it may be a profound brilliant brown and has come to an inside temperature of at slightest 205°F.
13. Put the hot bread on a rack for cooling. They ought to feel about ethereal and light, and they ought to cool in approximately 20 minutes. Heat the remaining rolls whereas these are cooling, but do not disregard to expel the paper and preheat the wood pellet smoker-grill to 500°F or higher some time recently preparing the moment clump.

10. Pita bread

Prep time: 3hrs25mins | Serve: 12 | Calories: 90.1kcal

Fixings

- Two glasses of warm water (105° to 115°F)
- Two tsps. nectar
- 1½ teaspoons dynamic dry yeast
- 4 glasses all-purpose flour, also more for working
- Half glass whole-wheat flour
- Two tsps. Legitimate salt
- Two tbsps. olive oil, also more for brushing

Informational

1. In a little bowl, include 12 mugs of the water and the nectar; whisk to combine. When the yeast is totally broken up, sprinkle it over the beat and blend. Permit standing for five minutes or until foamy.
2. Combine the flour, salt, and Two tbsps. Olive oil in a stand blender with the batter snare. Include the yeast blend and blend on moo speed. Include the remaining one and a half glasses of water continuously whereas proceeding to blend until all of the flour is joined. On a board that has been delicately tidied with flour, manipulate the mixture for approximately 5 minutes or until it is flexible, smooth, and now not sticky. Turn the batter to coat it with oil after putting it in a bowl that has been gently oiled. Permit it to rise until it has multiplied in estimate, approximately an hour, in a warm area, secured with a wet cloth or plastic wrap.
3. In a wood pellet, smoker-grill or cooker, set an awfully hot fire (500°F), or plan a hot roundabout fire in a wood pellet grill. Put the wood pellet smoker-grill rack within the least position in the event that employing a standard wood pellet smoker-grill.
4. To induce freed of the discuss bubbles, spread the batter out on a

delicately cleaned surface and work it. Make a log out of the batter, at that point cut it into 12 break even with pieces. Roll each piece of mixture into a ball, at that point utilize a rolling stick to straighten each ball into a plate that's 6 inches in breadth and 14 inches thick. Put the circles on a heating sheet that has been delicately lubed, and let rise revealed for 30 to 45 minutes, or until they have about multiplied in thickness.

5. For 5 to 10 minutes, prepare on a heating sheet or barbecue over backhanded warm until puffy and delicately brilliant. Expel from the warm and permit to cool for five minutes on wire racks.
6. Each pita ought to be part in half, at that point isolated with a fork on the cut line to make a take.

11. Spicy flatbread with meat filling, Turkish style

Prep time: 1hr15mins | Serve: 12 | Calories: 346kcal

Fixings

Mixture

- Half tsp. dynamic dry yeast
- Half a container of warm water (105° to 115°F)
- 1 Three-fourth glasses all-purpose flour, also more for manipulating
- ¼ teaspoon legitimate salt
- One tbsp. olive oil

Filling

- Two tbsps. olive oil, also more for sautéing
- 1 yellow onion, finely chopped
- 1 little unpeeled globe eggplant, cut into little dice
- Half tsp. legitimate salt, furthermore more for sprinkling
- ½ pound incline ground sheep
- Two tbsps. pomegranate molasses
- 1 huge tomato, peeled and diced
- ¼ teaspoon ground allspice
- Half tsp. ground cinnamon
- ¼ teaspoon crisply ground dark pepper1
- Two tbsps. Pine nuts, toasted
- One tbsp. naturally pressed lemon juice, or as required

Informational

1. In a wood pellet smoker-grill, begin a hot fire (475°F). Pour the yeast over one-fourth glass of warm water in a little bowl and whisk to combine the fixings for the mixture. Permit standing for five minutes or until foamy. In a huge bowl, blend the flour and salt.
2. Utilizing your hands or a stand blender, mix the fixings after including the olive oil. Include the remaining water as well as the yeast blend. On the off chance that employing a batter snare, manipulate the batter

for 5 minutes. In case employing a floured board, manipulate the mixture for 5 to 7 minutes until it is smooth and flexible. Turn the batter in an oiled bowl to equally disperse the oil.

3. Permit rising in a warm area for 30 minutes, or until it has multiplied in estimate, secured with a damp towel or plastic wrap.
4. To make the filling, combine the onion, eggplant, and olive oil in a bowl and season with salt. On a preparing sheet, spread. Cook for around 7 minutes, or until the eggplant is delicate, on the wood pellet smoker grill floor. Include the Half tsps. Salt and blend. The sheep should be cooked for around 5 minutes in a little cast-iron skillet within the wood pellet smoker-grill until it is browned. Toss absent any fat. Include the tomato, flavors, pine nuts, and pomegranate molasses, and turn the warm off. To taste, include lemon juice.
5. On a board cleaned with flour, partition the batter into 4 rise to pieces and roll into balls. Each ball should be squeezed into a 5-inch plate. Make a lean circle out of the mixture that's approximately 6 inches in distance across. Place on a preparing sheet secured with material paper. Each plate ought to have one-fourth of the meat filling within the center, extended out to approximately one and a half inches from the edge. To restrict the filling, overlap the batter up toward the center in increases of 4–5. Sprinkle with salt and delicately oil with olive oil.
6. Prepare the heating sheet for 12 to 15 minutes or until it, is beautifully brilliant. After 5 minutes of cooling, serve hot.

12. Spanish coca with smoky romesco and potatoes

Prep time: 1hr35mins | Serve: 12 | Calories: 705kcal
Fixings
Mixture

- 2½ teaspoons dynamic dry yeast
- Three-fourth glass of warm water (105° to 115°F)
- 1Three-fourth glasses of unbleached all-purpose flour, furthermore

more for

Manipulating

- ¾ teaspoon legitimate salt
- One tbsp. olive oil

Topping

- ¼ container olive oil, furthermore more for brushing
- 1½ teaspoons sweet pimentón (Spanish smoked paprika)
- Half tsp. legitimate salt
- ¼ teaspoon naturally ground dark pepper
- Half glass Smoky Romesco Sauce
- 8 green onions, trimmed to a light green range and cut into ¼-inch Cuts
- One tbsp. entirety new oregano clears out
- 2 huge Yukon Gold potatoes, cubed and simmered
- 2 hard-cooked eggs, cut into rounds

Enlightening

1. Pour the yeast over one-fourth container of water and blend to break down it to create the mixture. Permit to stand for around five minutes, or until foamy, at that point blend. Make a well within the center of the 134 mugs of flour and salt that have been filtered onto a work surface. Olive oil, the remaining water, and the yeast mixture should be included. Together with your fingertips, combine the fixings within the well, at that point include flour a small at a time to create a mixture. Work for 5 to 10 minutes, or until flexible, including flour as required. The mixture have to be be delicate but scarcely tasteless.
2. Turn the mixture in an oiled bowl to equitably convey the oil. Permit rising in a warm area for 45 to 1 hour, secured with a damp towel or

plastic wrap, or until it has multiplied in measure.

3. In a wood pellet smoker-grill or cooker, get ready a really hot fire (525 to 550 degrees Fahrenheit). For two minutes, gently manipulate the batter on a floured surface. Roll into a rectangle measuring 9 by 14 inches and alter along with your hands. It should be generally 1/2 inch thick. Exchange to an oiled heating sheet, at that point utilize your hands to create divots on the dough's surface to anticipate it from puffing up consistently.

4. To get ready the topping, combine the fourth container of olive oil, pimentón, salt, and pepper in a little bowl. Liberally brush the mixture with half of this blend. The romesco sauce ought to be connected indeed before the green onions and oregano. Olive oil ought to be brushed along the crust's edges. The batter ought to rise up after 10 to 15 minutes in a warm area.

5. In arrange to prepare the bread equitably, turn the container once amid the ten minutes it is within the wood pellet smoker-grill. Include the broiled potatoes on best, at that point heat for another 15 minutes or so, or until the outside is brilliant and fresh. After taking it out of the wood pellet smoker-grill, brush the crust's edges with olive oil. Cut or cut into serving-size squares, at that point beat with cut eggs. At room temperature or warmed, serve.

9

Seafood

1. Quenelles

Prep time: 11 mins | Serve: 4-6 | Calories: 210 kcal
  Fixings

- 1 pound cooked angle filets
- 2 egg whites
- Two mugs of overwhelming cream
- One tbsp. capers
- One tbsp. new tarragon
- One tsp. crisply ground dark pepper
- One tsp. arranged mustard
- Half tsp. salt

Informational

1. Put the egg whites and angle filets within the nourishment processor's bowl. Once everything is well combined, beat seven or eight times. Another, rub the sides.
2. Purée the other ingredients—cream, capers, tarragon, pepper, mustard, and salt—for 15 to 20 seconds, or until well mixed.
3. Utilize a spatula to exchange to a blending bowl. Scoop a liberal heap with a soup spoon, exchange it to another soup spoon, and shape it into an egg. Rehash with the remaining fixings and put on material or wax paper.
4. On a huge pot or wok, set over medium-high warm on a wood pellet smoker-grill in a wood pellet barbecue, and bring water to a bubble. With a opened spoon, carefully lower the quenelles into the water once it has come to a moderate bubble after diminishing the warm. 8 to 10 minutes of cooking, with one flip.
5. Put aside after exchanging to wax paper.
6. Utilize right absent in the event that utilized in Angle Drop Soup. For up to two days, quenelles can be put away in a secured fridge.

2. Angle drop soup

Prep time: 27 mins | Serve: 4-6 | Calories: 172 kcal

Fixings

- One tbsp. olive oil
- 1 little onion, finely chopped, around
- Half container 6–8 garlic cloves, minced (or to taste)
- One tbsp. Shrimp Glue
- One tsp. naturally ground dark pepper
- One tsp. ground turmeric
- Two glasses of Angle Stock
- Two glasses of dry white wine
- One tsp. angle sauce
- 1 pound angle filets, cut into bite-size pieces Quenelles
- 2 eggs, beaten softly
- 2–3 scallions or chives, finely chopped

Informational

1. On a wood pellet flame broil, warm the oil in a 4-quart pan over medium-high warm on a wood pellet smoker flame broil. Include the shrimp glue, pepper, and turmeric after cooking the onion and garlic within the oil for three to four minutes or until delicate.
2. After turning the warm down to moo, whisk for one diminutive.
3. In a wood pellet flame broil, include the stock and wine, at that point bring to a bubble over medium-high warm on a wood pellet smoker flame broil.
4. Include the angle sauce, turn the warm down to moo, and stew for five minutes.
5. When the angle is strong, include the pieces, cover, and stew for around 10 minutes. In the event that utilized, after the angle has cooked for 6 to 7 minutes, include the Quenelles.

6. Take off the cover, whisking with one hand whereas gradually sprinkling the eggs into the soup with the other.
7. Scoop the soup into warmed bowls, best with the scallions, and serve right absent.

3. Bluefish smoked over fennel

Prep time: 1 hour 35 mins | Serve: 4 | Calories: 93 kcal

Fixings

- 2–2½ pounds of bluefish filets
- Two tbsps. ocean salt
- Two tbsps. sugar
- One tsp. cayenne pepper
- ¼ glass drain
- ¼ fennel bulb part longwise

Informational

1. The filets ought to be put in a holder. Both sides of the filets ought to be secured with a blend of salt, sugar, and cayenne. The filets ought to be secured and chilled for 30 to 45 minutes after the drain has been included.
2. Lay the fennel within the foot of the smoke dish and include generally Two mugs of dried corn bits or wood chips on best. Preheat a barbecue for smoke cooking.
3. Deplete the filets after expelling them from the ice chest.
4. Near the cover after putting the filets on an oiled grind over the smoke skillet. After 20 minutes, turn the filets over and cover the container. Keep an eye out; fires may have to be put out in some cases. Cook the filets for 45 minutes or until they feel firm to the touch. Serve right absent.

4. Rosemary-smoked herring

Prep time: 1 hours | Serve: 8-10 | Calories: 123 kcal
Fixings

- 2 pounds of herring filets
- Two tbsps. ocean salt
- Two tbsps. sugar
- 6 expansive sprigs of rosemary
- Dill Mustard Sauce Lemon cuts

Enlightening

1. The salt and sugar ought to be connected after setting the filets in a holder. Put two rosemary stems around the filets and chill for one to two hours. After one hour, mix.
2. Set up a flame broil for smoke barbecuing and put two rosemary sprigs within the smoke dish with dried corn or wood chips on beat. Lay a bed of the extra rosemary sprigs on the grind, where you'll set the filets over it.
3. The filets should be taken out of the fridge, rubbed, and after that set on the rosemary bed on the flame broil after being brushed clean of additional salt and sugar. Put the cover on.
4. After around twenty minutes, flip the filets. Keep a tight eye out; fires seem have to be put out. The filets ought to be cooked for 45 minutes or until they are firm to the touch. Serve with lemon cuts and Dill Mustard Sauce.

5. Smoked bonito with green sauce

Prep time: 2hr 35 mins | Serve: 4-6 | Calories: 213 kcal
Fixings

- 2 pounds bonito filets
- Two tbsps. ocean salt
- Two tbsps. sugar
- One tbsp. coarse dark peppercorns
- Two tbsps. new parsley, finely chopped
- Juice of ½ lemon
- Pumpernickel squares Green Sauce

Enlightening

1. The filets ought to be put in a holder. The parsley, salt, sugar, and peppercorns ought to all be combined. Rub the blend all over the filets, at that point cover and chill for 30 to 45 minutes.
2. For smoke flame broiling, preheat the flame broil.
3. The filets ought to be taken out of the cooler, with most of the rub expelled and lemon juice sprinkled on best.
4. Near the top after setting the filets on an oiled grind over the smoke skillet. After around 20 minutes, flip the filets, at that point cover the skillet. Keep an eye out; fires may have to be be put out now and then. The filets ought to be cooked for 45 minutes or until they are firm to the touch.
5. Serve the Green Sauce warm with pumpernickel squares.

6. Smoked salmon pâté

SEAFOOD

Prep time: 1 hour 10 mins | Serve: 6-8 | Calories: 248 kcal

Fixings

- 1 pound salmon filet
- 1 container mirin or fruity white wine Juice of
- 2½ lemons (around ½ glass)
- Half container green olives, set and cut
- 1 /3 glass olive oil
- Two tbsps. finely chopped new dill
- Two tbsps. Finely chopped ruddy onion
- Two tbsps. finely chopped new thyme Toast or bread garnishes Lemon
- Wedges

Enlightening

1. Salmon ought to be secured and chilled whereas being drenched for an hour in mirin and 1/4 glass of lemon juice.
2. Set up a grill for smoking nourishment.

3. Deplete the angle after evacuating it from the fridge.
4. Over the smoke skillet, put the salmon on the hot side of the flame broil. The filets ought to ended up a light pink after 8 to 10 minutes of cooking with the cover on.
5. The salmon ought to be moved to a chopping board. Put the salmon in a huge blending bowl after chopping or chipping it into minor pieces.
6. The salmon chunks ought to be totally blended with the remaining lemon juice, olives, oil, dill, onion, and thyme. Serve with lemon wedges on bread or bread garnishes.

7. Smoked salmon spread

Prep time: 1 hours | Serve: 8-12 | Calories: 218 kcal

Fixings

- Juice of 1½ lemons (approximately ¼ glass)
- ¼ glass mirin
- Two tbsps. rice wine vinegar
- ½ pound Smoked Salmon, cut into chunks
- Half glass kalamata olives, set and cut
- Two tbsps. olive oil
- Two tbsps. finely chopped new oregano
- Two tbsps. Finely chopped scallions
- One tbsp. finely chopped new parsley, furthermore additional for embellish
- Pumpernickel or rye bread squares, cut in half
- Lemon wedges

Enlightening

1. Blend the vinegar, mirin, and lemon juice in a little bowl.
2. Pour the blend over the salmon chunks that have been set in a glass heating dish. For one hour, cover and chill.

3. Within the bowl of a nourishment processor, beat the olives, olive oil, oregano, scallions, and parsley five or six times to finely chop them.
4. Take the marinated salmon pieces out of the glass dish. They ought to be finely chopped after three or four beats within the nourishment processor bowl. Maintain a strategic distance from over-puréeing the blend by handling it as well altogether.
5. Spread the salmon blend over the bread parts, at that point include more parsley as a decorate. Lemon wedges and pumpernickel squares ought to be served nearby.

8. Curried trout timbales

Prep time: 41 mins | Serve: 6 | Calories: 221 kcal

Fixings

- 6 ounces Smoked Rainbow Trout cleaned and boned
- Juice of 1½ lemons (¼ glass)
- ¼ container new thyme stemmed
- 6 to 8 wild slopes or chives
- One tsp. curry powder
- ¼ teaspoon garam masala
- 1 container overwhelming cream
- 3 eggs

Enlightening

1. Set the wood pellet smoker-grill to 350°F. Within the bowl of a nourishment processor, beat the angle, lemon juice, thyme, inclines, curry powder, and garam masala five or six times to combine.
2. Purée for 15 seconds after scratching down the edges.
3. Include the eggs and cream. Purée until well combined.
4. At that point, partition the blend among six biscuit tins.
5. Some time recently exchanging the container to the wood pellet

smoker flame broil, put them in a roasting pan with water that's around two-thirds up the biscuit mugs. A toothpick embedded within the center of the timbales ought to come out clean after heating for 25 to 30 minutes.
6. Permit the blend to cool and firm up by turning off the warm and letting it sit for 10 minutes. To discharge the timbales, circle the edges of the mugs with the tip of a limit cut. Turn them delicately upside down over a enormous platter.
7. Serve right absent or chill after covering with plastic wrap.

9. Tickled pink shellfish

Prep time: 45 mins | Serve: 4 | Calories: 28 kcal

Fixings

- One and a half mugs of cognac or brandy
- One and a half glasses half-and-half
- Half glass clam juice
- Two tbsps. broken pink peppercorns
- One tsp. paprika
- 24 unopened clams
- Lemon wedges

Enlightening

1. Set up a grill for smoking nourishment. In a expendable or cast-iron skillet, combine the cognac, cream, clam juice, peppercorns, and paprika. Put the skillet over the fire instantly on beat of the smoke container. In arrange to avoid the fluid from shooting over, whisk or blend it each presently and after that.
2. Put the clams on the grill's cool side. Put the top on.
3. After around 15 minutes, as the shellfish start to open, altogether pry open each one to permit the smoky flavor to saturate.

4. Be cautious not to spill the oysters' characteristic liquids. Cook for a assist 30 minutes or until misty.
5. Put the shellfish on plates, best with a teaspoon of the sauce, and embellish with lemon wedges to serve.

10. Smoked shad roe–potato balls

Prep time: 10 mins | Serve: 15 | Calories: 155 kcal

Fixings

- ½ smoked little shad roe, almost
- Two glasses of pounded potatoes
- 1 egg ¼ container new thyme, stemmed
- Two tbsps. dissolved butter
- One tsp. salt1
- One tsp. naturally ground dark pepper
- Two tbsps. vegetable oil
- Romesco Sauce
- Horseradish Sauce

Enlightening

1. Within the bowl of a nourishment processor, beat the shad roe, potatoes, egg, thyme, butter, salt, and pepper five to six times, or until well combined. Exchange the blend to a plate after cleaning the sides.
2. Shape the mixture into 1 12-inch-diameter balls along with your hands. Put aside.
3. On a wood pellet flame broil set to medium-high warm, warm the oil for one miniature in a huge container or wok. Utilizing a spoon, tenderly lower the balls into the oil. They ought to be pivoted for 3 to 5 minutes or until all sides are browned.
4. Take out and wipe with paper towels. On the off chance that utilizing,

serve promptly with horseradish sauce or Romesco sauce.

11. Smoked whitefish

Prep time: 10 mins | Serve: 4 | Calories: 131 kcal

Fixings

- One tbsp. olive oil
- 2½ glasses cut shiitake mushrooms
- Three-fourth container asparagus tips
- Three-fourth container coarsely chopped green tomato
- ½ sweet white onion, coarsely chopped
- 4 garlic cloves, finely chopped
- Two tbsps. unsalted butter
- Two tbsps. orange blossom water
- One tbsp. shellfish sauce
- One tbsp. low-sodium soy sauce
- One tsp. coarsely ground dark pepper
- ¾ pound smoked whitefish, chipped into bite-size pieces
- ½ pound pasta, cooked and depleted

Informational

1. The mushrooms, asparagus, tomato, onion, and garlic are sautéed for 4 minutes, or until well cooked, in hot oil in a wok over a smoker flame broil.
2. Pepper, bloom water, shellfish sauce, soy sauce, and butter ought to be included. Sauté for a encourage 4 to 5 minutes, or until warmed. Include the chunks of smoked salmon and carefully combine.
3. Pour over the spaghetti.

12. Smoked salmon pizza with blended wild mushrooms

Prep time: 45 mins | Serve: 1 | Calorie: 845 kcal

Fixings

- 4 tbsps. olive oil
- ½ pound wild mushrooms
- 4–6 scallions
- 3–4 garlic cloves, finely chopped
- Two tbsps. new thyme
- Batter for a 12-inch pizza
- 2 little ready tomatoes, cut into rounds
- Salt and dark pepper
- 8 ounces of Smoked Salmon
- Two glasses of destroyed mozzarella
- Half container ground Asiago

Enlightening

1. The mushrooms, scallions, garlic, and Two tbsps. Of thyme ought to be sautéed in Two tbsps. Of the oil in a medium-sized skillet over medium-high warm on a wood pellet smoker-grill in a wood pellet barbecue for 6 to 8 minutes. Warm has been expelled; set aside.
2. Fire up the flame broil.
3. Roll out the batter into a 12-inch circle on a cutting board that has been cleaned with cornmeal and flour, and after that crease the corners all the way around. Exchange to a pizza skillet with gaps.
4. Put the tomatoes on the batter, at that point include the sautéed mushrooms.
5. Spread the salmon, cheeses, salt and pepper to taste, and the six thyme sprigs equally over the best. Include the barbecue to the dish. In the event that utilizing charcoal, diminish the warm or move the skillet

out of the coordinate warm. Put the top on. On the off chance that utilizing charcoal, which cooks significantly more rapidly than gas, cook for 10 to 12 minutes, but check regularly. Check to see in the event that the dough's edge has somewhat browned by tipping it up.

6. Near the cover and warm for a advance five minutes, or until the cheeses are liquefied, after moving the skillet to the warming rack. 20 minutes is the most extreme prescribed cooking time; in any case it may be shorter.
7. Cut after being exchanged to a cutting board and serve right absent.

13. Non-rising pizza batter

Prep time: 5 mins | Serve: 1 | Calorie: 259 kcal

Fixings

- 1Three-fourth mugs of all-purpose flour
- Two tbsps. preparing powder
- One tsp. salt
- 2/3 glass of water
- 1/3 glass olive oil
- A modest bunch of flour and cornmeal blend

Informational

1. In a expansive blending bowl, combine the salt, heating powder, and flour.
2. Oil ought to be sprinkled in after the water. Totally combine.
3. Put the mixture on a cutting board and cover it with the flour and cornmeal blend. Shape a ball after 3 to 4 minutes of manipulating, at that point roll it out to a thickness of 1/8 inch. Fill together with your favored fixings after pleating the edges.
4. Take after the recipe's headings whereas flame broiling on the wood pellet grill.

14. Gravad and smoked salmon with cilantro-mint rub

Prep time: 70 mins | Serve: 15 | Calories: 320 kcal

Fixings

- 1 little lime, washed and divided
- 4 glasses freely pressed cilantro, stemmed
- 1 glass light brown sugar
- Three-fourth glass finely chopped mint clears out
- ¼ container coarse salt
- One tsp. cayenne pepper
- ¼ container tequila
- 2–3 pounds salmon filet
- Dill Mustard Sauce
- Pumpernickel or rye bread
- Chopped dill for embellish
- Finely chopped ruddy peppers for embellish
- Lemon wedges for embellish

Informational

1. Beat the lime, cilantro, sugar, mint, salt, cayenne, and, on the off chance that utilized, tequila for 30 seconds within the nourishment processor's bowl. With a spatula, clean the sides, at that point beat for an additional minute.
2. On a chunk of plastic wrap, put the salmon skin-side down. Cover the filet totally with the rub employing a spatula. Three layers of the plastic wrap ought to be safely wrapped. Put the filet on a level plate or preparing dish, weigh it down with one or two clean, foil-wrapped pieces or enormous soup cans, and after that chill it for 12 hours whereas flipping it over once. You might got to deplete the filet once since it'll discharge fluid. For smoke flame broiling, preheat the flame broil.

3. Unwrap the salmon after expelling it from the cooler. For an hour, put the filet on an oiled barbecue over the smoke skillet. The filet ought to be moved to the cool side of the barbecue. Depending on your favored level of smoke concentrated, proceed to smoke for an extra hour or up to three hours.
4. Cut the angle, take it from the fire, and serve it with the Dill Mustard Sauce on the cuts of bread. Include lemon wedges, ruddy pepper drops, and dill to the dish as a embellish.

15. Smoked gravlax with an orange-dill rub

Prep time: 45 mins | Serve: 15 | Calories: 268 kcal

Fixings

- 1 container freely pressed dill
- 1 medium orange
- 1/3 container apple cider
- 1/3 container triple sec
- 2 to 3 pounds salmon filets
- Pumpernickel or rye bread
- Dill Mustard Sauce
- Chopped dill for decorate
- Finely chopped ruddy peppers
- Lemon wedges for embellish

Informational

1. Within the bowl of a nourishment processor, beat the dill, orange, cider, and triple sec for 30 seconds. Utilize a spatula to clean the sides, at that point beat for a advance 30 seconds.
2. On a chunk of plastic wrap, put the salmon skin-side down. Cover the filet totally with the orange rub employing a spatula. Three layers of the plastic wrap ought to be safely wrapped. Put within the fridge for

at slightest 12 hours or up to 3 days, turning once every day, on a level plate or preparing dish weighted down with one or two clean, foil-wrapped bricks or enormous soup cans. You might ought to deplete out any additional fluid that the filet removes.
3. For smoke flame broiling, preheat the barbecue.
4. Unwrap the salmon after evacuating it from the cooler.
5. For an hour, put the filet on an oiled barbecue over the smoke container.
6. Carefully move the filet to the cool side of the barbecue utilizing two spatulas. Depending on your favored level of smoke concentrated, proceed to smoke for an extra hour or up to three hours.
7. Cut after evacuating from the warm. Put the Dill Mustard Sauce over the bread squares, best with the ruddy peppers, lemon wedges, and chopped dill, and serve.

16. Smoked sable

Prep time: 1 hour | Serve: 10 | Calories: 73 kcal

Fixings

- 2 pounds sable or dark cod filets
- Two tbsps. good-quality extra-virgin olive oil
- One tsp. ocean salt
- Two tbsps. naturally ground dark pepper
- Lemon wedges
- Dill Mustard Sauce

Informational

1. Salt and pepper the filets on both sides after brushing them with olive oil. Put aside.
2. For smoke flame broiling, preheat the barbecue.
3. On the cool side of the flame broil, put the filets. Don't flip whereas

smoking for 1 to 112 hours or until the filets feel firm to the touch.
4. Near the cover. As it were sometimes lift the cover to check for unauthorized flares. In the event that required, soak with water.
5. At that point cut or break the smoked filets into bite-sized pieces after they have cooled for around half an hour.
6. Lemon wedges and Dill Mustard Sauce ought to be served nearby.

17. Catfish wrapped in collard greens

Prep time: 15 mins | Serve: 4 | Calories: 203 kcal

Fixings

- 8 whitened collard takes off
- 1 tomato, diced
- 1 container seeded and cut kalamata olives
- 6 scallions, finely chopped
- 4–6 garlic cloves, minced
- One tbsp. olive oil
- Salt and naturally ground dark pepper
- 4 catfish filets,
- 8 ounces each
- Lemon wedges for decorate
- Cooked brown rice

Informational

1. Fire up the flame broil. Four collard takes off ought to be spread out on a work region. Each leaf ought to be topped with half a tomato, olives, scallions, garlic, oil, salt, and pepper to taste. A filet ought to be put on best of each leaf. The remaining fixings ought to at that point be included, at the side extra salt and pepper in the event that required.
2. The ultimate four greens ought to be put on best of each course of

SEAFOOD

action and immovably squeezed with toothpicks.

3. Put the ingredients into an oiled, punctured pizza container, put the dish on the flame broil, and after that closed the cover. For 6 to 7 minutes, flame broil. With a spatula, delicately flip the burger over and cook for an extra 4 to 5 minutes, or until fair browned.
4. Four plates ought to each have one take. Some time recently including the lemon wedges as a embellish, take off the toothpicks. Include brown rice to the dish.

18. Sunnies dijon

Prep time: 18 mins | Serve: 4 | Calories: 4 kcal

Fixings

- ¼ glass mayonnaise
- Two tbsps. hot yellow mustard Juice of
- ½ lemon (around 1½ tablespoons)1
- ¼ container cornmeal
- One tsp. finely chopped new tarragon
- One tbsp. broken dark peppercorns
- 2–3 pounds of sunfish filets

Enlightening

1. Fire up the barbecue. In a expansive bowl, combine the mayonnaise, mustard, lemon juice, cornmeal, tarragon, and peppercorns.
2. The filets ought to be completely secured after being plunged within the blend.
3. Put the filets on the grill and, in case you'll , decrease the warm to medium.
4. Cook for 6–8 minutes with the top on. When cornmeal is fair beginning to brown, turn it over and sear for another 4 to 5 minutes. Serve right absent.

19. Barbecued butterflied trout

Prep time: 25 mins | Serve: 2 | Calories: 206 kcal

Fixings

- Two tbsps. shelled nut oil
- 1 container daintily cut shiitake or shellfish mushrooms
- 6–8 garlic cloves, finely chopped
- 1–2 serrano chili s, seeded, deveined, finely chopped
- 1 glass destroyed white cabbage
- 1 little carrot, peeled and julienned
- Half glass angle or chicken stock
- ¼ container low-sodium soy sauce
- 1 Juice of 1 lemon
- 1 butterflied trout
- One tsp. new oregano
- One tsp. salt
- One tsp. naturally ground dark pepper
- Cooked white rice

Enlightening

1. Fire up the flame broil. On a huge container or wok, warm Two tbsps. Of the oil over mediumhigh warm in a wood pellet flame broil. When the veggies are totally cooked, include the cabbage and carrot and proceed to stir-fry for an extra 4 to 5 minutes after the mushrooms, garlic, and chili s have been included.
2. Pour the stock in, and after 5 minutes, diminish it by a third. Mix within the soy sauce and turn the heat down to moo to preserve warmth.
3. Include the oregano, salt, and pepper, and after that sprinkle the remaining One tbsp. of oil and lemon juice over the butterflied angle.
4. A wire-mesh wicker container ought to be utilized to contain the

prepared angle.
5. After 4 to 5 minutes, flip the wicker container over and cook for an extra 5 minutes, or until the substance is murky.
6. Expel angle from the bushel, part it into two plates, and spread the warming sauce on beat. White rice ought to be served at once.

20. Steelhead trout in ruddy wine sauce

Prep time: 1 hour 5 mins | Serve: 4 | Calories: 150 kcal

Fixings

- Two tbsps. olive oil
- 1 little stalk of celery, finely chopped
- 1 little leek, white portion as it were, cleaned and finely chopped
- 1 little green chime pepper, seeded and finely chopped
- ½ pound mushrooms (shellfish, shiitake, or boletus)
- 1 container Beaujolais or other generous ruddy wine
- One tbsps. New oregano, finely chopped
- One tbsps. new thyme stemmed and finely chopped
- One tsp. tomato glue
- 1 entirety steelhead trout (3 to 4 pounds)
- 1 glass overwhelming cream
- One tsp. salt
- Two tsps. coarsely ground dark pepper
- Lemon wedges

Enlightening

1. Preheat a flame broil. On a wood pellet flame broil, preheat the oil over medium-high warm some time recently including the celery, leek, chime pepper, and mushrooms. For around 15 minutes, blend and bubble.
2. Tomato glue, Two tsps. Of oregano, Two tbsps. Of thyme, and wine

ought to all be included. 10 to 12 minutes ought to be cut in half. Turn off the warm, cover the skillet and save.

3. Put the angle on a lubed barbecue after brushing or cooking, showering it with a few oil. For 8 to 10 minutes, cook with the cover on. Turn the trout tenderly with two spatulas and cook for a advance 6 to 8 minutes, or until the angle feels firm to the touch.
4. Return the ruddy wine sauce to the stovetop and warm it to medium. To dodge burning, include the cream and blend frequently. It ought to take around 15 minutes to decrease the fluid by generally a third.
5. Include the angle to the ruddy wine sauce within the skillet, at that point cover the trout with the sauce. For approximately 5 minutes, stew the blend with the cover on moo warm until well warmed. After exchanging to a serving plate, cover with the remaining oregano, thyme, salt, and pepper.
6. Angle ought to be deboned and separated among plates. With the lemon wedges, serve.

21. Flame broiled freshwater roost with blood orange serving of mixed greens

Prep time: 38 mins | Serve: 4 | Calories: 260 kcal

Fixings

- 2 pounds roost filets (4 to 8 filets, depending on estimate)
- Juice of ½ orange (approximately 4 tbsps.)
- One tbsp. Unadulterated maple syrup
- Half tsp. ocean salt
- Chopped scallions for embellish
- Blood Orange Serving of mixed greens
- Cooked bulgur or pearl grain

Informational

1. The filets, orange juice, maple syrup, and salt ought to all be combined in one holder. 30 minutes of refrigeration beneath cover.
2. Fire up the flame broil.
3. The filets ought to be taken out of the holder, dried off, and put on an oiled flame broil. For 3 to 4 minutes, cook. When the filets feel firm to the touch, flip them over and cook for another 4 minutes.
4. Include scallions as a embellish. Serve bulgur and blood orange serving of mixed greens right absent.

22. Smoked lake trout with olive-mustard sauce

Prep time: 1 hour 40 mins | Serve: 4 | Calories: 120 kcal

Fixings

- 1–2 pounds lake trout filets
- One tbsp. olive oil
- 1 medium onion, coarsely chopped
- ½ little tomato, diced
- Half glass Gaeta or kalamata olives set and split
- Half container dry white wine
- ¼ glass new thyme, finely chopped
- Two tbsps. Dijon mustard
- One tsp. New oregano, finely chopped
- One tsp. crisply ground dark pepper Lemon wedges

Enlightening

1. Set up a grill for smoking nourishment. Put the filets on the smoker's cool side. For around 45 minutes, smoke with the cover closed. Turn and keep smoking for a encourage 45 minutes or until the substance feels firm to the touch.
2. Put the filets on the grill's best warming rack after turning off the warm, at that point cover the flame broil.

3. To plan the sauce, in a huge, revealed skillet over medium warm, sauté the onion, tomato, and olives for 4 to 5 minutes. Mix.
4. Wine, thyme, mustard, oregano, and pepper ought to be included steadily. Blend and cook for 4 to 5 minutes, or until decreased by half, with the top off.
5. Lay the angle in four pieces on warmed plates with the sauce spooned on the side. With the lemon wedges, serve.

23. Barbecued smallmouth bass wrapped in cornhusks

Prep time: 12 mins | Serve: 4 | Calories: 124 kcal

Fixings

- 2 ears of new corn
- 2 pounds of smallmouth bass filets
- 4 tbsps. unsalted butter
- Juice of 1 lemon
- Salt and dark pepper
- Lemon wedges

Informational

1. Warm up the flame broil. Peel the corn husks off with care, at that point lay them aside. Evacuate each cob's silk totally.
2. Cut the corn from the cobs in lines by cutting descending with a sharp cut whereas holding the cobs erect. Keep the cut corn aside and toss absent the cobs.
3. Per filet, spread out and press two or three husks level. Put a few corn on best of the clears out, at that point put a filet on beat of each "bundle" at an point to the husks.
4. Include the extra corn to the filets to cover them. Spread the butter bits on the corn.
5. Beside salt and pepper, squeeze a few lemon juice over each filet.

6. To make an envelope shape, overlay the husks over the best of the bundles on both sides and fasten them with toothpicks.
7. Lay on the flame broil for around 6 minutes; tenderly turn employing a spatula and cook for a assist 6 minutes, or until the husks are fair starting to burn.
8. At the side the lemon cuts, serve right absent.

24. Barbecued walleye with grapes and shaggy mane mushrooms

Prep time: 17 mins | Serve: 4 | Calories: 180 kcal

Fixings

- 1½ to 2 pounds walleye filets
- 2½ glasses shaggy manes, cleaned and cut
- Half container of solidified white grape juice
- Half container orange-flavored alcohol
- 4 tbsps. unsalted butter (½ adhere)
- 1 glass globe (or dark) grapes, cut in half
- Two tbsps. crisply ground dark pepper
- Pizzazz of 1 orange for embellish

Informational

1. Fire up the flame broil. Oil the skin side of the filets and the flame broil side. For 4 to 5 minutes, cook the filets. Cook for a further 3 to 4 minutes on the other side, or until the tissue feels firm to the touch. Put on the warming rack and keep up warmth.
2. Meanwhile, plan the sauce by softening the mushrooms in butter in a nonreactive pot. Include the alcohol and the grape juice. The fluid ought to be decreased by generally one-third after 5 to 6 minutes of cooking at medium-high warm.
3. For 1-2 minutes, blend within the grapes, pepper, and half of the

pizzazz.

4. The walleye ought to be cut into four pieces. Put the filets on beat of the sauce on four plates.
5. Serve right absent after including the remaining orange get-up-and-go as a embellish.

25. Smoked walleye with a dried mushroom–pumpkin seed rub

Prep time: 1hr 15 mins | Serve: 4 |Calories: 213 kcal

Fixings

- Three-fourth glasses of toasted pumpkin seeds
- Half container dried mushrooms
- ¼ container olive oil
- One tsp. ocean salt
- One tsp. naturally ground dark pepper
- One and a half pounds of walleye filets Juice of
- 1/3 lemon
- Lemon wedges

Enlightening

1. Set up the barbecue for smoking. Beat the pumpkin seeds, mushrooms, oil, salt, and pepper six to eight times, or until well combined, within the bowl of a nourishment processor. Put aside.
2. After oiling the fillets' foot skin, put them on a cutting board.
3. Apply lemon juice to the filets in a lean layer. Press the rub into the substance of the fillets, covering all surfaces along with your hands or a elastic spatula.
4. On the cool side of an oiled flame broil, put the filets tenderly. When the filets feel firm to the touch, near the cover and proceed smoking for 1 to 1 ½ hour without pivoting. As it were lift the top to explore

for uninvited flares.
5. Put the filets on four plates, isolate the lemon wedges on beat, and serve.

26. Smoked burbot with wild mushroom, plum & mint sauce

Prep time: 14 mins | Serve: 4 | Calories: 80 kcal

Fixings

- 2½ mugs wild mushrooms, cleaned and stemmed
- 1Three-fourth glasses dark plums, seeded and cut (4–5 medium plums)
- 1 glass new mint, coarsely chopped
- 4 tbsps. butter (½ adhere)
- ¼ glass apple cider
- ¼ container brownish harbour
- Salt and dark pepper
- 1 pound smoked burbot filet
- Cooked brown rice

Enlightening

1. On a wood pellet barbecue, in a non-reactive skillet over medium-high warm, sauté the mushrooms, plums, and mint for 3 to 4 minutes.
2. The fluid ought to be decreased by one-third after including the cider, harbour, and salt and pepper to taste.
3. When the angle is all secured, include the smoked burbot, decrease the warm to moo, and stew for almost 5 minutes.
4. Burbot ought to be taken out of the dish, separated into four parcels, and served right absent with brown rice.

27. Smoked walleye with ruddy pepper sauce

Prep time: 15 mins | Serve: 4 | Calories: 205 kcal

Fixings

- One and a half pounds of walleye filets
- 6 ounces brew
- ¼ container new basil
- Half tsp. ocean salt
- One tbsp. dark pepper
- Two glasses of Broiled Ruddy Peppers
- ¼ container angle or chicken stock
- Two tbsps. harbour wine
- Chopped ruddy chime peppers

Informational

1. Filets, brew, basil, salt, and pepper ought to be put in a glass or plastic holder. For one hour, cover and chill.
2. Set up a grill for smoking nourishment.
3. Wine, stock, and ruddy peppers ought to all be put within the nourishment processor's bowl. Four or five times, pulse. Purée after employing a spatula to rub down the edges.
4. The blend ought to be exchanged to a 2-quart pan and stewed for around 15 minutes, or until it has diminished by almost onethird, over medium warm. Whereas expelling the pot from the warm, take off it warmed.

28. Mixed eggs with smoked shad milt

Prep time: 4 mins | Serve: 2 | Calories: 316 kcal

Fixings

- Two tbsps. unsalted butter
- 6 eggs, beaten
- ¼ container entirety drain
- One tbsp. new tarragon
- Salt and dark pepper
- Half container smoked milt
- Fundamental Salsa

Enlightening

1. In a expansive skillet over medium warm on a wood pellet barbecue, dissolve the butter.
2. Within the butter, scramble the eggs with the cream, tarragon, salt, and pepper to taste. Put the milt in.
3. Cook the eggs for a advance 3 to 4 minutes, or until they have thickened and no fluid is unmistakable. Serve with Fundamental Salsa right absent.

29. Walleye hash browns

Prep time: 25 mins | Serve: 4 | Calories: 78 kcal

Fixings

- 1 pound walleye filet
- 2 medium Yukon potatoes
- Half glass of finely chopped ruddy onions
- ¼ glass overwhelming cream
- Two tbsps. all-purpose flour
- Two tbsps. Dijon mustard
- Two tbsps. ground Parmesan
- One tsp. canola oil
- 4 tbsps. unsalted butter

Enlightening

1. Fire up the barbecue. The filet ought to be flame broiled for 4 to 5 minutes on each side until dark and firm. Let the filet cool, at that point drop it and set it aside.
2. In a huge blending bowl, tenderly combine the chips filet, potatoes, onion, cream, flour, mustard, and Parmesan.
3. Making beyond any doubt to maintain a strategic distance from breaking it separated, frame the fabric into a sizable patty on a chopping board. It got to take after a monster hotcake.
4. In a enormous skillet, warm the oil and Two tbsps of butter over mediumhigh warm on a wood pellet smoker-grill. Carefully exchange the patties to the container utilizing two spatulas. For almost 10 minutes, sauté over medium warm on a wood pellet smoker-grill until brown.
5. Turn the patties gradually, at that point beat with the remaining butter. Sauté for a encourage 10 minutes or until the potatoes are well browned.
6. Cut into four wedges, at that point serve hot.

30. Smoked butterflied largemouth bass

Prep time: 1 hour 50 mins | Serve: 4 | Calories: 124 kcal

Fixings

- 1 entire bass, 2½ to 3 pounds, butterflied
- Curing arrangement of your choice
- 6–8 garlic cloves, finely chopped
- Half glass cilantro, chopped
- Two tbsps. tomato glue
- One tsp. salt
- One tbsp. dark pepper
- Essential Salsa

Informational

1. One hour some time recently cooking, infuse the curing arrangement all through the whole angle.
2. Set up a grill for smoking nourishment.
3. Combine the tomato glue, garlic, cilantro, salt, and pepper in a bowl to make a glue.
4. With a spatula, completely coat the bass by rubbing the glue into its plump surface.
5. Utilizing cooking shower or a brush, oil the grind and the skin of the angle. Near the cover and lie on the cool side of the barbecue. Cook for an extra 1 ¼ hours after turning the meat, or until the substance feels difficult to the touch.
6. Serve each side with two parcels of the Fundamental Salsa right absent.

31. Smoked apache trout

Prep time: 1 hour | Serve: 4 | Calories: 95 kcal

Fixings

- 4 to 8 trout filets Juice of
- 1 lemon juice
- Lemony Corn Salsa

Enlightening

- Set up a wood pellet grill for smoking nourishment. Lemon juice ought to be generously connected on the beat of the filets.
- Apply cooking shower or a brush to the grind and skin side (foot) of the filets. Put the filets on the grill's cool side and cover it.
- The angle ought to be smoked for almost two hours or until brilliant brown.
- Rapidly serve with Lemony Corn Salsa.

32. Smoked rainbow trout

Prep time: 1 hour 30 mins | Serve: 4 | Calories: 95 kcal

Fixings

- 2 entire trout,
- 2–3 pounds add up to Curing arrangement of your choice
- Dill Mustard Sauce

Informational

- Set up a grill for smoking nourishment. One hour earlier to cooking, infuse the curing arrangement all through the whole angle.
- With cooking shower or a brush, gently oil the grind and the angle on both sides. Put the angle on the grill's cool side and cover it. Cook for an extra 1 ¼ hours after turning the angle, or until the salmon is brilliant brown.
- Some time recently serving the angle with the Dill Mustard Sauce, expel and debone it.

33. Smoked pike with dried cherry and pear sauce

Prep time: 1 hour 15 mins | Serve: 4-6 | Calories: 240 kcal

Fixings

- 1 entirety pike, 1½ to 2 pounds
- 4 huge ready Bosc pears
- 1 container white vermouth
- ¼ container smashed dark peppercorns
- 4 tbsps. unsalted butter
- 1 container dried cherries
- Two tbsps. brandy
- Cooked white rice

- Sautéed broccoli rabe

Informational

- For smoke flame broiling, preheat the flame broil. Near the top after setting the angle on an oiled grind. It ought to be firm to the touch after cooking for 1 1/2 to 2 hours.
- Make the sauce whereas the pike is smoking. In a blending bowl, combine the pears and vermouth. Include the peppercorns, and marinate for one to two hours within the ice chest.
- Pike ought to be taken off the barbecue and kept warm. Take both pears out of the marinade and put them aside.
- In a wood pellet barbecue, soften the butter over medium-high warm on a wood pellet smoker-grill in a expansive pot. For three to four minutes, sauté the pears and cherries.
- Include brandy and half of the extra marinade. Cook for 6 to 8 minutes whereas diminishing the fluid until the sauce is somewhat thickened. After blending, turn off the warm.
- Serve the rice and broccoli rabe with the smoked salmon that has been scooped over.

34. Smoked yellow roost in grapefruit marinade

Prep time: 1 hour 15 mins | Serve: 4 | Calories: 60 kcal

Fixings

- ¼ container olive oil
- Half container grapefruit juice
- Two tbsps. finely chopped cilantro
- One tsp. cayenne pepper
- 8 roost filets Grapefruit wedges

Enlightening

- In a huge blending bowl, combine the oil, cilantro, grapefruit juice, and cayenne.
- Put the filets in glass preparing dish or 1-gallon zip-lock packs. Apply the marinade to the filets, at that point put within the ice chest for one to two hours.
- Set up a wood pellet grill for smoking nourishment.
- The filets ought to be taken out of the marinade and put on the cool side of the flame broil. For roughly an hour, near the top and let the smoke out. 200 to 250 degrees Fahrenheit ought to continuously be the insides flame broil temperature.
- On the off chance that the corn or wood chips run out, renew them. To induce a light brilliant color, smoke the angle for an extra 1 to 112 hours after turning.
- Serve nearby the cuts of grapefruit.

35. Maple syrup salmon steaks

Prep time: 1 hour 5 mins | Serve: 4 | Calories: 308 kcal

Fixings

- ¼ container unadulterated maple syrup
- ¼ container mirin or white wine
- ¼ container low-sodium soy sauce
- Two tbsps. olive oil
- Juice of ½ lemon and pizzazz of 1 lemon
- Two tbsps. broken dark peppercorns
- 2 pounds of salmon steaks

Enlightening

- In a non-corrosive holder, combine the peppercorns, oil, maple syrup, mirin, soy sauce, and container. Steaks ought to be marinated for 30 minutes within the fridge.

- Fire up the flame broil.
- Salmon steaks ought to be taken out of the marinade, depleted, tapped dry, and the marinade ought to be spared. The steaks ought to be cooked for 4 minutes on one side and 4 minutes on the other, or until the steaks feel to some degree delicate to the touch. Flame broil for less time for uncommon meat and more time for well-done.
- Whereas the steaks are being turned, cook the marinade in a little pot over medium-high warm on a wood pellet smoker-grill until it bubbles, at that point decrease the warm and stew for 5 minutes. Cut the warm off right absent.
- Salmon steaks ought to be topped with sauce.

36. Columbia stream chinook with cherry balsamic sauce

Prep time: 25 mins | Serve: 4 | Calories: 30 kcal

Fixings

- 1 glass of new cherries
- Half glass angle or chicken stock
- ¼ container new thyme stemmed
- Two tbsps. brandy
- One tsp. new lemon juice
- Two tbsps. brown sugar
- 1½ teaspoons balsamic vinegar
- 1½–2 pounds salmon filets
- Lemon wedges

Enlightening

1. Fire up the grill. The cherries ought to be finely minced after three or four beats within the nourishment processor bowl.
2. Over medium warm on a wood pellet smoker-grill, stew the stock,

thyme, brandy, and lemon juice for 10 to 12 minutes, or until they have diminished by half.
3. When everything is adequately cooked, include the vinegar and brown sugar, blend, and stew for 2 to 3 minutes. Keep warm but expel from warm.
4. The salmon filets ought to be to some degree delicate to the touch. Put the salmon filets on the lubed barbecue and cook for 4 to 5 minutes. At that point, flip them over and cook for another 4 to 5 minutes.
5. Four servings ought to be made. Make pools of warmed sauce by scooping it into the four plates' centers. The salmon ought to be put quickly on the sauce.
6. With the lemon wedges, serve.

37. Hoisin-grilled coho

Prep time: 1 hour 8 mins | Serve: 4 | Calories: 178 kcal
Fixings

- Get-up-and-go of 1 lemon
- juice of ½ lemon
- ¼ container low-sodium soy sauce
- Two tbsps. broken dark peppercorns
- 2 pounds of coho filets
- Half glass hoisin sauce
- Chopped chives for embellish
- Chopped ruddy pepper for decorate

Informational

1. In a little bowl, combine the peppercorns, soy sauce, lemon get-up-and-go and juice.
2. 30 minutes ought to pass whereas the filets are marinated.
3. Fire up the flame broil.

4. The filets ought to be taken out of the marinade, depleted, and dried.
5. Apply half of the hoisin sauce on the coho's two sides with a seasoning brush.
6. For 4 minutes, sear the filets straightforwardly over the fire. Turn, at that point brush with the remaining sauce. Cook for a advance 4 minutes, or until fair delicate to the touch. For uncommon or well-done angle, flame broil it for a shorter period of time.
7. Serve the angle promptly after isolating it among four dishes and including the chives and ruddy peppers as enhancements.

38. Salmon and boletus kebabs

Prep time: 1 hour 38 mins | Serve: 4 | Calories: 209 kcal

Fixings

- ¼ glass olive oil
- ¼ glass parsley
- ¼ glass new thyme
- Two tbsps. lemon juice
- Two tbsps. dark pepper
- One tsp. salt
- One and a half pounds of salmon filets
- 1 to One and a half pounds of mushrooms
- 8 wooden sticks
- Lemon wedges

Informational

1. In a huge bowl, combine the oil, parsley, thyme, lemon juice, salt, and pepper.
2. Include the salmon pieces, completely combine, cover, and chill for an hour. Fire up the flame broil.
3. After taking the blend out of the cooler, hurl within the bits of

mushroom to equally disseminate the marinade. In a colander, deplete.
4. For eight kebabs, organize three pieces of salmon and three pieces of mushrooms on sticks in an substituting mold.
5. On an oiled barbecue, put the damp sticks, and cook for four minutes.
6. When the filets feel to some degree soft to the touch, turn them over and cook for another 4 minutes.
7. On each plate, orchestrate two sticks and a lemon cut.

39. Flame broiled wild lord salmon with smoked lobster–tarragon

beurre blanc Prep time: 45 mins | Serve: 4-6 | Calories: 260 kcal

Fixings

- 1 lobster,
- 1 ¾ pounds
- Half container dissolved butter
- Juice of ½ lemon
- 2 pounds of salmon filets
- ¼ glass ruddy onion
- Two tbsps. white vinegar
- Two tbsps. water
- ¼ container overwhelming cream
- Two tbsps. new tarragon
- 4 tbsps. butter
- Salt and dark pepper
- Lemon wedges
- Blood Orange Serving of mixed greens

Enlightening

1. Set up a grill for smoking nourishment. On a huge chopping board,

flip the lobster onto its back. Make a cut with a sharp cut nearly to the tip of the tail's center without cutting through the shell. Open the depression by carefully part separated the tail along with your hands.
2. Butter and lemon juice ought to be sprinkled into the depth.
3. Put the lobster over the smoke dish on the flame broil with its back confronting up. When the meat feels firm to the touch, near the cover and smoke it for around 25 minutes. The lobster must not be turned over.
4. Utilizing tongs, take the lobster from the flame broil. Whereas saving the coral and its fluids within the fridge, exchange to a chopping board and expel the substance from the tail and claws.
5. Cut the meat into 3/4-inch pieces, at that point chill until required.
6. On a wood pellet barbecue, over medium-high warm on a wood pellet smoker-grill, bring the onions, vinegar, and water to a bubble. At that point, lower the warm and stew the blend for 3 to 4 minutes, or until it has decreased by around half.
7. Blend within the cream and tarragon, and cook for 1–2 minutes, or until the fluid is decreased by half.
8. Once the butter has softened, expel the skillet from the warm and whisk in each piece until smooth.
9. Return the fluid to the container after straining it through a cheesecloth or strainer.
10. The lobster substance ought to be taken out of the ice chest and put aside.
11. Lay the salmon on the hot side of the barbecue and re-heat it. Cook for a encourage 4 to 5 minutes after turning, or until the nourishment feels marginally delicate to the touch. After evacuating the salmon from the warm, put it on a warming rack or take off it alone.
12. Blend and increment the warm to medium-high after including the lobster pieces and liquids to the pan with the beurre Blanc. For 3 to 4 minutes, stew, secured, mixing frequently, or until the lobster substance is well warmed.
13. Put the salmon on warmed plates, cut each piece into serving-size

pieces, and best with beurre whiten. Serve the Blood Orange Serving of mixed greens right absent.

40. Flame broiled halibut in coconut drain and soy sauce

Prep time: 22 mins| Serve: 4 | Calories: 115 kcal

Fixings

- 4 halibut steaks,
- One tbsp. vegetable oil
- 4–6 cloves of garlic
- ¼ container ginger
- ¼ glass jalapeño peppers
- 1–2 anchovy filets
- Three-fourth container chicken stock
- Half container coconut drain
- 1/3 container tomato sauce
- ¼ glass dim soy sauce
- Naturally ground dark pepper
- ½ tomato, diced
- One tbsp. unadulterated maple syrup
- Two glasses of rice noodles or wheat noodles
- One tbsp. sesame oil
- 6–8 huge scallions
- Lemon wedges

Informational

1. Fire up the flame broil. Halibut ought to be barbecued for around three-quarters as long as wanted, or 3 to 4 minutes on each side, and after that kept warm on the grill's warming rack.
2. Garlic, ginger, jalapenos, and anchovies are sautéed in oil in a huge

container or wok over medium warm on a wood pellet smoker-grill for 3 to 4 minutes.
3. Include the stock, coconut drain, tomato sauce, soy sauce, and dark pepper to taste; stew for 7 to 8 minutes or until the fluid has diminished by half over medium warm on a wood pellet smoker barbecue.
4. Cook for a advance three to four minutes after including the diced tomato.
5. The noodles ought to be warmed through in sesame oil. Blend in generally a third of the pan's sauce after including it.
6. The remaining sauce ought to be included to the skillet with the warmed, cooked halibut steaks. Spoon the sauce over the steaks and blend to coat. Stew the steaks for one to two minutes or until well-coated.
7. The halibut ought to be topped with scallions and served with noodles and lemon wedges.

41. Lemon sorbet–glazed mahi-mahi

Prep time: 23 mins | Serve: 4 | Calories: 244 kcal

Fixings

- Two glasses of solidified lemon sorbet
- Juice of 1 huge lemon and pizzazz of 1 huge lemon
- 2 pounds mahi-mahi filets, 1 inch thick
- Chopped new cilantro for embellish

Enlightening

1. Fire up the flame broil. On a 4-quart pan or huge pot over medium-high warm on a wood pellet smoker-grill in a wood pellet barbecue, dissolve the sorbet for 4 to 5 minutes.
2. Include the lemon juice and half of the get-up-and-go, diminish the warm to a stew for roughly 8 minutes, and after that decrease by

one-third.
3. Take the nourishment off the stove and take off it to cool.
4. Spoon half of the cooled sauce over the filets, flipping them to cover them as you are doing so.
5. Put the steaks on the barbecue, at that point cook them for four to five minutes.
6. Cook for another five minutes or until the angle is firm to the touch, at that point turn it over and brush the remaining sauce on best.
7. Include the remaining lemon get-up-and-go and cilantro as embellish.

42. Fish kebabs

Prep time: 15 mins | Serve: 4 | Calories: 150 kcal

Fixings

- ¼ container lemon juice
- One tbsp. olive oil
- Two tbsps. dried marjoram
- Two tbsps. dried oregano
- Two tbsps. dried thyme
- Half tsp. ocean salt
- One tbsp. dark pepper
- 16 pieces of fish filets
- 24 pieces of green chime pepper
- 24 pieces of ruddy chime pepper
- 24 pieces of ruddy onion
- 16 cherry tomatoes
- 6 wooden sticks

Informational

1. Fire up the barbecue. Combine the lemon juice, oil, marjoram, oregano, thyme, salt, and pepper in a huge blending bowl. Hurl the

angle chunks with the peppers, onions, tomatoes, and other fixings.
2. As before long as all four sticks are full, interchange setting a bit of angle, a green pepper, a ruddy pepper, and an onion on each stick. Put eight cherry tomatoes on each two sticks. Put aside.
3. Put all of the sticks on an oiled flame broil, barring the one with tomatoes. The tomato sticks ought to be included to the flame broil and turned after 4 to 5 minutes. Angle kebabs ought to be flame broiled for a encourage 4 to 5 minutes, or until the angle feels firm to the touch, at that point evacuated. Cut the flame broiling time in half for fish that's medium-rare. After five minutes, expel the tomato kebabs.
4. Serve each guest one angle stick and four tomatoes after evacuating the tomatoes from their sticks.

43. Dark cod with stamped orange sorbet sauce

Prep time: 46 mins | Serve: 4 | Calories: 50 kcal

Fixings

- One and a half mugs of orange sorbet
- Half glass finely chopped new mint
- Juice of 1 huge orange also get-up-and-go
- One and a half pounds of dark cod filets

Enlightening

1. Fire up the flame broil. On a wood pellet barbecue, liquefy the sorbet in a 4-quart pan over medium-high warm on a wood pellet smoker flame broil.
2. Include the orange juice, mint, and 50 percent of the pizzazz. Cook revealed for 7 to 8 minutes, or until diminished by one-third, over medium warm on a wood pellet smoker barbecue. Set alone for cooling.

3. Spoon the sauce over the filets after setting them in a shallow dish.
4. Turn and coat totally. 30 minutes ought to be went through on cooling.
5. The filets ought to be taken out of the marinade and set on the flame broil. 4 minutes to cook. Brush more marinade on beat as you turn.
6. Cook for a encourage 4 minutes, or until the salmon chips effectively when tried.
7. Serve with the remaining orange get-up-and-go as a decorate after partitioning into four break even with servings.

44. Tilapia and coffeehouse stuffing

Prep time: 15 mins | Serve: 4 | Calories: 230 kcal

Fixings

- 2 bagels, cut into little pieces
- 1 scone, broken into pieces
- 1 croissant, broken into pieces
- ¼ little ruddy onion, coarsely chopped
- 1 medium-sized orange, cut into chunks
- 4 huge eggs Salt and dark pepper
- 4 pieces of aluminum thwart
- 2 pounds tilapia,
- 1 inch thick, cut into four break even with pieces
- 1 lemon, quartered

Enlightening

1. Fire up the flame broil. For 10 to 15 seconds, or until the fixings are well combined but not puréed, beat the bagel, scone, croissant, onion, orange chunks, eggs, salt, and pepper within the bowl of a nourishment processor. This may require to be completed in two or three clumps. In a dish, set the stuffing aside.
2. The four distinctive thwart pieces ought to be spread separated. Put a

cut of tilapia on each and spread the stuffing over each filet in a layer that is 12 inches thick (you'll require around a glass for each). Deliver each of them a lemon quarter's worth of juice. On the off chance that you've got any remaining stuffing, you will solidify it for afterward utilize. to ingest a dim lager, like India Pale Brew The foil's beat ought to be squeezed together. The thwart bundles ought to be put on a flame broil set to tall warm. For around 10 minutes, cook.

3. Check to see in case the filling is adequately cooked; on the off chance that not, return to the barbecue for an extra 4–5 minutes (whereas delicately turning over).
4. For a more happy appearance, expel from the flame broil and let the visitors open the bundles and take the substance out on their possess.

45. Fish steaks and blood oranges in thwart

Prep time: 1hr 10 mins | Serve: 4 | Calories: 191 kcal

Fixings

- 4 fish steaks, 6–8 ounces each1
- 1/3 glass low-sodium soy sauce
- Juice of 1 new blood orange
- ¼ glass finely chopped new ginger
- Two tbsps. new lime juice
- Two tbsps. immaculate maple syrup
- Salt and dark pepper
- Get-up-and-go of 1 blood orange
- 8 blood orange cuts

Enlightening

1. In a huge blending bowl, combine the fish steaks, soy sauce, orange juice, ginger, lime juice, and maple syrup. Combine, cover, and chill for around 30 minutes. Fire up the barbecue.

2. Expel four 12 by 12-inch pieces of aluminum thwart from the roll.
3. Take the fish steaks out of the marinade and orchestrate one on each thwart square. Sprinkle each with salt and pepper, at that point best with two orange cuts and orange get-up-and-go. The thwart is safely creased together.
4. Barbecue for 4 to 5 minutes, at that point flip it over and cook it for an extra 5 minutes, or until it feels firm to the touch.
5. Each thwart bundle ought to be opened and served right absent.

46. Barbecued fish burgers

Prep time: 24 mins | Serve: 4 | Calories: 230 kcal

Fixings

- One and a half pounds of new fish
- 2 eggs, beaten
- 4–6 little gherkins or cornichons
- Salt
- One tsp. dark pepper
- One tbsp. olive oil
- Half glass finely chopped sweet white onion
- Two glasses of new corn
- ¼ glass dry white wine
- Juice 1 lemon and pizzazz of that lemon
- 1½ tablespoons dill
- Lemony Corn Salsa

Informational

1. Fire up the barbecue. Flame broil the fish for three to four minutes on the lubed grind. Barbecue the angle for a encourage 3 to 4 minutes, or until it starts to drop somewhat.
2. Cool after expelling. With a enormous fork, pound the eggs, gherkins,

salt, and pepper into the broken-up fish in a expansive blending bowl. Put aside.
3. In a wood pellet flame broil, warm the oil in a huge pot over mediumhigh warm on a wood pellet smoker flame broil. When the onion is delicate, include it and cook for 2 to 3 minutes. For 4 to 5 minutes, include the corn, wine, lemon juice, and dill. Get freed of the warm.
4. Blend the fish with the fluid and get-up-and-go well. Make four patties out of the blend. Put the patties in a wire-mesh bushel over the flame broil or on an oiled, punctured pizza dish. The patties ought to be brilliant brown and strong to the touch after 3 to 4 minutes of browning.
5. Serve with the Lemony Corn Salsa on toasted cheeseburger buns.

47. Curried barbecued pompano

Prep time: 20 mins | Serve: 4 | Calories: 72 kcal

Fixings

- One tbsp. olive oil
- 1 medium onion, finely chopped
- 4–5 cloves garlic, finely chopped
- One tbsp. finely chopped galangal
- Half glass of light coconut drain
- 2 sticks lemongrass
- One tsp. chili powder
- One tsp. curry powder
- One tsp. ground turmeric
- Half tsp. ground cinnamon
- One and a half pounds pompano filets, almost 1 inch thick
- Juice of ½ lemon
- Lemon wedges

Informational

1. On a wood pellet barbecue, warm the oil in a expansive dish over medium-high warm on a wood pellet smoker flame broil. For 3 to 4 minutes, sauté the onion, garlic, and galangal.
2. Lemongrass, chili powder, curry powder, turmeric, and cinnamon ought to all be included. Cook for roughly 5 minutes or until the fluid has been cut in half. Low-heat setting.
3. Fire up the flame broil. Put the filets on a flame broil that has been gently lubed, cover with lemon juice, and cook for 4 to 5 minutes. When the angle feels firm to the touch, turn it over and cook for a encourage 4 to 5 minutes.
4. The filets ought to be taken off the flame broil, secured with warm sauce, partitioned into four parts, and served right absent with lemon wedges.

48. Striped bass with cattail shoots and morels

Prep time: 17 mins | Serve: 4 | Calories: 80 kcal

Fixings

- 8–10 cattail shoots, green tops expelled
- 6–8 morels, cleaned and trimmed
- Half container olive oil furthermore One tbsp.
- Half container of new thyme stemmed and cleaned
- Half tsp. salt
- One tsp. naturally ground dark pepper
- One and a half pounds striped bass filet
- Salt and dark pepper
- Two tbsps. butter
- Juice of 1 little lemon

Informational

1. Fire up the smoker flame broil. Cattails ought to have their harsh outside expelled; at that point, they ought to be cut askew like scallions. Put aside.
2. Set aside the morels after cutting them into bite-sized pieces.
3. In a little bowl, combine 12 glasses of the oil, thyme, salt, and pepper.
4. The bass filet ought to be coated with a seasoning brush or spoon some time recently being set on the barbecue.
5. Meanwhile, warm the remaining One tbsp. of oil and the butter in a skillet over medium warm on a wood pellet smoker-grill. Till the mushrooms are delicate, sauté the morels for 3 to 4 minutes. Diminish the warm, include the cattail shoots, and cook for an extra two to three minutes. Turn down the warm and remain cozy.
6. Flame broil the bass for 4 to 5 minutes, at that point flip it over and cook it for an extra 4 to 5 minutes, or until it feels firm to the touch.
7. Put on warmed plates after being isolated into four parts. Another to the bass, put a spoonful of cattails and morels. Include more salt and pepper to taste and sprinkle the lemon juice over the bass. Serve right absent.

49. Striped bass with curried shrimp sauce

Prep time: 33 mins | Serve: 4 | Calories: 190 kcal

Fixings

- 1 huge sweet white onion, finely chopped
- 3–4 garlic cloves, peeled
- Two tsps. finely chopped new ginger
- One tsp. chili powder
- 2½ tablespoons canola oil
- One and a half pounds of striped bass filets
- 1 medium tomato, diced1
- One tbsp. Shrimp Glue
- Juice of ½ lemon

- Cooked white rice

Enlightening

1. Within the bowl of a nourishment processor, beat the onion, garlic, ginger, and chili powder five or six times. Purée for 1 to 2 minutes, until smooth, scratching down the sides as essential.
2. In a wood pellet barbecue set to medium-high warm, warm the oil in a medium skillet. When thickened, include the puréed fixings, blend, lower the warm to moo, cover the dish, and stew for around 15 minutes.
3. Prepare a barbecue within the in the interim.
4. The filets ought to be cooked for three to four minutes on an oiled grind. Cook for a encourage 4 to 5 minutes or until the nourishment is firm. Go to the warming rack on the flame broil.
5. Cooking the tomatoes within the skillet for three to four minutes some time recently including the shrimp glue and mixing for a assist diminutive.
6. Include the filets to the skillet and cover with the sauce. Include the lemon juice, cover, hold up for one to two minutes, at that point turn off the warm.
7. Serve the angle promptly over white rice after partitioning it into four parts and topping each with sauce.

50. Bluefish with tomato and basil

Prep time: 40 mins | Serve: 4-6 | Calories: 156 kcal

Fixings

- 2 pounds of bluefish filets
- Juice of 2 limes and pizzazz of 1 lime
- Two tsps. ocean salt
- 4–5 medium tomatoes

- 1 container cleaned and coarsely chopped new basil
- ¼ container good-quality extra-virgin olive oil
- One tbsp. naturally ground pink and green peppercorns
- 3–4 garlic cloves, minced

Informational

1. Put the filets in a non-corrosive holder and include One tsp. of salt and Two tbsps. Of lime juice. 30 minutes ought to be went through cooling.
2. In a sizable blending bowl, combine the tomatoes, basil, oil, peppercorns, garlic, and get-up-and-go with the remaining Two tbsps of lime juice, One tsp. of salt, and the other fixings. Mix well and save.
3. Fire up the barbecue. Bluefish filets ought to be taken out of the marinade, depleted, and set on the smoker flame broil.
4. The angle ought to be firm to the touch after cooking the filets for 5 minutes on one side and 5 minutes on the other.
5. Put the filets on warmed plates, beat with sauce, and serve right absent.

51. Heated new wild sockeye salmon

Prep time: 15-20min | Serve: 6 | Calories: 14.5kcal
Fixings

- Two wild sockeye salmon filets, skin on
- Two tsps. Fish Flavoring
- Three-fourth tsp. ancient inlet flavoring

Informational

1. Utilize cold water to wash salmon filets and dry them with paper towels.
2. Season the filets with a little number of flavors.

3. Set smoker-grill up for backhanded warm and warm any pellets to 400°F.
4. On a Teflon-coated fiberglass tangle or specifically on the flame broil grates, put the salmon skin-side down. Heat, the salmon for fifteen to twenty minutes or until it chips effectively with a fork.
5. Some time recently serving, let the salmon rest for five minutes.

52. Pacific rockfish

Prep time: 90min | Serve: 6 | Calories: 70 kcal

Fixings

- Four to seven Pacific rockfish filets
- Three tsps. simmered garlic
- 3 tsps. olive oil
- 2 tbsps. Creole Fish Flavoring

Enlightening

- Cover filets with olive oil and flavoring.
- Set your smoker flame broil up to 225°F.
- To keep the filets from following to the flame broil grates, put them on a non-stick container.
- The filets ought to be smoked for generally 90 minutes or till the substance effortlessly pieces with a fork.
- Earlier to serving, permit the filets to rest for five minutes.

53. Shrimp-stuffed tilapia

Prep time: 15-20min | Serve: 4 | Calories: 160kcal

Fixings

- 1½ teaspoons smoked paprika

- Five new, cultivated tilapia filets
- One and a half tsps. Fish Flavoring
- Two tbsps. extra-virgin olive oil

For stuffing:

- One pound shrimp
- Half glass mayonnaise
- 1 container Italian bread pieces
- One huge egg
- One tbsp. salted butter
- Two tsps. parsley
- One glass of ruddy onion
- One and a half tsps. salt and pepper

Informational

1. Make the filling with shrimp by finely chopping them.
2. Liquefy the butter in a utensil over medium-high fire, at that point sauté the ruddy onion for around 3 minutes, or until straightforward. Put aside and permit to warm up to room temperature.
3. In a sizable bowl, blend together the cooled sautéed onion, other fixings and shrimps.
4. The shrimp stuffing ought to be secured and kept within the cooler until required. Utilize the shrimp stuffing in two days.
5. Olive oil ought to be connected to the filets on both sides.
6. Put one-third of a glass of the stuffing on the back of each filet. The tilapia fillet's turn around shows ruddy striping.
7. Spread out the stuffing on the fillet's foot half. To keep the tilapia in put, overlap it in half and affix it with two or more toothpicks.
8. Tidy each filet with the Ancient Inlet flavoring or smoked paprika and fish flavoring.
9. Set your wood pellet smoker/grill up for circuitous warm and warm

any pellets to 400°F.
10. Put the stuffed filets on a barbecuing dish that's nonstick.
11. Till the tilapia pieces effectively and comes to an inner temperature of 145°F, prepare them for 30 to 45 minutes.
12. Some time recently serving, let the angle rest for five minutes.

54. Cold-hot smoked salmon

Prep time: 16hours | Serve: 6 | Calories: 30kcal

Fixings

- 5 pounds of new sockeye (ruddy), Chinook (Ruler), coho (silver), or
- Atlantic cultivated salmon filets
- 4 mugs Salmon and Trout Brine

Enlightening

1. Cut salmon filets into 3 to 4-inch square pieces so that they will smoke/cook at the same rate.
2. Put the salmon pieces into a 1-gallon food-grade plastic pack or bringing holder and refrigerate for 8 hours. Turn the salmon each 2 hours to form beyond any doubt it remains submerged.
3. Expel the salmon from the brine and delicately pat the pieces dry with a paper towel.
4. Air-dry the brined salmon within the fridge, uncovered, for 8 hours to permit the pellicle to make.
5. Set up your wood pellet barbecue or smoker for circuitous warm. Set up your pellet smoker flame broil for cold smoking in case your flame broil has the capability.
6. Put the salmon pieces on Teflon-coated fiberglass mats after evacuating them from the fridge.
7. Utilizing birch pellets, warm your wood pellet smoker/grill to 180°F.
8. Depending on the exterior temperature, a smoker-grill temperature

of 180°F ought to deliver cold smoke in your smoker box at 70° to 100°F.
9. Utilize the taking after smoker-grill temperatures to smoke the salmon, which ought to deliver the taking after smoke box temperatures:
10. Set point for the pellet smoker-grill at 180°F: Salmon ought to be smoked for an hour at a box temperature of 80 to 90 degrees. Set point for the pellet smoker-grill at 225°F: Salmon ought to be smoked for one hour at 110°F.
11. Set point for the pellet flame broil at 250 °F: Salmon ought to be smoked for two hours at 120°F.
12. Set point for the pellet smoker/grill at 350°F: Smoke salmon for 2 to 4 hours at 150° to 160° F.
13. The smoker box must keep up a temperature underneath 175°F.
14. Keep smoking the angle until it comes to a temperature of 145° Fall through its thickest locale.
15. Some time recently serving, take the salmon from the flame broil and let it rest for ten minutes.
16. Any remaining smoked salmon ought to be vacuum-sealed and solidified for up to six months. Smoked salmon tastes way better when vacuum-sealed and solidified since of the birch smoked flavor.

55. Hot-smoked teriyaki fish

Prep time: 5-7hours | Serve: 6 | Calories: 120kcal

Fixings

- 2 (10-ounce) new fish steaks
- Two mugs of Mr. Yoshida's Conventional Teriyaki Marinade and
- Cooking Sauce, or any other teriyaki marinade

Enlightening

1. The fish ought to be cut into cuts that are consistently 2 inches thick.

2. Put the marinade and fish cuts in a 1-gallon sealable plastic pack, and set the pack on a shallow heating dish in case it spills. Turn the fish each hour whereas letting it sit within the ice chest for three hours.
3. Expel the fish from the marinadeafter three hours and rapidly dry it with a paper towel.
4. Until pellicles shape, let the fish air-dry, revealed, within the fridge for 2 to 4 hours.
5. Utilize birch pellets to preheat your wood pellet smoker/grill to 180°F and set it up for circuitous cooking.
6. The fish ought to be smoked for an hour either on a Teflon-coated fiberglass tangle or straightforwardly on the flame broil grates.

56. Smoked salmon & Dungeness crab chowder

Prep time: 70 min | Serve: 6 | Calories: 50kcal

Fixings

- 4 gallons furthermore 5 mugs of water
- 3 new Dungeness crabs
- 1 container shake salt
- 3 mugs new Smoked Salmon
- 3 mugs sea clam juice
- Five celery stalks, diced
- 1 little yellow onion, diced
- 2 huge reddish brown potatoes, peeled and diced
- One can of sweet corn, depleted
- One bundle of clam chowder dry soup blend
- Four bacon cuts, cooked and disintegrated

Enlightening

1. Shake salt and 4 gallons of water ought to rapidly come to a bubble. New Dungeness crabs ought to be included to the bubbling water.

Cover the crabs and bubble them for 20 minutes when the water returns to a bubble.

2. Crabs ought to be taken out of the water and cleared out to cool. Once they have cooled, appropriately clean the crabs and evacuate the meat from the shells.
3. Crisply smoked salmon ought to be chipped.
4. Bring the clam juice, remaining 5 glasses of water, diced celery, diced potatoes, and diced onion to a difficult bubble in a sizable, revealed pot over tall warm. After it bubbles, diminishes the warm to a medium stew, cover, and let the dish cook for 10 minutes.
5. To evacuate any protuberances, blend within the clam chowder or velvety potato blend after including the corn and some time recently bringing the blend back to a bubble.
6. Blend the chowder habitually whereas stewing on moo for 15 minutes.
7. Include the bacon disintegrates five minutes some time recently serving.
8. Include 12 glasses of chipped smoked salmon and 12 mugs of Dungeness crabmeat to the beat of each bowl of chowder as decorate.

57. Birch wood–smoked boned trout

Prep time: 4 hours | Serve: 6 | Calories: 100kcal

Fixings

- Four new boneless entirety trout
- Five glasses of Salmon and Trout Brine

Enlightening

1. Put the brine and the trout in a 2-gallon sealable plastic sack or brining holder. Refrigerate the pack for two hours, moving the angle each 30 minutes to keep it submerged, and put it on a shallow dish in case it spills. In case there's a spill, put the sack in a little dish.

2. Trout ought to be taken out of the brine and dried with a paper towel.
3. To assist the pellicle shape, let the brined angle discuss dry for two hours in the fridge, revealed.
4. Set up your wood pellet barbecue or smoker for circuitous warm. Set up your pellet smoker barbecue for cold smoking in case your barbecue has the capability.
5. With birch pellets, warm the barbecue to 180 degrees. Depending on the exterior temperature, a smoker-grill temperature of 180°F ought to give a cold-smoke temperature in your smoker box of 70°F to 100°F.
6. The trout was cold-smoked for 90 minutes.
7. Exchange the cold-smoked boned angle to the wood pellet smoker-grill range after 90 minutes, and raise the temperature of the flame broil to 225°F.
8. Cook the angle until it comes to an inside temperature of 145°F at its thickest point.
9. Some time recently serving, take the trout from the barbecue and let it rest for five minutes.

10

Cooking with Clay Pots and Cast Iron Smokers and Grills

1. Tiella of sheep with fennel, pecorino, and potatoes

Prep time: 60min | Serve: 4-6 | Calories: 40kcal

Fixings

- Two pounds incline boneless sheep bear
- One container of new bread pieces
- Two narrows clears out
- Two mugs of entirety drain
- One-fourth tsp. fennel seeds
- Half glass parsley
- Two cloves of garlic, cut, and 1 clove of entirety
- Salt and pepper
- Five tbsps. olive oil
- Two and a half pounds of bubbled potatoes
- One sprig rosemary
- One ruddy onion, cut
- Flour for tidying
- Three-fourth container ground cheese

Informational

1. In a sizable pot, combine the narrows takes off, drain, sheep, garlic, fennel and rosemary. For four to six hours, cover and take off in a cool area. In a wood smoker barbecue, get ready a medium-hot fire (425°F). In a preparing dish, warm Two tbsps of the olive oil over medium warm. Sauté the onion for 10 to 15 minutes, or until it turns pale brown. The sheep ought to be taken out of the drain shower and tapped dry with paper towels. Keep the drain and aromatics on hand. Sprinkle a few flour over the sheep after flavoring it with salt and pepper.
2. Over medium warm, include the sheep and brown it for around 10 minutes on all sides. Peel the potatoes and cut them crosswise into

1/8-inchthick pieces as you hold up. Set aside a few drain and drench the potatoes in it. Include a bit of additional salt and pepper to the meat once it has browned.

3. Put the meat and onion in a side dish. Evacuate any oil by tilting the container.
4. To expel the browned parts from the pan's foot, include a couple of tablespoons of water and mix. Put the fluid aside. The garlic clove ought to be rubbed inside an oven-safe 212-quart clay dough puncher some time recently being gently lubed. Spread the onion cuts around the stove. Whereas preserving the drain, deplete the potatoes on best of the onions, put one-half of the depleted potatoes and season with pepper. All of the parsley, half of the cheese, and half of the bread scraps ought to be conveyed over the meat in one layer. On best, organize the extra depleted potatoes.
5. Pour the drain blend over the potatoes after including the container fluid that was spared. The potatoes will have a few zone for development in case you press down on them. Over moo warm, gradually bring the skillet to a bubble for around 15 minutes. The remaining two tbsps. Olive oil, bread scraps, and cheese ought to all be connected to the potatoes' best. The dish ought to be freely secured with aluminum thwart and put on the oven's foot rack to prepare for roughly 15 minutes.
6. Move to a cooler range of the broiler (around 325°F) and carry on heating for anextra 114 hours. Cook for an extra 30 minutes, or until brown and dried up, after expelling the thwart. After 30 minutes of rest, serve warm.

2. Soufflé casserole of chard, goat cheese, and new herbs

Prep time: 60min | Serve: 8 | Calories: 40kcal

Fixings

- Two mugs of ground Parmesan cheese
- 1 little bunch of chard takes off
- Two tbsps. olive oil
- ¼ container cut shallots
- 1 container chopped arugula takes off
- One tbsp. New marjoram takes off
- One tbsp. new mint takes off, torn into little pieces
- Legitimate salt and finely ground white pepper
- Béchamel sauce
- One and a half mugs of low-fat drain
- 1 huge cove leaf
- 1 shallot, cut
- Two tbsps. unsalted butter
- 3 green onions (white portion as it were), meagerly cut
- Two tbsps. all-purpose flour
- Half tsp. Dijon mustard
- Legitimate salt and naturally ground white pepper
- 4 huge egg yolks, beaten
- 1 container disintegrated new goat cheese
- 6 expansive egg whites
- ¼ container minced new flat-leaf parsley

Informational

1. In a wood smoker-grill or cooker, plan a medium warm fire (375°F). Butter and Parmesan cheese are sprinkled over an 8-cup gratin dish.
2. The chard stems ought to be expelled, diced, and kept aside. The chard

takes off ought to surrender generally Two glasses when chopped.
3. The diced chard stems and shallots ought to be sautéed in a cast-iron skillet with olive oil over medium warm for 5 to 7 minutes or until delicate. Include salt and pepper to taste, along side the chard clears out, arugula, and herbs. Greens ought to be sautéed for 5 minutes to shrivel them. Turn off the warm and take off the pot alone.
4. In a pot over medium warm, combine the drain, inlet leaf, and shallot to make the béchamel sauce. After bringing to a moo bubble, turn off the warm and let the blend soak for 15 minutes. Toss absent the shallots and cove leaf.
5. Put aside. In a pot over medium warm, liquefy the butter. For one miniature, include the green onions and sauté. Mix for three minutes after including the flour. Include the Dijon mustard and blend. Mix within the soaks drain slowly, as you need the sauce to be thick. Include salt and pepper to taste. Turn off the warm and take off the pot alone.
6. Egg yolks and béchamel sauce ought to be combined. Include the shriveled greens along side a squeeze of salt and pepper. Incorporate 1/4 container of goat cheese. The egg whites ought to be beaten until firm; reflexive crests frame in a huge bowl. Overlap the primary half of the egg whites into the bechamel blend some time recently including the moment. Put the soufflé blend in the dish that has been arranged.
7. Include the remaining goat cheese and parsley over the best. Put on a grind within the stove and heat for 25 to 30 minutes, or until brilliant and difficult to the touch. Serve warm.

3. Crab gratin with potatoes, leeks, and spinach

Prep time: 60min | Serve: 8 | Calories: 40kcal

Fixings

- ¼ container olive oil
- 3 little leeks (white portion as it were), cut crosswise and washed

- 8 ounces new or solidified crabmeat, flushed and depleted
- Two tsps. Dijon mustard
- ¼ teaspoon chili powder
- ⅛ teaspoon white Worcestershire sauce
- 1 (10-ounce) bundle solidified chopped spinach, defrosted and depleted
- Two tsps. chopped new tarragon
- Half tsp. legitimate salt
- Squeeze of crisply ground white pepper
- Mornay sauce
- Two tbsps. unsalted butter
- Two tbsps. flour
- Two glasses drain
- One tsp. naturally ground nutmeg
- One tsp. ground lemon get-up-and-go
- Half tsp. salt
- ⅛ Teaspoon naturally ground white pepper
- 1 container destroyed Gruyere cheese
- Two tbsps. dry sherry
- Half glass of toasted bread scraps
- Three-fourth glass destroyed Gruyere cheese
- 2 pounds unpeeled ruddy or Yukon Gold potatoes, exceptionally meagerly cut
- Legitimate salt and crisply ground white pepper

Informational

1. In a wood smoker-grill or cooker, plan a medium warm fire (375°F). Leeks ought to be sautéed for approximately 7 minutes or until shriveled in a little skillet with half the olive oil warmed over medium warm. Crabmeat, mustard, chili powder, and Worcestershire sauce are combined in a bowl; set absent.
2. The spinach ought to be sautéed within the remaining olive oil until the larger part of the dampness has vanished over medium warm.

Include the tarragon, white pepper, and salt after stirring.

3. Mix within the crab blend after turning the warm off.
4. Dissolve the butter in a skillet over medium warm to get ready the Mornay sauce. Include the flour once it stops frothing, and stew for 3 minutes whereas blending. Salt, pepper, nutmeg, drain, and get-up-and-go ought to all be whisked in.
5. Include the sherry and Gruyère. Until thickened, cook whereas blending.
6. Take the dish off the warm, at that point put it over a container of stewing water.
7. Combine the bread scraps and Half a glass of the Gruyère in a little bowl. Apply olive oil to an 8-cup clay casserole or gratin dish. Clean the bread scrap blend over the dish's foot. One-third of the potatoes ought to be utilized to line the dish with the covering longwise cuts.
8. Blend the crab blend with one-third of the Mornay sauce. Sprinkle the potatoes within the gratin dish with a small salt and pepper, at that point best with half of the crab blend.
9. Third more of the potatoes ought to be included some time recently the remaining crab stuff is secured. The extra potatoes are layered on best of the remaining Mornay sauce.
10. For 25 to 30 minutes, heat. 14 container Gruyère ought to be put on beat, and the potatoes ought to be prepared for 10 minutes or until the cheese has browned. Some time recently serving, evacuate fromthe broiler and permit stand for 10 minutes.

4. Three-cheese prepared penne with pancetta

Prep time: 60min | Serve: 6 | Calories: 140kcal
Fixings

- Three-fourth glass furthermore Two tbsps. ground pecorino Romano cheese
- 2½ mugs overwhelming cream

- Ground get-up-and-go of 1 lemon
- Three-fourth glass destroyed Italian fontina cheese
- ¼ glass ricotta cheese
- Puree from 1 head of broiled garlic
- One tsp. legitimate salt
- Half tsp. ruddy pepper drops
- ¼ glass olive oil
- 4 ounces pancetta, chopped
- 1 container new bread pieces
- Two tbsps. new thyme clears out
- 1 pound penne rigate pasta
- 4 tbsps. chopped new flat-leaf parsley for decorate

Informational

1. Plan a medium warm fire (400°F) in a wood smoker-grill or cooker. Liberally butter an 8-cup casserole and clean it with the Two tbsps.
2. Pecorino Romano. Combine the cream, lemon pizzazz, remaining Threefourth glass pecorino Romano, the fontina and ricotta cheeses, pureed garlic, salt, and ruddy pepper drops in a expansive bowl.
3. Warm the olive oil in a little skillet over medium warm and sauté the pancetta until fresh. Employing a opened spoon, exchange to paper towels to deplete, saving the fat. Coarsely disintegrate the pancetta.
4. Combine the bread scraps and thyme in a little bowl and dampen with the saved cooking fat from the pancetta. Softly salt. In a expansive pot of salted bubbling water, cook the pasta for 10 minutes. Deplete and include to the cream mixture.
5. Hurl within the disintegrated pancetta (or take off to sprinkle over the breadcrumb topping, in case you select). Fill the arranged dish with the pasta mixture and sprinkle on the bread-crumb blend. Prepare within the customary stove or on a grind within the wood smoker-grill until the pasta is bubbly, brilliant brown, and a bit fresh on the edges, 15 to 20 minutes. Serve hot, embellished with parsley.

5. Eggplant, ruddy pepper, and goat cheese gratin

Prep time: 60min | Serve: 6-8 | Calories: 140kcal

Fixings

- One and a half pounds little globe eggplants, cut into ⅓-inch-thick cuts
- Two tbsps. olive oil
- Salt, for sprinkling, additionally ½ teaspoon
- 2 ruddy chime peppers
- 3 medium tomatoes
- 1 head garlic
- Two tbsps. new thyme clears out
- Half tsp. herbs de Provence (discretionary)
- Squeeze of sugar
- Squeeze of naturally ground dark pepper
- 1 glass toasted bread scraps
- Two tbsps. almond meal1
- 12 ounces new goat cheese, daintily cut
- ⅓ container oil-cured olives, smoker-grilled and split
- Half container new entire flat-leaf parsley takes off
- 2 huge eggs
- One and a half cups of Greek goat's drain yogurt
- 2 little squeezes of saffron strings, doused in many tablespoons of hot water

Informational

1. In a wood smoker-grill or cooker, prepare a medium warm fire (400°F). Either instantly on the wood smoker barbecue or on the cooktop, sauté the eggplants within the olive oil in a skillet over medium warm.
2. Cook until delicate, approximately 2 minutes on each side. To deplete, put the eggplant aside on paper towels. Each side with a small salt.

The red peppers, tomatoes, and garlic ought to be put on the foot of the broiler or cooker, near to the hot ashes, whereas there are some hot coals within the fire. As the skins rankle and burn, pivot them frequently.

3. Cook for 5 to 7 minutes for tomatoes and 10 minutes for peppers, or until the skins are totally broiled.
4. Cook thegarlic for 5 to 7 minutes, or until the cloves are delicate and the peel has browned to some degree. Crush the skins off of the simmered garlic cloves and utilize a fork to pound the cloves into a glue in a little bowl. The simmered peppers and tomatoes ought to be put in a bowl, secured with plastic wrap, and permitted to sweat for ten minutes. The tomatoes and peppers ought to have their skins removed. Remove the stems and seeds from the peppers, at that point chop them into pieces that are nearly the same measure as the eggplant and set them aside. Cut the tomatoes open, at that point utilize your file finger or a delicate crush to evacuate the seeds. In conjunction with the pounded garlic, herbs, herbs, sugar, 12 teaspoon salt, and pepper, dice the tomatoes.
5. Clean the bread pieces and almond supper with olive oil some time recently setting them in a clay casserole. Keep the remaining bread crumb mixture aside. One-third of the tomato blend is used to line the casserole.
6. Cuts of eggplant, goat cheese, ruddy pepper, and bread scraps are at that point included, taken after by half of the olives. Each layer ought to be prepared.
7. The tomato combination, parsley, and goat cheese served as the ultimate embellish. Rehash the layering prepare.
8. Combine the yogurt, eggs, and Half tsps. Salt in a bowl. Pour the custard over the complete casserole after blending within the saffron alcohol. In a wood smoker barbecue, prepare the casserole for 25 minutes or until the best is bubbling and brown. Some time recently partitioning into parts and serving, turn off the warm and permit the dish to stand for 10 minutes.

6. Moroccan tagine of halibut, potatoes, and artichokes

Prep time: 1hour 15min | Serve: 4 | Calories: 140kcal

Fixings

- Sauce
- One 1Half container of new cilantro clears out
- Half glass of new flat-leaf parsley clears out
- 4 cloves garlic
- Half onion
- ¼ container extra-virgin olive oil
- Two tbsps. naturally pressed lemon juice
- One tsp. naturally ground dark pepper
- One tsp. paprika
- Half tsp. ground cumin
- ¼ teaspoon ground cinnamon
- One tsp. salt
- 4 (5-ounce) halibut, ocean bass, genuine cod, or other firm angle steaks, each
- cut ½ to ¾ inch thick
- 8 child artichokes
- Two tbsps. naturally pressed lemon juice
- Two tsps. extra-virgin olive oil
- 2 unpeeled potatoes, exceptionally daintily cut
- Salt and dark pepper
- 16 oil-cured dark olives
- Half glass canned Italian plum tomatoes, chopped and juice saved,
- or 2 ready ruddy tomatoes, daintily cut
- ¼ glass chopped new cilantro clears out
- ¼ glass chopped new flat-leaf parsley clears out

Enlightening

1. In a wood smoker-grill or cooker, get ready a medium warm fire (350°F). Mix all the fixings together in a blender to make the sauce until they frame a glue. In case fundamental, include a small additional olive oil. On the other hand, finely chop the parsley, onion, garlic, and cilantro some time recently combining with the rest sauce components. Coat the angle on both sides with the remaining sauce. For at slightest one hour or up to three hours, cover and chill. The flavors will be able to merge as a result.
2. Cut off and dispose of the artichoke stems. Up until the base of the takes off, which are pale yellow, break off the external takes off. Kill the best third of the clears out. At the base, smooth the spiked edges. The artichokes ought to be quartered the long way. The artichokes and lemon juice ought to be combined in a bowl of water. The potatoes ought to begin with be included to the foot of the tajine with olive oil. Salt and pepper the potatoes with a squeeze of each. The angle is put on best of the potatoes. Put the angle within the center of the artichokes and olives.
3. Final but not slightest, include generally Half container of the diced tomatoes and their juices on best of the remaining sauce. Sprinkle on a few salt and pepper. Include the cilantro, parsley, and a small more salt and pepper on beat to total the dish. For approximately 1 hour and 15 minutes, broil the potatoes secured within the stove until fork-tender. Bring the tajine to the table and raise the cover to serve. Each individual should be given a chunk of angle, a few artichokes, olives, and potatoes employing a serving spoon or spatula.

7. Prepared risotto with asparagus and Swiss chard

Prep time: 60min | Serve: 6 | Calories: 140kcal
Fixings

- Two tbsps. olive oil
- 1 onion, finely chopped Squeeze of legitimate salt, additionally

- 1½ teaspoons
- One and a half mugs Arborio rice
- 2½ glasses vegetable or chicken stock
- Half container of dry white wine
- 1 expansive bunch of chard takes off, chopped, stems cut out and saved (around 4 glasses)
- 1 pound lean asparagus lances, trimmed and cut into 2-inch inclining cuts
- ¼ teaspoon naturally ground nutmeg
- One and a half glasses ground Parmesan cheese

Enlightening

1. In a wood smoker-grill or cooker, plan a medium warm fire (375°F). A 6-quart Dutch broiler or casserole dish ought to be warmed with olive oil over medium warm. Include the onion and a sprint of salt, and cook for three minutes, or until the onion is straightforward. Blending to equally disseminate the oil, include the rice. Include the stock, wine, chard stems and takes off, asparagus, nutmeg, and 1 1Two tbsps. Of salt after mixing.
2. Put within the broiler without a cover, at that pointstew. After 5 minutes, smooth the beat and blend in half the cheese.
3. The remaining cheese ought to be sprinkled on beat before the aluminum thwart is cozily secured. Reposition the preparing skillet to the center of the oven's floor. Heat for approximately 20 minutes, or until the rice is delicate and has doused up most of the fluid. Whereas not soupy, the rice ought to be wet. For the ultimate 10 minutes of heating, take the foil off to induce a flawless brilliant hull and smoky flavor. Serve right absent.

8. White Tuscan beans with frankfurter

Prep time: 60min | Serve: 6 | Calories: 140kcal

Fixings

- 3 mugs dried cannellini beans, flushed, picked over, and splashed overnight
- ½ pound Italian frankfurter of choice
- One tsp. legitimate salt
- 6 cloves garlic, daintily cut
- 1 (3-inch) sprig of rosemary
- ¼ container extra-virgin olive oil, furthermore more for sprinkling
- Two glasses of balsamic vinegar (discretionary)

Enlightening

1. In a wood smoker-grill or barbecue planned for cooking with round-about warm, make a medium-hot flame(350°F). Put the drenching beans in a sizable clay bean pot after depleting them. Include water until the beans are 2 inches over the surface. Bring to a bubble beneath cover within the stove or over backhanded warm on the barbecue. Put the wiener, cut side down, in a clay broiler, after cutting it in half longwise. Deplete after simmering in the stove until the fat has rendered. Then again, barbecue the frankfurter over tall warm.
2. Cut or break the cooked wiener into sensible pieces. Put aside. The beans ought to be salted, at that point moved to a cooler portion of the broiler or flame broil where they ought to be tenderly stewed for around an hour or until the beans begin to mollify. In case the beans are obvious over the decreased fluid, include more water. Include 1/4 container of olive oil, garlic, and rosemary. Once the beans are cooked through, and the garlic is delicate, cover the dish and proceed to cook, turning once in a while. On the off chance that all of the fluid has vanished, include extra water. The beans have to be fair scarcely

impudent. Evacuate the rosemary, at that point include 1 glass of the beans and purée until smooth in a nourishment processor. Combine the complete beans with the pureed beans. When the frankfurter is amazingly delicate, include it and proceed to cook. Meanwhile, warm the balsamic in a nonreactive pot to a stew. Cook for 20 to 25 minutes, or until decreased by generally two-thirds. After expelling the beans from the container, generously sprinkle olive oil over them. In case craved, sprinkle warmed dishes with the balsamic decrease.

9. Bouillabaisse

Prep time: 60min | Serve: 8 | Calories: 140kcal

Fixings

- 4 glasses water
- 6 mugs of angle stock
- 12 ounces (16 to 20) shrimp within the shell
- Two tbsps. olive oil
- 1 yellow onion, chopped
- 3 stalks of celery, coarsely chopped
- 3 carrots, peeled and coarsely chopped
- 4 cloves garlic, minced
- Half container dry white wine or vermouth
- One tsp. legitimate salt
- Half tsp. new ground white pepper
- Half tsp. saffron strings
- One tsp. new thyme clears out
- 2 inlet clears out
- 2½ pounds halibut, cod, or tilapia filets, cut into 1½-inch pieces
- 4 ounces scallops, depleted of fluid
- 1 dozen mussels, scoured
- Two tbsps. chopped new flat-leaf parsley

Informational

1. In a wood smoker-grill, stove, or flame broil, plan a medium-hot flame(350°F). In a stockpot, combine the water and stock; warm to a stew over coals or on the broiler floor of a wood smoker barbecue. Put the shrimp shells within the stockpot after shelling them. Keep warmed and set aside. On a flame broil grind or the floor of a wood smoker barbecue, warm the olive oil in a Dutch broiler over medium-high warm.
2. For five minutes, include the onion, celery, and carrots and sauté. For two minutes after including the garlic, sauté. Three-quarters of the stock ought to be included to the sautéed veggies once the shells have been expelled from the warm soup. Bring to a bubble the wine, together with the salt, pepper, saffron, thyme, and cove takes off. Stew for 15 minutes in a cooler portion of the broiler; expel the narrows clears out. Bring the blend back to a bubble, include the angle, and stew for five minutes.
3. Cook for 2 minutes after including the remaining fluid, scallops, and mussels. Three more minutes will be included after including the shrimp.
4. To taste and season as fundamental. For one miniature, gradually bring to a bubble. Unopened mussels ought to be tossed absent. Serve in dishes after including the parsley.

10. Two-bean pozole with cumin crème fraiche

Prep time: 60min | Serve: 8 | Calories: 140kcal

Fixings

- 2 ruddy chime peppers
- 2 poblano chili s
- 6 glasses vegetable stock
- Two tbsps. olive oil

- 2 onions, diced
- 4 carrots, peeled and diced
- 2 stalks of celery, diced Legitimate salt and naturally ground pepper
- 2½ mugs cooked Yellow Indian legacy beans, depleted
- 2½ mugs cooked Ojo de Cabra treasure beans, depleted
- 3 glasses cooked white hominy (canned or crisply made white pozole)
- 2 ancho chili s
- 6 cloves simmered garlic
- 1 (14½-ounce) can of smashed tomatoes, ideally fire-roasted
- Two tbsps. new thyme takes off
- One tbsp. Chopped new sage
- Two tbsps. Chopped new oregano, or Two tsps. dried Mexican oregano
- 1 container dry sherry
- New cilantro clears out, for decorate Cumin Crème Fraîche

Informational

1. In a wood smoker-grill or cooker, get ready a medium warm fire (375°F). Put the poblano chili s and chime peppers on the grind of the cooker or on the broiler floor when there are a few hot ashes within the fire. As the skins rankle and burn, turn them frequently. Cook for 5 to 7 minutes for poblanos and 10 minutes for peppers, or until the skins are totally simmered. For 10 minutes, put the poblanos and peppers in a bowl, cover with plastic wrap and sweat.
2. Poblanos and peppers ought to have their skins evacuated some time recently being cut open and having the stems and seeds taken out. In a pot on the stove, within the stove, or in a weight cooker, bring the vegetable stock to a stew. In a 6-quart Dutch stove, warm the olive oil over tall warm until it scarcely starts to smoke. Include the vegetables and sauté for around 3 minutes, or until the onions are straightforward. Sauté the chime peppers and poblanos for one miniature whereas flavoring with salt and pepper to taste. To the pot, include the hominy and beans after depleting. 4 cups of stock ought

to be included. Put within the oven with a cover.

3. On the stovetop, within the broiler, or within the cooker, warm a little cast-iron skillet over tall warm. The ancho chili s ought to be toasted within the hot, dry skillet for approximately five minutes until they are fragrant and somewhat darker in color. Cut open after cooling and evacuating the stems and seeds. Expel from the dish. Crush the skins off of the broiled garlic cloves and utilize a fork to pound the cloves into a glue in a little bowl. Put aside. The beans ought to be stewing for 30 minutes some time recently including the tomatoes, ancho chili s, broiled garlic, thyme, sage, and oregano. In case more stock is required to keep the beans secured, include the sherry. After 20 minutes, checkthe fluid level and include more stock, in case vital, some time recently proceeding to bubble for another 40 minutes.
4. Expel the cover, on the off chance that fundamental, and cook without it for 15 minutes.
5. To taste and season as vital. Some time recently serving, expel from the broiler and permit stand for 10 minutes. Cumin Crème Fraîche and cilantro ought to be included to the serving dishes.

11. Cumin crème Fraiche

Prep time: 10min | Serve: 1| Calories: 40kcal

Fixings

- ounces crème Fraiche
- One tbsp. cumin seeds, toasted and ground
- Ground get-up-and-go and juice of 1 lime
- Legitimate salt

Enlightening

- In a bowl, combine the crème Fraiche, cumin, get-up-and-go, and juice. Mix to combine. To taste, include salt.

12. Smoky French onion soup

Prep time: 10min | Serve: 8| Calories: 40kcal

Fixings

- Two tbsps. olive oil
- Two tbsps. unsalted butter
- 5 pounds of onions, meagerly cut
- 10 mugs wealthy chicken or meat stock
- Half container Madeira wine
- Two tbsps. Worcestershire sauce
- Half tsp. naturally ground nutmeg
- 2 huge sprigs of thyme
- 1 cove leaf 3
- Legitimate salt and naturally ground white pepper
- Two glasses of destroyed Gruyère cheese
- 8 cuts baguette, toasted

Informational

1. Plan a wood smoker flame broil or cooktop for roundabout warm cooking. In a 4-quart Dutch stove or clay pot, warm the olive oil over medium warm some time recently including and softening the butter. For around 40 minutes, include the onions and cook them over backhanded warm, regularly blending, until they mellow and scarcely begin to brown. Put the pot on tall warm and include a Half container of the stock. Cook, scratching up any browned bits from the pot's foot as you blend until the stock is totally gone.
2. Include another Half container of stock along side the Madeira and Worcestershire sauce. And after that hurl within the nutmeg. Proceed by including a half container of stock and bubbling it twice more until it dissipates. Include the thyme, cove leaf, and salt and pepper to taste, together with the remaining 8 mugs of stock. For 20 minutes, stew. To

taste and season as vital. Take off the narrows leaf and thyme sprigs.
3. Warm the broiler to 400 degrees. Pour the soup into expansive, protects bowls or containers. A cut of toast ought to be set on beat of the soup after the cheese has been sprinkled over it.
4. The remaining cheese ought to be sprinkled on the toast. Put the bowls on a heating sheet and heat for 10 to 15 minutes, or until the soup bubbles and the cheese is softened and brilliant. Serve warm.

13. Curried lentil and vegetable cassoulet

Prep time: 10min | Serve: 8| Calories: 40kcal

Fixings

- 4 tbsps. olive oil
- 1 glass diced carrots
- Half glass finely diced celery
- 6 to 8 cauliflower florets, divided
- 4 shallots, peeled and quartered
- Legitimate salt
- 2 cloves garlic, meagerly cut the long way
- Two tsps. ground new ginger
- 1¼ container dried brown lentils
- 1 narrows leaf
- Two tsps. cumin seeds, toasted
- 1 container dry white wine
- 2½ mugs vegetable stock
- One tsp. ground turmeric
- Two tsps. garam masala
- ¼ teaspoon cayenne pepper
- 2 to Two tbsps. extra-virgin olive oil

Enlightening

1. In a wood smoker-grill or cooker, get ready a medium warm fire (375°F). Put the carrots, celery, cauliflower, shallots, and Two tbsps of olive oil in a bowl. Put on a preparing sheet with a edge and sprinkle with salt.
2. Broil for 20 to 25 minutes, or until delicate and faintly caramelized.
3. Take out of the broiler, at that point put aside. Any liquids cleared out on the heating sheet ought to be poured into a little bowl and set aside. The garlic and ginger ought to be sautéed for 5 minutes within the remaining olive oil over medium warm in a Dutch broiler or clay container.
4. Include the wine, saved vegetable juices, narrows leaf, cumin, lentils, and 1 container of the stock. After 5 minutes of cooking, whisk within the cayenne, turmeric, and garam masala. Include another glass after the stock has about totally been ingested. Rehash for 10 to 15 minutes, or until the lentils are delicate (you will not require all of the stock). Stew for a advance miniature after including additional virgin olive oil and salt to taste.
5. Cook for an extra 10 minutes after including the broiled vegetables, at that point turn off the warm. Get freed of the inlet leaf. Serve soup in shallow dishes.

14. Fava bean, potato, and escarole soup

Prep time: 10min | Serve: 8| Calories: 40kcal

Fixings

- ¼ container olive oil
- 3 to 4 medium leeks (white portion as it were), finely chopped (Two glasses) and washed
- 1 pound of unpeeled ruddy or yellow potatoes, cut into ½-inch dice
- Legitimate salt
- 8 mugs vegetable or chicken stock
- 6 cloves whitened garlic

- 1 pound youthful escarole clears out, expansive stems expelled
- 2 pounds fava beans, steamed, shelled, and cleaned (see Cleaning Leeks)
- 15 expansive new mint takes off
- 20 new basil takes off from
- ½ bunch of new flat-leaf parsley
- ¼ glass new chervil or tarragon takes off (discretionary)
- Crisply ground white pepper
- One tbsp. naturally pressed lemon juice1
- ¼ glass Tuscan extra-virgin olive oil
- Half glass crème Fraiche for sprinkling Simmered Garlic Bread garnishes

Enlightening

1. In a wood smoker-grill or cooker, get ready a medium warm fire (375°F). In a clay pot or Dutch broiler, warm the olive oil over medium warm.
2. Leeks ought to be included and cooked for five minutes or until straightforward. Include the potatoes and blend. After 2 minutes of cooking, include salt and sufficient stock to cover. For 10 minutes, include the garlic and stew. With the cover on, stew for 5 minutes after including the escarole and Half a container of stock. Cook the fava beans, 1 glass at a time, for 5 minutes.
3. Include half of each herb after turning off the warm. Utilize an inundation blender or a nourishment processor to puree. To taste, include salt and pepper. Set aside to cool somewhat or refrigerate for 30 minutes. Mix one more after including the remaining herbs. Include the lemon juice and additional virgin olive oil after blending. To taste and season as fundamental. For the best flavor, serve the soup in shallow bowls at room temperature.
4. Pour crème Fraiche over each plate some time recently including the remaining fava beans and a number of bread garnishes.

15. Broiled garlic bread garnishes

Prep time: 10min | Serve: 8| Calories: 40kcal

Fixings

- 1 demi baguette or little natural bread such as Pugliese, cut or torn into little 3d shapes
- 3 cloves broiled garlic, pounded
- ⅓ container olive oil
- Legitimate salt

Enlightening

1. Combine the bread, olive oil, and garlic in a bowl. To taste, include salt. Spread out on a sheet skillet coated with material paper and toast in a 375°F stove. Expel from the broiler, and put in a bowl until embellish is required.

11

Baking and BBQ with Wood Pellet Grill

1. Shiitake and Simmered Garlic Tart

Prep time: 10min | Serve: 8| Calories: 10kcal

Fixings

- Savory tart batter
- 1Three-fourth mugs of unbleached all-purpose flour
- Half tsp. fine ocean salt
- 1Two tbsps. cold unsalted butter, cut into little pieces
- One tbsps. cold water

Filling

- 3 unpeeled cloves of garlic
- Two tbsps. olive oil, additionally more for sprinkling
- 8 ounces shiitake mushrooms, stemmed and finely chopped
- Fine ocean Salt and dark pepper
- 3 expansive eggs
- 1¼ glasses half-and-half

Enlightening

1. In a wood smoker barbecue, get ready a medium-hot flame(450°F). In a bowl, combine the flour and salt to form the mixture. Rub or cut the butter into the flour along with your hands or a baked good blender until a few of the butter is in drops and other pieces are the estimate of peas. One tablespoon at a time, mix within the water until all the fixings are dampened. Make a ball out of the mixture. It'll still have a few butter streaks and a somewhat unforgiving appearance.
2. Cut the mixture in half, frame each half into a circle, and cover in plastic wrap on a floured surface. Put within the ice chest for up to 3 days or at slightest an hour. Furthermore, the batter can be solidified for a month. One plate is rolled out into an 11-inch circular. It ought to be 1/8 inch thick.
3. Fit it into a 9-inch tart container with a separable foot after exchanging it there. Roll the best with a rolling stick to induce freed of the additional mixture.
4. Whereas planning the filling, chill the lined container. Cut the stem

closes off of the garlic cloves, place them in a shallow preparing dish, and best with olive oil to create the filling.

5. Cook for approximately 20 minutes or until delicate. Whereas that's happening, warm the Two tbsps. Of olive oil in a enormous skillet until it sparkles.
6. Salt and pepper the mushrooms after counting them. Around 5 minutes of cooking and ceaseless blending will cause the mushrooms to mellow, sparkle, and squeak. Turn off the warm and permit it to cool.
7. After taking the garlic out of the stove, let it cool for ten minutes.
8. Clove contribute ought to be pressed out onto a work surface and finely chopped. Put it interior a bowl. Include the eggs and half-and-half by whisking. Include salt and pepper to taste.
9. Put the mushrooms on the foot of the tart dish that has been lined, and after that pour the custard on best. Put the dish on a preparing sheet with material paper. When the outside is brilliant brown, and the custard is puffy and brilliant brown, slide the heating sheet onto the oven's hearth and heat for 35 to 40 minutes. Put a wire rack to cool on. At room temperature or warmed, serve.

2. Fresh potato, artichoke, leek, and gruyere tart

Prep time: 10min | Serve: 8| Calories: 44.8kcal

Fixings

- 4 leeks (white portion as it were), divided longwise
- ¼ glass olive oil
- 1pound infant artichokes
- Two tbsps. naturally crushed lemon juice
- Half glass of dry white wine
- Two tsps. new thyme takes off
- Legitimate salt and crisply ground white pepper
- 1 pound ruddy potatoes, exceptionally meagerly cut

- 2 expansive eggs
- One and a half glasses ricotta cheese
- Half container drain
- Half tsp. cayenne pepper
- Two tsps. ground lemon get-up-and-go
- Two tsps. minced new chives
- Two mugs of destroyed Gruyère cheese
- ¼ glass pine nuts, toasted

Enlightening

1. In a wood smoker flame broil, get ready a medium-hot flame(425°F). Leeks ought to be cut in half crosswise and well washed. In an broiler or cooker, warm Two tbsps. Of the olive oil, at that point cook the leeks for approximately 7 minutes, or until they are straightforward. Put aside in a bowl after exchange.
2. Cut the artichokes longwise after expelling the external clears out. Cuts of artichoke ought to be submerged in a dish of ice and lemon juice.
3. Artichokes ought to be depleted and dried with paper towels. Cut artichokes ought to be sautéed for approximately five minutes at medium-high warm within the same clay dough puncher with the additional olive oil from the spills. To expel the browned parts from the pan's foot, include the wine and blend. Cook for three minutes, or until the dampness is gone, after including the thyme and salt and pepper to taste. Turn off the warm and take off the pot alone. Salt and hurl the potato cuts in a bowl with the remaining olive oil. 5 cuts ought to be spared for the tart's best. On the stovetop, preheat a 10-inch clay bread cook or container with a inclined foot over medium-high warm. After taking the skillet from the warm, layer the foot and sides with potato cuts that are overhanging one another.
4. Include a little pepper. Put within the stove or cooker, and heat for around 15 minutes, or until brilliant. From the broiler, evacuate. Beat

the eggs and ricotta together until well combined in a bowl. Cayenne, lemon pizzazz, chives, drain, and salt to taste ought to all be included. Leeks are put inside the potato hull after half of the Gruyère. The artichokes ought to be set on best, taken after by the ricotta blend, the remaining Gruyère, and a scrambling of pine nuts. Beat with the potato cuts you set aside. Once more, prepare for another 25 minutes, or until fair scarcely browned. Take out of the broiler, at that point permit to cool for 15 minutes. Serve after cutting into wedges.

3. Tuscan torta with spinach, chard, and raisins

Prep time: 10min | Serve: 9| Calories: 44.8kcal
Fixings

- Batter
- One bundle of dynamic dry yeast
- Two and a three-fourth glasses of flour
- Half tsp. sugar
- One-fourth glass of olive oil
- One huge egg, softly beaten
- One glass of warm water
- One tsp. legitimate salt

Filling

- Two tbsps. unsalted butter
- Half glass drain
- One bunch parsley
- One container of whole-milk ricotta cheese
- 2 bunches of green onions, cut
- Two bunches of chard, coarsely chopped
- Four glasses of stuffed spinach clears out
- Half glass brilliant raisins

- One-fourth tsp naturally ground nutmeg
- Legitimate salt
- Two glasses of pressed arugula clears out
- Half glass of new basil clears out
- Naturally ground dark pepper
- Two huge eggs, beaten
- Half glass destroyed Gruyère cheese
- One-fourth glass ground pecorino cheese

Informational

1. In a wood smoker barbecue, get ready a medium warm fire (375°F). To plan the batter, combine the yeast with the sugar and water in a medium bowl. Mix to blend the fixings. Permit standing for five minutes or until foamy. Include the salt, egg, and oil by whisking. Until the batter is as well firm to handle with a spoon, whisk within the flour, a Half container at a time. The batter ought to be turned out onto a floured work surface and manipulated for 4 minutes or until it is versatile and smooth. When vital, sprinkle flour over the batter to avoid staying.

2. Combine the fixings on moo speed in a stand blender prepared with a dough snare, and after that manipulate the batter for five minutes at tall speed. The batter ought to be set in an oiled bowl, turned to coat, and secured with plastic wrap or a wet cloth. Permit rising for 45 minutes or until it has multiplied in estimate in a warm area. The chard ought to be chopped into bite-sized pieces to deliver the filling. On the stovetop or the floor of the wood pellet barbecue, soften the butter over medium warm some time recently including the chard. About 10 minutes of broiling is required to create the chard delicate. Salt it delicately. Including a small water will offer assistance a dry dish. Include the parsley, basil, arugula, spinach, green onions, and salt to taste. Cook for about 5 minutes over medium warm until delicate. Salt & pepper to taste, beside the raisins. Two tbsps.

3. The beaten eggs are set aside. Ricotta, drain, and the remaining beaten eggs ought to be combined in a huge bowl and completely mixed with a whisk. Include the greens, nutmeg, and cheeses after mixing. To taste and season as vital.
4. Isolate the batter into 2 pieces and put them on a delicately cleaned surface. To form an 11-inch circular thatis 1/8 inch thick, roll out one piece. Fit the mixture into a 9-inch, 3-inch-deep spring shape tart container.
5. Embed the filling. The moment piece of mixture is rolled out to the same thickness. Cut the mixture into 34-inch-wide strips employing a ravioli cutter. The strips ought to be dispersed 12 inches separated over the tart's surface. Weave the strips on the other hand to make a cross section. Cut any remaining dough 1 inch underneath the best of the skillet. Together with your fingers or a fork, pleat the dough's edges after collapsing it up over the strips. Apply the spared, beaten egg to the cross section and edge. Prepare for 25 to 30 minutes, or until brilliant brown, on a heating sheet. Evacuate the spring from the edge after letting the cake cool for 10 minutes on a wire rack. Permit it cool for 20 to 30 minutes some time recently serving wedge-shaped.

4. Wild mushroom, fennel, chard, and gruyère tart

Prep time: 10min | Serve: 11| Calories: 152kcal
Fixings

- Outside
- Three-fourth glasses fine cornmeal
- Two glasses of all-purpose flour
- 1½ teaspoons salt
- Half tsp. sugar
- 7 tablespoons cold unsalted butter
- Two tbsps. olive oil
- 8 to 10 tablespoons of ice water

Filling

- 1 fennel bulb, trimmed
- 4 huge chard takes off, thick stems expelled
- One tsp. fennel seeds
- ¼ glass olive oil
- 1½ teaspoons legitimate salt, furthermore more for flavoring
- ¼ container dry white wine
- 8 ounces blended chanterelle and clam mushrooms, stemmed
- Half tsp. crisply ground pepper, also more for flavoring
- ¼ teaspoon naturally ground nutmeg
- 2 expansive eggs
- 1 huge egg yolk
- Half glass drain
- Three-fourth container overwhelming cream
- 1 glass destroyed Gruyère or Italian fontina cheese

Informational

1. In a wood smoker barbecue, get ready a medium warm fire (375°F). Cornmeal, flour, salt, and sugar ought to be combined in a nourishment processor and beat to make the outside. Butter ought to be cut into 1-inch 3d shapes, included to the processor in small sums at a time, and beat until the measure of a little pea. Include One tbsps. of the cold water after including the olive oil continuously whereas the machine is running until it is combined. On the off chance that the batter is still as well dry to come together, add just sufficient water to form a ball of batter that pulls absent from the bowl's sides. Maintain a strategic distance from exhausting the batter. Wrap in plastic wrap, shape into a plate, and chill for at slightest two hours or overnight.
2. Cut the fennel bulb the long way into quarters to deliver the filling.
3. Cut each quarter into the long way cuts that are 14 inches thick after expelling and disposing of the center. Shred the chard takes

off into little pieces. Fennel seeds ought to be delicately pulverized in a mortar or with a wide chef's cut. Cut fennel ought to be blended with Two tbsps. Of olive oil and Half tsps. Salt. Spread out on a rimmed preparing sheet, best with white wine, and cook for almost 25 minutes, or until fork-tender and somewhat caramelized. Cut the mushrooms into bite-sized pieces by tearing them the long way. Include the pulverized fennel seeds, Two tbsps. Of olive oil, Half tsps. Each of the salt and pepper, and proceed broiling as you did with the fennel. The chard leaves should be included to the simmered mushrooms, combined, and after that put back within the broiler for 5 to 7 minutes or until the chard is wilted.

4. Turn off the warm and permit it to cool. Salt and pepper to taste, and nutmeg may well be utilized. Take the nourishment off the stove and take off it to cool briefly. Increment the temperature of the cooker or stove to 400°F. Roll the batter to a 13-inch-diameter, 18-inch-thick circular between 2 sheets of plastic wrap or material paper. Fill an 11-inch tart skillet with a separable foot with the mixture. Prebake the batter for 12 minutes with fork pricks on the foot and sides. Some time recently including the filling, evacuate it from the broiler and let cool for five to ten minutes. In a bowl, combine the eggs, egg yolk, drain, cream, and Half tsps. Salt.

5. Put the preparing sheet on beat of the tart container. The mushroom-chard blend ought to be utilized to line the shell some time recently including the broiled fennel on best. Pour the custard over the blend after scrambling with half of the cheese. Include the remaining cheese on best and prepare for 25 to 35 minutes, or until firm and brown. Permit cooling for 15 minutes on a wire rack. Serve after being evacuated from the tart skillet and cut into wedges.

5. Puff baked good pissaladière

Prep time: 10min | Serve: 8-10| Calories: 44kcal

Fixings

- Dissolved onions
- ¼ glass olive oil
- One and a half pounds of yellow onions, cut into wedges ⅛ inch thick
- Three-fourth container white balsamic or Champagne vinegar
- Two tbsps. sherry vinegar
- Crisply ground white pepper
- Two tsps. sugar
- Two tsps. new thyme clears out
- 1 sheet solidified puff cake, defrosted within the fridge
- 1 expansive egg yolk beaten with One tbsp. overwhelming cream
- 1 glass Oven-Roasted Tomatoes, cut into limit strips
- 4 cloves broiled or whitened garlic, minced
- Half container niçoise olives, smoker-grilled and cut
- Two tbsps. new thyme takes off
- Legitimate salt
- Anchovy filets depleted and splashed in drain (discretionary)
- Half container ground matured goat cheese, such as certain

Informational

1. In a wood smoker barbecue, plan a medium warm fire (375°F). To get ready the dissolving onions, warm the olive oil in a huge skillet over medium warm, at that point sauté the onions for around 7 minutes, or until they are translucent.
2. Include a little white pepper in conjunction with the vinegar. Decrease the warm, whisk within the sugar, and proceed cooking for 20 to 25 minutes, or until the fluid has about totally diminished and the onions have "liquefied" into a stick. Get freed of the warm. Include the thyme

and mix. Put aside.

3. Roll out the puff cake 1 inch more extensive all around on a floured surface.
4. Place on a parchment-lined preparing sheet. The puff pastry's sides ought to be cut into 34-inch-wide strips. To make a baked good edge, brush the yolk blend along the crust's edges and include the cut pieces.
5. Beginning with the dissolved onions and wrapping up with the anchovies, equally disperse the fixings over the insides. Apply the yolk blend to the edge. Put on a grind and heat for 15 minutes, or until brilliant brown.
6. After taking it out of the broiler, instantly sprinkle it with goat cheese. Cut into segments, at that point warm serve.

6. Milanese risotto, leek, and asparagus tart

Prep time: 10min | Serve: 8-10| Calories: 44kcal

Fixings

- 2½ mugs extra risotto Milanese or other risotto
- 1Three-fourth mugs Asiago or pecorino romano cheese, coarsely ground
- 5 tablespoons olive oil, furthermore more for coating
- Two tbsps. new thyme clears out
- 12 to 14 stalks of asparagus, trimmed, peeled, and cut into 4-inch pieces
- Legitimate salt
- 4 leeks (white portion as it were), cut longwise into eighths
- Ground get-up-and-go of ½ lemon
- Half tsp. crisply ground white pepper
- 3 huge eggs, beaten
- 5 sprigs thyme

Informational

1. In a wood smoker flame broil, get ready a medium warm fire (375°F). Include 1 container of the Asiago cheese to the risotto. In a clay casserole or 10-inch ovenproof skillet, warm Two tbsps. Of the olive oil. The risotto blend ought to totally cover the foot and edges of the skillet or dish. 12 glasses of the cheese are at that point sprinkled on beat in conjunction with One tbsp. of thyme takes off. Heat for 15 to 18 minutes, or until brown, in the stove.
2. The asparagus ought to be generously coated in salt and olive oil some time recently being simmered for around 15 minutes on a preparing sheet. Leeks ought to be cut into 14-inch slices crosswise and well washed. Leeks ought to be sautéed within the remaining Two tbsps. Of olive oil for approximately 7 minutes or until delicate. Salt to taste, at that point set absent after including the leeks, lemon get-up-and-go, and the remaining two tsps. Of thyme takes off to the prepared hull, organize the asparagus in a starburst design. Include the pepper and a small salt. Over the filling, pour the eggs. The remaining cheese and a fan of thyme sprigs ought to be placed on beat. Prepare for almost 25 minutes, or until the cheese incorporates a brilliant brown hull and the eggs are set. Take the nourishment out of the stove and grant it 10 to 15 minutes to stand.
3. Turn out by laying a cutting board on best, at that point turning the tart over and setting it on the board. The tart ought to presently be turned over one more so that the asparagus side is on best of a enormous plate. Warm wedges ought to be served.

7. Provincial Corn, Tomato, and Basil Tart

Prep time: 45min | Serve: 8-10| Calories: 4.4kcal
Fixings

- One and a half pounds of yellow tomatoes, cut into ¼-inch-thick cuts
- One and a half pounds of ruddy tomatoes, cut into ¼-inch-thick cuts
- Legitimate salt

- Batter
- 1 glass new corn parts (approximately 2 ears)
- One tbsp. crisply pressed lime juice
- Two tbsps. new goat cheese, at room temperature
- One and a half mugs all-purpose flour
- ¼ container fine yellow cornmeal
- Half tsp. legitimate salt
- 4 tbsps. cold unsalted butter, cut into 3d shapes

Filling

- Half container destroyed new basil takes off
- Half container destroyed Italian fontina cheese
- One tbsp. entire new oregano clears out, minced
- 4 tbsps. new bread scraps
- Half tsp. legitimate salt, also more for flavoring
- ¼ teaspoon broken dark pepper
- 1 egg for wash
- Half tsp. coarse ocean salt
- ¼ container disintegrated new goat cheese

Enlightening

1. In a wood smoker flame broil, get ready a medium-hot flame(400°F). On paper towels, orchestrate the tomato cuts in a single layer and sprinkle with a small salt. After ten minutes, tenderly crush to extricate more juice. Goat cheese, juice, and 1/4 container ought to be handled in a nourishment processor to create the mixture. Salt, flour, and cornmeal are combined in a huge bowl and whisked to combine. Employing a baked good cutter, join the butter into the blend until it takes after a coarse feast. Until a delicate mixture shapes, include the corn fixings and work altogether. 3 or 4 tender times of manipulating. The mixture ought to be put on plastic wrap, at that point secured

with more plastic wrap, into a 6-inch circle, and squeezed. Roll out the mixture into a 14-inch circle whereas it's still coated.
2. Put the batter on a heating sheet coated with paper, and after that chill it for 45 minutes or solidify it for 10 minutes, depending on your inclination, until it is firm and the plastic wrap is straightforward to expel.
3. Combine 14 mugs of basil, fontina, and oregano to form the filling.
4. Two tbsps.Of the bread scraps and Half tsps. Ofkosher salt ought to be combined in another bowl. Make a 1 1 2-inch border around the cheese blend some time recently putting it on the rolled-out batter. Sprinkle with the breadcrumb blend. Over the cheese, put half of the tomatoes in an covered design. Include the final of the corn bits, season with salt, and best with the final of the bread scraps. Sprinkle a few salt and crisply broken dark pepper on best of the moment layer of tomatoes. Tenderly crease the dough's borders toward the center to take after a galette, at that point press to seal. Sprinkle with half tsps. Of course, ocean salt after brushing with egg wash.
5. After 20 minutes of heating, evacuate from the broiler and sprinkle the goat cheese scraps over the center. Delicately press the cheese into the tomatoes. Within the stove once more, heat the dish for an extra 20 minutes or until the outside is brilliant. After taking it out of the stove, hold up for at slightest 20 and conceivably indeed up to 45 minutes. Cut and serve the tart at room temperature after scrambling the remaining basil clears out over it.

8. Spinach, mushroom, and feta pie

Prep time: 45min | Serve: 8| Calories: 44.5kcal
Fixings

- Spinach-onion filling
- Two tbsps. olive oil
- 1 bunch of green onions, coarsely chopped, counting a few green parts

- 1 (10-ounce) bundle of solidified spinach, defrosted and depleted
- ¼ container dry white wine
- One tbsp. capers, washed and depleted
- Half tsp. legitimate salt, additionally more for flavoring
- ¼ teaspoon naturally ground white pepper, also more for flavoring
- 1½ teaspoons minced new dill
- 6 ounces residential feta, disintegrated (flushed on the off chance that in brine)
- 8 ounces shellfish mushrooms, torn into bite-sized pieces
- 8 ounces shiitake mushrooms, stemmed and chopped
- ¼ glass olive oil
- Half container (1 adhere) of unsalted butter
- 1 container toasted bread pieces
- One tbsp. minced new dill clears out
- One tsp. dried thyme
- Half tsp. sweet pimentón (Spanish smoked paprika)
- Ground pizzazz of 1 lemon
- One tsp. salt
- 12 sheets of solidified phyllo cake, defrosted within the fridge

Enlightening

1. In a wood smoker barbecue, get ready a medium warm fire (375°F). Apply olive oil to an 8-inch spring shape dish. In a sauté container set over medium warm, include the olive oil and onions to get ready the filling. For a assist 5 minutes, include the spinach and proceed to sauté. Cook the white wine until it has generally vanished after being included. Include the salt, white pepper, and capers. Include the dill, at that point turn the warm off and permit the blend cool. Include the feta and blend.
2. The mushrooms ought to be sautéed or prepared independently until about dry in Two tbsps, Of olive oil and a small salt. Get freed of the warm. In the event that vital, season with white pepper and extra salt.

Put separated in different bowls. In a little pan over medium warm, soften the butter and include the remaining olive oil. Keep warmed and set aside. In a bowl, blend the salt, pimentón, pizzazz, dill, and thyme with the breadcrumbs.

3. Put aside. Put the phyllo on a work surface, at that point cover it with a soggy paper towel and a kitchen towel. Lay one cake sheet the long way on a cutting board, at that point begin brushing the edges with the butter blend from the center out. Sprinkle the bread scrap blend generously over the dish. Put another sheet over the beat and proceed to brush the surface with the butter blend. Include more of the breadcrumb blend liberally. Include a third sheet on beat, at that point brush it one more. Evacuate two inches or so from one brief side. Put the stacked sheets carefully within the spring shape skillet, squeezing them all the way to the foot and hanging the additional sheets over the pan's borders. Include the shiitake mushrooms to the space.

4. Three more phyllo sheets, the remaining butter blend, and the bread scraps ought to be layered on best as some time recently. Expel two inches or so from one brief side. These sheets ought to be carefully situated within the spring frame skillet, squeezing down over the mushrooms and hanging the additional sheets over the pan's borders. Half of the spinach-onion blend ought to be included. Re-do the phyllo layering and trimming prepare. As some time recently, layer within the dish some time recently including the shellfish mushrooms. Repetition of trimming, layering, and phyllo layers within the skillet is required. Include the remaining spinach-onion mixture to the center. Include the breadcrumb blend on beat. To make the beat hull and cover the spinach-onion filling, overlay all the abundance hanging phyllo into the center. Brush the beat generously with the butter blend, at that point prepare for 25 to 30 minutes, or until fresh and brilliant on beat. After expelling from the oven, let the spring frame dish cool for 15 minutes some time recently evacuating the prepared great. Warm wedges ought to be served.

9. Juicy smoked salmon

Prep time: 45min | Serve: 8-10| Calories: 44.5kcal

Fixings

- 1 (2-pound) salmon filet, skin on, stick bones expelled
- One tbsp. or so coarse ocean salt, or as required
- One tsp. coarsely ground juniper berries (discretionary)
- Two tbsps. minced new dill for embellish
- Two tbsps. capers, for decorate

Informational

1. Set up the wood pellet flame broil for circuitous cooking. Utilize a plate setter with the legs raised and a grind in put to isolated the angle from the warm source within the BGE situation. In case wanted, drench 1 glass of apple wood chips in water for thirty minutes some time recently scrambling them over the charcoal ten minutes after it is lit. Near the BGE's top whereas clearing out the best and foot vents somewhat slightly open.
2. To cook on a wood pellet flame broil, lay a pizza stone over the flares, taken after by 2 fire brick pavers dispersed around 8 inches separated on either side of the pizza stone. Open the lower vents to 1/2 inch whereas closing the top. After two minutes, put the salmon filet on a pizza screen or punctured pizza container. Put on the grind after flavoring with juniper berries and ocean salt. Pizza dish or barbecue screens ought to be adjusted on the fire brick pavers whereas utilizing a flame broil. 190°F for 30 to 35 minutes with the top closed or until the substance feels to some degree firm to the touch but shows up damp. As it were negligibly ought to the flesh's color have changed since it to begin with begun smoking. Bear in intellect merely are smoking, not broiling, the angle. With a fork, delicately peel absent a bit of the meat from the thickest portion of the angle to check its

doneness.

3. It ought to have a uniform color and be very damp. As it were negligibly will the color have changed since it was put on the fire. Take it out of the broiler or flame broil, at that point permit it to cool to some degree. To serve, cut meagerly; evacuate with a cut or angle fork, taking off the skin on.
4. Refrigerate angle scraps with the skin on for up to a week after cooking. Serve with capers and dill as garnishes.

10. Olive oil–poached fish with fennel, orange, and olive serving of mixed greens

Prep time: 45min | Serve: 8-10| Calories: 44.5kcal

Fixings

- One and a half pounds center-cut albacore fish or yellowtail
- Fine ocean salt for rubbing
- 4 cloves garlic, cut into thick cuts
- 1 inlet leaf
- Two tsps. capers depleted and flushed
- 4 strips of orange pizzazz
- 2 fennel bulb fronds
- ⅛ teaspoon white peppercorns
- Olive oil to cover (approximately 3 glasses)
- Serving of mixed greens
- 1 little fennel bulb, trimmed, cored, meagerly cut the long way
- Half glass picholine olives, smoker-grilled and coarsely chopped
- 1 orange, peeled and sectioned, juice saved
- Two tsps. Herbs de Provence
- Two tbsps. coarsely chopped new flat-leaf parsley
- Legitimate salt and crisply ground dark pepper

Dressing

- ¼ container saved poaching oil (from Olive Oil–Poached Fish)
- Two tbsps. Champagne vinegar
- Legitimate salt
- Two glasses of infant arugula
- Two tbsps. chopped new flat-leaf parsley for decorate
- Ocean salt, for tidying

Enlightening

1. In a wood pellet flame broil, begin a moo warm fire (190° to 210°F) and utilize a grind to set up for cooking with backhanded warm. Pat the fish dry after flushing. Rub ocean salt all over some time recently letting it stand for an hour at room temperature. Choose a coated pottery preparing dish that's 8 inches wide and fits the angle firmly. Include the white peppercorns, fennel fronds, orange get-up-and-go, garlic, cove leaf, capers, and capers to the dish.
2. Include sufficient olive oil to cover the fish some time recently putting it on best. Wrap with aluminum thwart immovably. Put on a grind and poach for 45 to 55 minutes, or until completely cooked, in an encased stove or broiler over roundabout warm. Combine all of the salad's components meanwhile, flavoring with salt and pepper to taste at room temperature, and set aside. After 35 minutes, check the angle for doneness; it need to be firm to the touch on the exterior and pink on the interior. Turn off the warm and let the nourishment cool for five minutes.
3. Break or cut the angle into serving-size pieces after depleting it, sparing the olive oil. 3 to 4 tbsps. of the olive oil from the poaching ought to be whisked with vinegar some time recently dressing the serving of mixed greens. To taste and season as essential. Put a few arugula on each plate, at that point include a few poached salmon pieces and the serving of mixed greens. Sprinkle with ocean salt and

include the parsley as a decorate. Wine-Poa.

11. Wine-Poached Shrimp with Smoky Tomato Sauce

Prep time: 45min | Serve: 6| Calories: 44.5kcal

Fixings

- 18 huge shrimp within the shell, scored down the back and deveined
- Two mugs of dry white wine
- Two glasses of light vegetable or shrimp stock
- 2 cloves garlic, peeled Half tsp. fennel seeds
- 1½ teaspoons legitimate salt
- Smoky Tomato Sauce

Informational

1. In a wood pellet flame broil, plan a low-medium warm fire (225°F) for cooking. Warm up the wine and stock together in a pan. Put the shrimp in a little preparing dish, at that point pour the stock and wine over them. The broth ought to presently contain garlic, fennel, and salt.
2. Firmly cover the dish and prepare for 15 to 20 minutes, or until the shrimp are a uniform pink color. Take the shrimp out of the fluid, permit them to cool to some degree, and after that take the shells off. Re-heat the dish within the stove and cook until the fluid has been decreased by onethird.
3. For the sauce, set aside 1/4 glass of it. Fair some time recently serving, include the shrimp to the remaining decreased fluid.

12. Smoky tomato sauce

Prep time: 45min | Serve: 6| Calories: 44.5kcal

Fixings

- 4 tomatoes, seeded and split
- 2 unpeeled shallots, divided
- Three-fourth container olive oil
- Legitimate salt
- Half tsp. crisply ground dark pepper
- ¼ container diminished poaching fluid (from Wine-Poached Shrimp)
- Juice of 1 lemon
- Two tbsps. white balsamic vinegar
- Naturally ground white pepper
- 1 container chopped new basil clears out
- ¼ glass chopped fresh mint clears out

Enlightening

1. Make a wood pellet barbecue fire that's 400 degrees Fahrenheit hot. On the other hand, in the event that you're heating the shrimp, sauté the tomatoes and shallots nearby them. To stamp and cook them, put them on a flame broil container or grind.
2. Hurl the tomatoes, shallots, salt, and dark pepper with Two tbsps. Of olive oil in a bowl to coat. For 15 minutes, or until the skins have shriveled and the tomatoes have relaxed, flame broil the tomatoes and shallots with the cut side down. Expel off the barbecue, at that point spread out to cool to the touch on a preparing sheet. After expelling the tomato and shallot skins, cut the vegetables. Juices included combined in a bowl and saved.
3. In a bowl, combine the poaching fluid, vinegar, and lemon juice. To make an emulsion, blend within the remaining 12 mugs of olive oil steadily. Include salt and white pepper to taste and mix into the tomato

blend. Add the chopped herbs and mix. For the flavors to merge, set aside for 20 minutes. Plunge the shrimp within the sauce.

13. Beer-Braised Brief Ribs

Prep time: 45min | Serve: 4| Calories: 44.5kcal

Fixings

- 3 pounds brief ribs, cut into 2-inch pieces with the bone joined
- Legitimate Salt and dark pepper
- Two tsps. olive oil
- 2 expansive onions, cut
- 2 carrots, peeled and chopped
- 1 stalk celery, chopped
- 2 cloves garlic, peeled
- 2 Roma tomatoes, chopped
- One tsp. caraway seeds
- Two tsps. sweet Hungarian paprika 1 (12-ounce) bottle dim lager
- Two mugs wealthy chicken or hamburger stock, also more as required 8 sprigs thyme
- 2 cove clears out

Informational

1. In a wood pellet barbecue, plan a medium-hot fire (400°F). The brief ribs ought to be dried. Sprinkle pepper on best of the meat after equally applying salt. On a flame broil or the foot of a wood-fired broiler, warm the olive oil over medium-high warm in a sizable, overwhelming broiling container or clay dough puncher. Include the meat, at that point brown it completely all over. Brief ribs ought to be moved to a enormous plate and cleared out alone. The simmering container ought to presently contain the onions, carrots, celery, and garlic.
2. Cook the vegetables within the broiler for almost 20 minutes, mixing

twice or three times, or until they are delicate and fair beginning to brown.

3. Mixing to rub off the browned bits from the pan's foot, include the tomatoes, caraway seeds, paprika, lager, Two mugs of stock, thyme, and inlet takes off. Join the brief ribs back into the dish, cover it, and heat for around 2 12 hours within the front, cooler portion of the stove, once in a while observing to see in the event that additional stock or water is required. To caramelize the meat and minimize the fluid, reveal the brief ribs and prepare for 30 minutes. Exchange the brief ribs to a dish with care, at that point wrap them in thwart. Press the cooked vegetables with the back of a expansive spoon to discharge additional fluid as you pour the braising fluid from the dish through a sifter. Toss the vegetables absent.

4. Skim the fat from the surface of the fluid after pouring it into a little pan and bringing it to a bubble. Once all the fat has been disposed of, and the sauce has been diminished to the suitable thickness, keep delicately stewing and skimming. Brief ribs can have their bones cleared out in or expelled some time recently cooking.

14. Solitary Star Grilled Brisket

Prep time: 45min | Serve: 4| Calories: 41.5kcal

Fixings

Rub

- Three-fourth container sweet Hungarian paprika
- ¼ glass naturally ground dark pepper
- ¼ container coarse ocean salt or legitimate salt
- ¼ glass sugar
- Two tbsps. chili powder
- Two tbsps. garlic powder
- Two tbsps. onion powder
- Two tsps. cayenne pepper

- 1 (10-to 12-pound) packer-trimmed hamburger brisket

Brew clean

- 1 (12-ounce) can or bottle of brew brew
- Half glass cider vinegar
- 4 tbsps. canola oil
- Two tbsps. Worcestershire sauce
- ½ onion, slivered, or 2 to 4 garlic cloves, minced

One tbsp. Rub (over)

- 1½ teaspoons coarsely ground pepper
- Salted jalapeno cuts, new jalapeno cuts, Tabasco sauce, or other
- hot sauce (discretionary)
- Half container water
- Genuine Texas brisket sauce (discretionary)
- One and a half glasses of grilled brisket drippings from cut brisket
- (over), supplemented with
- bacon drippings on the off chance that required
- Two tsps. Worcestershire sauce
- One tsp. cayenne pepper

Enlightening

1. In a little bowl, blend all the fixings for the rub the night some time recently you proposed to barbecue. For the clean, spare One tbsp. of the rub. The remaining rub ought to be conveyed equitably and altogether rubbed into the brisket. Refrigerate the brisket overnight in a sizable selfsealing plastic sack. Expel the brisket from the fridge and let it sit at room temperature, revealed, for 45 minutes some time recently beginning the barbeque. Turn on the smoker and raise the temperature to between 180° and 220°F. Put all the fixings in a pot

and cook over moo warm to form the clean. Put the brisket fat side up within the smoker so that the fluids can offer assistance treat the meat.
2. Cook for 10 to 16 hours, or 60 to 75 minutes per pound of brisket, until amazingly delicate. Treat the darkening chunk with the clean approximately each hour. Take the meat out of the smoker and let it rest for 20 to 30 minutes at room temperature. Partitioned the slimmer foot area from the beat greasy segment. The two regions are isolated by a fat layer that's simple to see. Both parcels ought to have any additional fat evacuated some time recently being meagerly cut against the grain. In any case, keep an eye on the grain as you work since it can alter course. As you cut, collect all of the meat drippings.
3. Combine all the fixings for the sauce in a bowl, at that point utilize a little sum to dampen the meat some time recently serving the remaining sauce on the side.

15. Slow-roasted part turkey with citrus-chili coat

Prep time: 45min | Serve: 8-10| Calories: 14.5kcal

Fixings

1 half turkey, approximately 6 pounds

BRINE (Discretionary)

- 8 glasses water
- ⅔ container salt
- ⅔ container sugar

Caja turkey rub

- 1 container olive oil
- Two tbsps. pimentón (Spanish smoked paprika)
- ⅓ glass pressed light brown sugar
- One tbsp. onion powder

- Squeeze of chipotle chili powder
- 6 cloves garlic, minced
- ½ tablespoon cumin seeds, toasted and ground
- One tbsp. legitimate salt
- ½ tablespoon crisply ground dark pepper

Citrus-chili coat

- Two tbsps. olive oil
- One tbsp. minced garlic
- One tbsp. cascabel chili powder
- ¼ container light corn syrup
- ¼ glass orange bloom nectar
- ¼ container ponzu sauce, or Two tbsps. each crisply pressed lime juice and lemon juice
- Two tbsps. naturally pressed lime juice
- Two tbsps. naturally crushed orange juice

Informational

1. To brine the turkey, combine all the brine fixings in a expansive nonreactive holder and submerge the turkey totally. Refrigerate for at slightest 4 to 6 hours or overnight. Wash and let it come to room temperature. To form the rub, combine all the rub fixings in a bowl. Rub the part turkey liberally with the rub and set aside at room temperature for 30 minutes. To form the coat, warm the olive oil in a pan over medium warm and sauté the garlic for 30 seconds.
2. Include the chili powder and sauté for 30 more seconds. Increment the warm, include the remaining fixings, and cook until decreased to a light syrup. Strain and let cool to room temperature. Put the turkey, skin side up, within the La Caja China box roaster on a rack over a drip dish.
3. Cover with the top, include charred wood, and light. On the off chance

that you're simmering this turkey in a Huge Green Egg or wood-fired stove, get ready a medium-hot fire (325°F) and cook secured on a rack. After 1 hour, evacuate the cover, turn the turkey over, cover once more, include more char wood as required, and cook for 15 minutes.

4. Expel the cover and brush both sides of the turkey with the coat. Put a test thermometer into the turkey breast, return the cover, and cook until the thermometer registers 170° to 175°F. Evacuate from the warm and set aside on a heating sheet. Brush once more with the coat and let rest for around 20 minutes. Carve and serve.

16. Milk-braised pork with mushroom-artichoke ragù

Prep time: 45min | Serve: 6| Calories: 64.5kcal

Fixings

- 1 (3-to 4-pound) boneless pork bear, a few fat trimmed
- Legitimate salt and crisply ground dark pepper
- Two tbsps. olive oil
- 2 onions, coarsely chopped
- 3 juniper berries, pulverized
- 2 inlet takes off
- 2 sprigs of rosemary or savory
- 2 cloves garlic, daintily cut
- 3½ mugs entirety drain

MUSHROOM-ARTICHOKE RAGÙ

- Two tbsps. olive oil
- 2 pounds mushrooms (chanterelles, cremini, or shiitakes), cut (on the off chance that utilizing shiitakes, stem the primary)
- One and a half glasses new or defrosted solidified artichoke hearts
- 3 cloves garlic, daintily cut
- 1 glass dry white wine

- One tsp. legitimate salt
- Half tsp. crisply ground dark pepper
- Ground get-up-and-go of 1 lemon
- ¼ teaspoon crisply ground nutmeg
- Half container walnuts, toasted and chopped

Informational

1. In a wood pellet flame broil, get ready a medium fire (325°F). Put salt and pepper on the pork to season it. In a Dutch stove or expansive container, warm the olive oil over medium-high warm until it gleams. Pork ought to be included and burned until well-browned all over. Put the pork on a platter and save. Expel all of the fat from the pot but for 3 tablespoons. Once more over medium warm, include the onions, juniper berries, inlet takes off, and rosemary and cook for approximately 5 minutes, or until the onions are delicate.
2. After including it, sauté the garlic for almost 3 minutes, or until it turns faintly yellow. Include the drain and put the pork back within the pot. For a 2-hour braise, cover the dish and cook it within the stove, flipping the pork 2 or 3 times. Meanwhile, get ready the ragù by sparkling the olive oil in a little Dutch stove or overwhelming casserole over medium warm. Include the artichoke hearts and mushrooms, cover, and stew for 15 minutes within the stove. Expel the cover and mix within the wine, garlic, salt, and pepper. For 10 more minutes of cooking, cover the container and put it back within the stove. Mix once in a while. After 15 minutes, evacuate the cover and proceed cooking the artichoke hearts until they are delicate and portion of the liquids have gone. After taking it out of the stove, include the lemon get-up-and-go. To taste and season as vital. Keep warmed and set aside.
3. After two hours, reveal the pork and stew for another 30 minutes, or until the meat is delicate to the fork. Put aluminum thwart over the broil some time recently exchanging it to a dish. Take the juniper

berries, rosemary, and cove takes off out of the smooth sauce. Expel any additional fat by skimming the best. The cooking prepare will have caused the drain to curdle. The sauce ought to be mixed with an inundation blender until it is smooth.

4. Include the walnuts and nutmeg. Warm through within the stove one more. To taste and season as fundamental. The sauce ought to be spooned on best of the cut meat some time recently serving. Include the ragù to the dish.

17. Sheep Braised in Yogurt with Onions and Tomatoes

Prep time: 45min | Serve: 4| Calories: 34.5kcal

Fixings

2½ pounds boneless sheep stew meat, cut into 1-inch 3d shapes

MARINADE

- 1 glass plain whole-milk yogurt
- Juice of 1 lemon
- One tsp. cumin seeds
- Half tsp. salt
- 4 tbsps. olive oil, also more for rubbing
- Legitimate salt and naturally ground dark pepper
- 3 huge unpeeled cloves of garlic
- 5 expansive ready tomatoes
- 2 poblano or expansive jalapeno chili s
- 1 pound white onions, destroyed (4 glasses)
- One tbsp. cumin seeds
- Squeeze of ruddy pepper drops
- One tsp. ground allspice
- Half tsp. ground ginger
- Sprinkle of ruddy wine vinegar
- 3 glasses chicken stock

- 5 glasses whole-milk yogurt, depleted overnight through a fine-mesh strainer
- 5 teaspoons cornstarch
- Chopped new flat-leaf parsley for embellish

Informational

1. Put the sheep in a sizable plastic sack that self-seals. The marinade fixings ought to be combined, at that point included to the sack. Sheep ought to be marinated for two hours at room temperature or all night within the ice chest. In the event that refrigerated, hold up 30 minutes for it to reach room temperature some time recently utilizing it. In a wood pellet flame broil, get ready a medium warm fire (325°F). Dry off the meat by depleting it. Olive oil and salt and pepper cleaning are connected. In a dry cast-iron skillet over tall warm, broil the garlic, tomatoes, and poblano chili s until the skins are simmered and rankled.
2. Put on a plate and permit to cool until the touch. Amphibians and chili s ought to be peeled and seeded. Chop everything up finely. In a nonreactive skillet over medium warm, warm the olive oil until it gleams. Include the onions, ginger, allspice, ruddy pepper drops, and cumin, and sauté for 5 minutes. Put the sheep on best of the blend after including the vinegar and chopped vegetables. To the stock, include 11Two glasses. Over the sheep, spoon a few of the onion blends. Cook the vegetables for 45 minutes, or until they have somewhat dissolved, in the stove, secured safely with a top or aluminum thwart. Combine the depleted yogurt and cornstarch in a bowl.
3. Combine the sheep with the extra stock and the yogurt blend that has been depleted. For a encourage 30 minutes, or until the sheep is delicate to the fork, cook secured within the stove. At this point, the sauce will show up to be coagulated. The sauce ought to be smoothed out with a hand blender some time recently being returned to medium warm, revealed, for 15 minutes to thicken. Evacuate the sheep to a

platter. Include the sheep that has been braised, cover with a few of the sauce, and warm the dish in the broiler revealed. With the sauce on beat and parsley as adecorate, serve the sheep hot over the couscous.

18. Provençal Chicken

Prep time: 45min | Serve: 6| Calories: 4.5kcal

Fixings

- 1 glass toasted bread scraps or panko (Japanese bread pieces), finely ground
- Two tsps. herbs de Provence
- One tsp. Legitimate salt, furthermore more for flavoring
- Half tsp. crisply ground dark pepper, furthermore more for flavoring
- 3 bone-in chicken breasts, split crosswise
- 3 bone-in chicken thighs, divided crosswise
- ¼ glass olive oil
- 6 shallots, peeled and divided
- 8 unpeeled cloves of garlic
- 12 smoker-grilled prunes
- Two tbsps. picholine or other green olives with smoker-grills
- One tbsp. capers depleted and washed
- One tbsp. fennel seeds
- 1 glass dry rosé or white wine
- One tbsp. nectar
- 1 orange, cut into 6 wedges, juice saved

Informational

1. In a wood pellet flame broil, get ready a medium warm fire (325°F). In arrange to hold the warm all through the cooking handle when employing a woodfired stove, keep a little fire (one small log) blasting within the distant cleared out raise of the stove. In a bowl, blend

together the bread pieces, herbs de Provence, and One tsp. Salt, and Half tsps. Pepper.
2. Pat the chicken dry some time recently coating it with the bread scraps and putting it on a preparing skillet. The chicken ought to be browned equally on all sides in a sizable cast-iron dish or shallow clay preparing dish that has been warmed over medium warm. Exchange the chicken to a shallow ceramic heating dish or a cast-iron skillet with a ceramic coating. Include the fennel seeds, shallots, garlic, prunes, olives, and capers. Pour the fluid over the chicken after combining the wine, nectar, and any orange juice that was set aside. Incorporate more pepper and salt. Prepare for 45 minutes, or until the chicken is cooked and the stew is bubbling, closely secured with a overwhelming ovenproof top or aluminum thwart.
3. For an extra 15 minutes, caramelize the chicken, evacuate the cover, organize the orange wedges around the chicken, and skin side up. Some time recently serving, take the dish out of the broiler and let it rest for ten minutes.

19. Clambake in a Box

Prep time: 45min | Serve: 20| Calories: 3.5kcal

Fixings

- Six chicken parts refrigerated
- Hot dried up bread
- Twenty ears corn
- Two glasses of unsalted butter
- Four dozen clams
- Three pounds potatoes

Informational

1. Put six to eight inches of ocean growth interior the China box roaster.

Put the chicken on the side of the pig rack and put it on beat. A test thermometer ought to be embedded into the chicken breast. Light the charcoal by putting the grind and cover on it. One hour of broiling.
2. To hold all the clams, develop a cheesecloth or burlap sack with two layers. Open the box's top, at that point put the sack on the rack following to the chicken without touching it. On the other side of the chicken, organize one or two punctured pizza container or screens and after that include the potatoes and corn.
3. Include a moment, lean layer of ocean growth over everything. As teaching, supplant the cover and include another layer of charcoal. 45 minutes of simmering time, or until the test thermometer peruses 175°F confirm the doneness of the potatoes. With the cover off, permit steam to elude for around 15 minutes. Serve the supper straight from the box, or spread ocean growth on a dish, arrange the food on it, and after that serve. For plunging, serve with warm, dried up bread and softened butter.

20. Overnight meat chili Colorado

Prep time: 45min | Serve: 8-10| Calories: 44.5kcal

Fixings

- 6 dried ancho chili s
- 6 cuts of bacon, diced
- 1 expansive onion, chopped (Two mugs)
- 5 pounds hamburger brisket, trimmed and cut into 3-inch 3d shapes
- Legitimate salt, for flavoring, additionally One tsp.
- Crisply ground dark pepper
- 1 habanero chili, stemmed and seeded (discretionary)
- 6 cloves garlic, peeled
- Two tsps. cumin seeds
- One tsp. dried oregano
- One tsp. ground coriander

- Two tbsps. chili powder
- 1 (14½-ounce) can of fire-roasted diced tomatoes with green chili s
- 1 (12-ounce) bottle of Mexican lager
- Chopped stems from 1 bunch of cilantro
- 4 gentle green chili s, fire-roasted, peeled, seeded, and diced, or 1 (7-
- ounce) can dice fireroasted
- Green chili s

Garnishes

- Half container of new cilantro takes off
- 1 container finely chopped sweet ruddy onion
- One cut avocado
- Destroyed Monterey Jack cheese
- Warm corn or flour tortillas for serving

Enlightening

1. Cut the ancho chili s into pieces. Put the chili s in a bowl after expelling the seeds and stems. To drench for at slightest 30 minutes or up to a few hours, cover with bubbling water. In a wood-fired broiler, get ready a medium warm fire (350°F). Over medium warm, cook the bacon in a enormous Dutch stove until it begins to brown. After including, sauté the onion for 5 minutes. Include salt and pepper to taste when planning the meat.
2. Include the meat after turning off the warm within the pot. Mix the doused chili s with around 12 mugs of the dousing fluid (spare the remaining fluid to include to the pot afterward on the off chance that required).
3. Include the chili powder, habanero, garlic, cumin, oregano, and coriander, at the side One tsp. of legitimate salt. Pour over the meat after being mixed into a puree with the tomatoes, ale, cilantro stems, and green chilies. To equitably coat the meat and combine the fixings,

mix well. Place within the stove with the pot secured. To keep the warm within the chili for up to 12 hours or until the meat is tender to the fork, near the stove entryway. The pot is out of the broiler. In order to expel the coagulated fat, either skim the additional fat from the chili's surface or chill the chili overnight within the fridge. Utilize salt and pepper to taste to season.
4. Warm up the chili delicately. Warm tortillas for rolling and plunging, along with the garnishes on the side, ought to be served in bowls.

21. Wood-smoked cheese fondue

Prep time: 45min | Serve: 6-8| Calories: 14.5kcal

Fixings

- Two and a half mugs of dry white wine
- One and a half tbsps. Cornstarch
- Legitimate salt
- Three glasses of destroyed Italian fontina cheese
- One tbsp. water
- One-fourth tsp. nutmeg
- Three tbsps. Kirsch alcohol
- Three mugs of destroyed Gruyère cheese
- 1 lounge of artisan bread
- Six cloves of garlic, meagerly cut

Informational

1. In a wood pellet flame broil, plan a medium warm fire (325°F). In a modest clay or cast-iron pot with a cover, combine the wine and garlic. For around 20 minutes within the broiler, cook the garlic with the cover on.
2. Once the garlic has liquefied, expel the cover and heat for a assist 10 minutes. Take the garlic out of the broiler and pulverize it. To thicken

the blend, combine the water and cornstarch to form a slurry.
3. Include the cheeses after mixing, at that point put the dish back within the stove to soften them. Mix everything together some time recently including the discretionary Kirsch, nutmeg, and salt to taste. On the off chance that the sauce has diminished as well much, include a small water. Take out of the stove, at that point keep hot on a hibachi or tabletop burner. A small plate and a fondue fork ought to be given for each person. A bit of bread ought to be set on a fondue fork, plunged into the cheese, and after that brought up and spun to expel the additional cheese.

22. Braised Cauliflower, Potato, and Onion Curry

Prep time: 45min | Serve: 6-8| Calories: 4.5kcal

Fixings

- Two tbsps. canola oil
- 2 onions, chopped
- ½ jalapeno chili, seeded and minced
- ¾-inch piece of new ginger, peeled and minced
- 4 cloves garlic, minced
- One tsp. brown mustard seeds
- Half tsp. cumin seeds
- 1½ teaspoons coriander seeds
- 2 entirety cloves
- 4 entire peppercorns
- One tsp. legitimate salt
- Half tsp. ground turmeric
- Half tsp. Indian (hot) paprika
- One and a half glasses coconut drain
- Half container water
- 1 pound of potatoes, peeled and cut into huge pieces
- 1 head cauliflower (2 pounds), broken into bite-sized florets

Enlightening

1. In a wood pellet flame broil, plan a medium warm fire (325°F) in a little skillet over medium warm, and warm Two tbsps. Of the oil, at that point sauté the onions for 3 minutes, or until they are translucent. Cook the ginger and jalapeno for two minutes after including them. Include the garlic, blend, and stew for an extra two minutes. Put aside. The mustard seeds, cumin, coriander, cloves, and peppercorns ought to be sautéed in the remaining One tbsp. oil in a coated clay pot over medium warm until fragrant. Take out the flavors, at that point set aside the skillet.
2. Mix the blend of onions, sautéed flavors, salt, turmeric, and paprika. Pour in 1 container of the coconut drain or sufficient to create a lean glue whereas the machine is working. Put the blend and water in the already utilized coated clay pot for the flavors. Include the potatoes after mixing, cover, and prepare for 7 minutes. At this point, the potatoes ought to as it were be somewhat cooked.
3. Add the remaining coconut drain along side the cauliflower. In the event that additional water is required to lean, do so. For around 20 minutes, or when the veggies are cooked, and the flavors are well-balanced, cover and warm the dish within the broiler. To permit the feast to consolidate a few of the taste of the wood, reveal and heat for a encourage five minutes.
4. Whether hot or cool, serve.

12

Wood Pellet Barbecue Desserts and Sweets

1. Apple-Prune Galette

Prep time: 45min | Serve: 6-8| Calories: 144.5kcal

Fixings

Batter

- 1¼ glass unbleached all-purpose flour
- Half tsp. fine ocean salt
- Two tbsps. sugar
- 9 tablespoons cold unsalted butter, cut into little pieces
- 4 tbsps. cold water

Filling

- 6 or 7 smoker-grilled prunes, coarsely chopped
- 1 pound flavorful preparing apples, such as Gravenstein or Braeburn
- Two tbsps. sugar
- Two tbsps. Calvados, Armagnac, or Cognac
- One tbsp. sugar, for sprinkling

Enlightening

1. In a wood pellet barbecue, plan a hot fire (450°F). Combine the flour, salt, and sugar in a bowl to form the batter. Whisk the blend together. Rub or cut the butter into the flour together with your hands or a baked good blender until a few of it is in chips and the rest is the estimate of peas. To damp the dry fixings, include the water One tbsp. At a time whereas blending. Make a ball out of the batter. Indeed with a few butter streaks, it'll still show up a touch miserable. The batter ought to be separated into two parts, each of which ought to be straightened into a plate and wrapped in plastic. Put within the ice chest for up to 3 days or at slightest an hour. The additional mixture circle can be solidified for up to a month. Cover the prunes with

hot water and let them drench for 15 minutes to deliver the filling. Peel and center the apples, at that point cut them into 1/8-inch pieces while the prunes are drenching. Erase the prunes. They ought to be combined with the apples in a bowl, beside the sugar and booze. Roll out 1 disc of the mixture into a 14-inch circle on a board cleaned with flour. Exchange the circle to a pizza peel secured in cornmeal. Put the natural product within the center, taking off a 2-inch mixture border uncovered. As you go around, crease the mixture to seal as you overlap it over the natural product. Include One tbsp. of sugar to the batter that has been collapsed over. Straightforwardly exchange the galette from the peel onto the woodfired oven's hearth. Prepare for 25 to 30 minutes, or until the outside is brilliant and the apples are delicate to the tip of a cut.

2. Apricot Tart with Lavender Crème Anglaise

Prep time: 45min | Serve: 6-8| Calories: 44kcal

Fixings

- Baked good batter
- 2¼ glasses all-purpose flour
- ⅓ container almond flour or finely ground almonds
- Two tbsps. sugar
- Half tsp. finely ground nutmeg
- One tsp. salt
- Three-fourth glass (1½ sticks) cold unsalted butter, cut into little pieces
- Half container ice water

Filling

- 12 ounces dried California or Turkish apricots
- ¼ container amaretto or Terrific Marnier alcohol
- 2½ mugs water

- Three-fourth glass orange jelly furthermore Two tbsps. water
- ¼ container turbinate sugar
- Half container cut almonds
- Lavender Crème Auglaize

Informational

1. In a wood pellet barbecue, plan a medium warm fire (350°F). The dry fixings ought to be combined in a huge bowl or nourishment processor to deliver the mixture. When the butter is the estimate of peas, rub or chop it utilizing your fingertips or a baked good blender. Include half of the ice water continuously whereas mixing until the mixture shapes a ball. As it were include a small additional water in the event that fundamental. Maintain a strategic distance from exhausting the batter. Shape the batter into a plate on a floured surface, wrap it in plastic wrap, and chill for 30 minutes or overnight. In a little pot, combine the apricots, amaretto, and water. Cook over moo warm for around 20 minutes or until the apricots are ready and soft. Turn off the warm, deplete, and after that save. On a delicately cleaned surface, roll out the batter to a 12-inch circular that's almost 1/8 inch thick. Fit into a separable foot 10-inch tart pan. Roll the best with a rolling stick to induce freed of the additional mixture. Pie weights or dried beans ought to be put interior the tart shell after it has been lined with material paper. Prebake the container for 15 minutes within the stove. Some time recently filling, evacuate from the broiler and permit cool for 10 minutes. Embed a little piece of wood into the fire to raise the oven's temperature to 375°F. The apricots ought to fan out over the hull, with each cut covering the others by a half-inch.
2. Orange preserves and water are warmed to a spreadable consistency over moo warm. Overlay over best of the apricots. Best with the almonds once the turbinado sugar is sprinkled on. Prepare for 20 to 30 minutes, or until brown, on a heating sheet. After taking it out of the broiler, let it cool for at slightest 15 minutes. Evacuate from

the tart container once it has cooled, parcel, and serve with the crème anglaise on beat.

3. Lavender crème anglaise

Prep time: 45min | Serve: 6-8| Calories: 75kcal
Enlightening

- Two mugs of overwhelming cream
- 1 glass half-and-half
- ⅓ container finely ground Lavender Sugar
- ⅓ container wildflower nectar
- Two tbsps. dried lavender buds
- 4 expansive egg yolks

Enlightening

1. In a nonreactive pot, blend the cream, half-and-half, sugar, and nectar. Mixing with a elastic spatula or wooden spoon will offer assistance the sugar and nectar break down when the blend is warmed over mediumlow warm to fair underneath the bubbling point. Include the lavender after expelling it from the warm. For 10 minutes, cover and let soak.
2. Squeezing the lavender with the back of a huge spoon to discharge the juice, pour the blend through a fine-mesh strainer into a dish. Toss absent the lavender. Refill the pot with the flavored cream. Warm the skillet to fair underneath bubbling point over a medium-low warm source. Egg yolks are whisked in a little bowl. To mood, the eggs, steadily whisk 1 glass of the hot cream into the yolks. Mix persistently as you include the blend to the skillet with the remaining cream, cooking the custard until it thickens and coats the back of a wooden spoon. Eggs will turn sour in the event that the blend is permitted to bubble. Evacuate from the warm and pour into a sizable stainless

steel bowl after passing through a finemesh screen. For a number of minutes, delicately blend the custard to permit it to cool. Until prepared to serve, cover with plastic wrap, squeezing it solidly on the custard's surface. It may be put away for the night.

4. Breakfast Focaccia with Grapes and Figs

Prep time: 45min | Serve: 6-8| Calories: 75kcal

Fixings

Mixture

- One tbsp. dynamic dry yeast
- Two glasses of warm water (105° to 115°F)
- Half glass olive oil
- Two tsps. legitimate salt
- 4 mugs all-purpose flour

Topping

- 4 tbsps. blood orange olive oil (see Citrus Olive Oil)
- One tbsp. Minced new rosemary
- Two tbsps. vanilla turbinado sugar (see Vanilla Turbinado Sugar)
- Half container ruddy seedless grapes split
- Half container figs, quartered
- ¼ glass Candied Orange Peel

Informational

1. Pour the yeast over the warm water in a expansive bowl to create the mixture. Blend to combine the yeast, at that point permit it to stand for 5 minutes or until foamy. Salt and 1/4 glass of olive oil ought to be combined. To make a delicate mixture, whisk, at that point include half a glass of flour at a time.

2. At that point, roll the mixture into a ball on a board that has been softly cleaned with flour. Put the mixture in a sizable, softly oiled bowl and turn it to equitably disperse the oil. One to eleven and a half hours ought to pass as the bowl rises in awarm area with a soggy towel or plastic wrap covering it. In a wood pellet flame broil, get ready a medium-hot fire (425°F). A 12 by 17-inch preparing container ought to be gently oiled. Extend the batter to cover as much of the container as you'll be able after setting it there. Extend once more and dimple the best. 15 minutes ought to be apportioned for resting; cover with a towel. Sprinkle the rosemary and One tbsp. of vanilla turbinado sugar over the mixture after brushing it with Two tbsps of orange olive oil. Tenderly press the candied orange peel, figs, and grapes into the batter. Rehash the batter dimpling. For another 15 minutes of rest, cover with a towel. Put within the broiler after including the ultimate small vanilla turbinado sugar. Heat for 20 to 25 minutes or until brilliant brown. After taking it out of the broiler, sprinkle it with the extra orange olive oil. After 10 minutes, take off the heating container and cool encourage on a wire rack. Cut into rectangles or squares that are fitting for serving.

5. Candied orange peel

Prep time: 45min | Serve: 1| Calorie: 12.5kcal

Fixings

- 1 orange, cleaned
- 1 glass straightforward syrup
- Half container sugar

Enlightening

1. Peel the fruit's get-up-and-go and a parcel of the white smoker-grill in strips employing a vegetable peeler. Peel is cut into 1/8-inch-wide

strips. Put in a non-reactive pan and include the straightforward syrup to cover. Cook for 15 minutes after bringing to a moo stew on a wood pellet barbecue. Spread after depleting on a preparing sheet lined with paper. Hurl with the sugar, then leave it out within the open to dry for the night. Include to an sealed shut holder along side half the sugar. For afterward utilization as a embellish or as flavored sugar, spare the remaining citrus oil-infused sugar in a distinctive bump.

13

Wood Pellet Barbecuing and Simmering

1. Flame broiled cilantro-mint naan

Prep time: 1hr25mins | Serve: 10 | Calories: 416kcal
Fixings

Batter

- Two tsps. sugar
- Four tsps. heating powder
- Half container whole-milk yogurt
- Five mugs flour
- Four tsps. legitimate salt
- One and one-fourth mugs of warm water
- One-fourth container of shelled nut oil or canola oil
- One huge egg

Filling

- Half container of new mint clears out
- 1 clove of garlic, chopped
- One tbsp. chopped new ginger
- One and a half mugs cilantro
- One tbsps. shelled nut oil or canola oil
- One-fourth container of crude cashews
- One tsp. legitimate salt
- Four ounces of clarified butter for brushing

Informational

1. Make the mixture by blending water, oil and all dry fixings. Spread like a naan. Presently apply the butter blend with garlic seasonings and herbs.
2. Cook on a wood pellet barbecue.

2. Tuscan barbecued pizza with escarole

Prep time: 1hr | Serve: 10 | Calories: 505kcal

Fixings

- 2 cloves garlic, minced
- 4 tbsps. extra-virgin olive oil, also more for brushing
- Three-fourth container destroyed mozzarella cheese
- Three-fourth glass destroyed Italian fontina cheese
- ¼ glass pine nuts Takes off from 1 head escarole, cut into 1-inch-wide strips
- Two tsps. balsamic vinegar
- Squeeze of ruddy pepper drops, Salt and dark pepper
- Joanne Weir's Pizza Batter
- Half glass set niçoise olives, coarsely chopped

Enlightening

1. Plan a wood pellet barbecue with a hot fire (475 to 500°F). In a little bowl, combine the garlic and Two tbsps. Of the olive oil.
2. Set aside for 30 minutes. In a bowl, blend the fontina and mozzarella.
3. Pine nuts ought to be warmed in a sizable skillet over tall warm for one to two minutes, sometimes turning, until brown. Take out of the skillet and put aside.
4. Within the same container, warm the remaining Two tbsps of olive oil on medium. Escarole is included, and it is cooked for 1 to 2 minutes whereas being mixed once in a while. Ruddy pepper pieces and vinegar are included.
5. Utilize salt and pepper to taste to season. Put aside. Make two rise to balls of mixture by isolating the blend into two rise to pieces. Do not exhaust the mixture. One ball ought to be rolled into a 10- to 11-inch circle. Put the mixture on a preparing sheet that has been softly oiled and sprinkles olive oil over the beat. Proceed by utilizing the moment

mixture ball.

6. Bring the batter, fixings, and barbecue to the table. Put one pizza circular on the flame broil with the oiled side up. Cook the flame broil for 5 minutes with the cover on. The demonstrated side ought to be brushed with the garlic-infused oil to inside a half-inch of the edge some time recently flipping the pizza over. Expel the pizza from the warm source. On beat of the oil, sprinkle half of the combined cheeses. Spread similarly on beat and sprinkle with the remaining escarole, pine nuts, and olives. Heat with the cover on for approximately 7 minutes, or until brilliant and fresh. Make a second pizza by rehashing the method with the remaining fixings.

3. Joanne weir's pizza batter

Prep time: 1hr30mins | Serve: 10 | Calories: 283.8kcal

Fixings

- Two tsps. dynamic dry yeast
- Three-fourth container additionally
- Two tbsps. warm water (105° to 115°F)
- Two mugs of unbleached bread flour
- One tbsp. extra-virgin olive oil
- Half tsp. salt

Informational

1. Blend the yeast with one-fourth glass of warm water and one-fourth container of flour in a little bowl. Set aside for 30 minutes.
2. Include the salt, container also half a teaspoon of warm water.
3. The mixture ought to be well-mixed.
4. Turn out onto a floured surface and work for 7 to 8 minutes, or until the batter is flexible, smooth, and marginally tasteless to the touch. Put in a bowl that has been delicately oiled, turning to coat.

5. Permit rising until it has multiplied in volume, almost 1 to one and a half hours, in a warm area, secured with a wet towel or plastic wrap.
6. On the other hand, let the batter rise overnight within the fridge.
7. Bring the batter to room temperature the taking after day.

4. Flame broiled flank steak with ruddy peppers and fontina cheese

Prep time: 35mins | Serve: 6 | Calories: 460kcal

Fixings

- 1 (1½-to 2-pound) flank steak
- Legitimate Salt and dark pepper

Gremolata stuffing

- 1 container coarsely chopped new flat-leaf parsley
- ¼ glass julienned new basil
- 6 cloves garlic, whitened and minced. Ground get-up-and-go of 1 lemon
- ⅓ container bread scraps or panko (Japanese bread scraps)
- Half tsp. ruddy pepper pieces
- Half tsp. legitimate salt
- Two tbsps. olive oil, for dampening
- 2 ruddy chime peppers, broiled and peeled (see Wood-Roasted Ruddy Pepper Wine Sauce)
- Two glasses of pressed spinach takes off
- 8 ounces Italian fontina or Monterey Jack cheese, daintily cut Olive oil, for brushing
- Wood-Roasted Ruddy Pepper Wine Sauce

Informational

1. In a wood pellet smoker-grill or barbecue, construct a hot fire that's between 475° and 500°F. By cutting nearly through the steak on a level plane (once more, with the grain), taking off the two sides connected by a half-inch, you'll be able butterfly it. Salt and pepper the cut meat delicately after opening it up and smoothing it. The meat ought to be beat to a sensibly uniform thickness. Put aside.
2. Put all the fixings for the gremolata stuffing in a bowl. Two tbsps.
3. They are set aside for decorate.
4. The broiled ruddy peppers were isolated into 4 thick pieces. Over the opened steak, organize the spinach clears out. Put the ruddy pepper pieces to begin with, at that point the cheese pieces. Include a few gremolata stuffing on best. The steak ought to be safely rolled longitudinally. Each three inches or so, tie the coiled steak with kitchen string. Apply olive oil to the surface and sprinkle with a small salt and pepper.
5. Within the wood pellet smoker-grill or on the barbecue, put the meat on a grind and turn it after almost 10 minutes to brown all sides. When an instant-read thermometer put within the center peruses 120° to 130°F, expel the skillet from the warm source and proceed to cook for another 20 to 25 minutes. When it comes to 130° to 58°Con, an instant-read thermometer is put within the center, exchanged to a carving board, tent softly with aluminum thwart, and permitted rest for 10 minutes. Cut into rounds 12 inches thick, beat with the gremolata you spared, and serve with the wine sauce.

5. Flame broiled pork loin stuffed with chard, fennel, and olives

Prep time: 3hrs50mins | Serve: 6 | Calories: 542kcal

Fixings

Brine

- ⅓ glass salt
- ⅓ glass sugar
- 4 mugs water, at room temperature
- 1 (3-pound) pork loin, boned

Stuffing

- 4 to 6 expansive Swiss chard takes off, stemmed
- ¼ glass olive oil, furthermore more for brushing
- 1 pound green garlic or leeks, trimmed and cut the long way
- 1 medium fennel bulb, meagerly cut and chopped
- 1 container picholine olives, set and finely chopped
- 1 glass dry white wine Ground get-up-and-go of 1 orange
- Half glass chopped new flat-leaf parsley
- Two tsps. fennel seed
- Legitimate salt and naturally ground white pepper Olive oil, for brushing
- Toasted Walnut Sauce

Enlightening

1. In a wood pellet flame broil, begin a hot fire (450°F). Break down the salt and sugar within the water to form the brine. Refrigerate for two to three hours after including the pork loin to the brine. The pork loin ought to be flushed, dried with paper towels, and let warm up.
2. The chard clears out ought to be whitened for one miniature in salted

water some time recently being put promptly in a dish of ice water to create the stuffing. Clears out ought to be depleted and dried on paper towels. Green garlic is included to a sauté dish that has been warmed with one-fourth container of olive oil over medium warm on a wood pellet smoker flame broil. Include the fennel bulb and stew for a advance 7 minutes, or until the fennel is delicate. Cook until delicate, approximately 5 minutes. Wine and olives are included.

3. Cook the wine nearly to evaporation. Add salt and pepper to taste, in conjunction with the orange get-up-and-go, parsley, and fennel seed. Put aside.

4. After unrolling the pork, cut any abundance fat. Cut the pork into thirds longwise, halting around 12 inches from the interior. Lay the pork level after opening. Setting plastic wrap over the pork, smooth it with a little dish or level meat pounder to an rise to thickness of around 12 inches. Include a small pepper and salt for flavoring. To line the pork, spread the chard takes off that have been whitened. To inside half an inch of the edges, cover the chard with the fennel stuffing blend.

5. Beginning with one long side, roll the pork up jelly-roll fashion and tie with kitchen string each two inches.

6. Apply a lean layer of olive oil and liberally season with salt and pepper. Put the pork on the barbecue and turn it around after roughly 10 minutes, or until all the sides are brown and fair scarcely fresh. Put the cook on the grill's side, absent from the flares.

7. For 20 minutes, or until the cook is equitably browned and an instantread thermometer put into the substance(not the stuffing) peruses 145°F, cover the container and cook, pivoting the meat roughly each 5 minutes. After moving the meat to a cutting board, cover it freely with aluminum thwart and grant it 15 minutes to rest. Cut the meat into 1-inch-thick circles after expelling the strings. Serve with the walnut sauce on beat.

6. Toasted walnut sauce

Prep time: 20mins | Serve: 4 | Calories: 542kcal

Fixings

- 2 cuts of day-old white artisan bread, such as Pugliese, levain, sweet baguette
- 2 to 3 glasses of entire drain
- Two mugs (8 ounces) walnut parts or pieces, toasted
- 4 cloves broiled garlic
- One tbsp. new thyme clears out
- Legitimate salt and crisply ground white pepper
- ⅓ container olive oil
- Ruddy pepper drops (discretionary)

Enlightening

1. Put fair sufficient drain on the bread to cover it. Include the blend of walnuts, garlic, and thyme to a nourishment processor.
2. To create a glue, beat. Include white pepper and salt to taste.
3. Include the olive oil whereas the machine is running. To deliver a saucelike consistency, include drain as required. To taste, include ruddy pepper pieces.
4. Use right absent or store within the ice chest for up to a week.

7. Mediterranean sheep kebabs with pomegranate coat

Prep time: 2hrs40mins | Serve: 8 | Calories: 433kcal

Fixings

- Marinade
- Half glass chopped onion
- Legitimate salt

- One and a half teaspoons of ground cumin
- Two tsps. sweet Hungarian paprika
- Half tsp. chopped new ginger
- Four cloves of garlic, chopped
- One tsp. naturally ground dark pepper
- One tbsp. tomato glue
- Twenty-four cove takes off
- Two tbsps. olive oil
- Two tbsps. pomegranate molasses or concentrate
- Three pounds of boneless sheep bear
- One-fourth glass of chopped pistachio nuts
- Thirty-six dried Turkish apricot parts

<u>Informational</u>

1. Blend and blend all veggies and herbs, and flavors together to form a rub. At that point, beat to combine the tomato glue and pomegranate molasses. Sprinkle the olive oil into the machine whereas it is running to blend.
2. The sheep ought to be put in a dish, secured with half of the marinade, and let stand for two hours at room temperature or overnight within the fridge. The leftover portion of the marinade ought to be set aside for a barbecuing coat.
3. In a wood pellet flame broil, begin a hot fire.
4. Some time recently cooking, take the sheep out of the fridge 30 minutes in advance.
5. 30 minutes of water drench time for 16 wooden sticks. On the sticks, on the other hand string the sheep, narrows takes off, and apricot parts.
6. Salt the sheep fair a bit. The saved marinade ought to be bubbled for five minutes in a little dish.
7. For medium-rare, barbecue the sticks for almost four minutes on each side. Whereas cooking and after it has been taken off the warm,

proceed to brush on the marinade. Put the sticks in a line on a plate and best with pistachios.

8. Flame broiled duck breasts with lavender-herb rub

Prep time: 50mins | Serve: 6 | Calories: 297.4kcal
Fixings

- Two tbsps. herbes de Prwood pellet smoker-grille
- Two tbsps. new or dried lavender buds
- One tbsp. coriander seeds
- One tsp. fennel seeds
- Half tsp. broken dark peppercorns Ground pizzazz of 1 orange
- 2 (1-pound) Muscovy duck breasts
- Legitimate salt
- One tbsps. olive oil
- Two tbsps. crisply pressed orange juice
- Crisply ground white pepper
- 3 glasses infant greens

Informational

1. Employing a zest processor, crush the herbs and flavors to a really fine powder. Orange pizzazz and the ground herbs and flavors ought to be combined in a little bowl.
2. Score the duck breasts with five corner to corner lines divided approximately an inch separated, as it were going profound sufficient to cut the skin but not the substance.
3. Apply the herb blend equitably to both sides of the duck breast and work a few of it into the skin-side score marks. Utilize right once or, to upgrade the tastes, cover in plastic wrap and chill for up to a day.
4. Get ready a wood pellet barbecue with a hot fire (450–475°F). Evacuate the duck from the fridge and permit it to sit at room temperature for

30 minutes some time recently cooking. Salt, the duck, breasts fair a small.
5. For 3 minutes, flame broil the duck skin-side down over tall warm until the skin is fair starting to caramelize. Keep a water sprayer near by to offer assistance avoid any potential duck fat flare-ups. Exchange to a cast-iron skillet with the skin sides down. Cook for 8 minutes, or until greatly uncommon, on the side of the flame broil, absent from the flares. Turn the breasts over and deplete off any remaining duck oil. Medium-rare requires 3 to 4 minutes of cooking. Expel from the fire, cover freely with thwart, and permit to cool for five minutes. Cuts ought to be 14 inches thick when cut on the corner to corner and exchanged to a carving board.
6. In a little bowl, combine the orange juice with the olive oil and season with salt and pepper to taste. Isolate the child greens among 6 dishes and mix with the vinaigrette fair some time recently serving. Include 3 cuts of duck on beat of each. Any remaining vinaigrette ought to be sprinkled over the duck.

9. Tandoori chicken

Prep time: 50mins | Serve: 6 | Calories: 263kcal
Fixings

- 4 chicken thighs
- 4 chicken breasts
- Marinade
- 1 glass nonfat yogurt, depleted through a fine-mesh strainer for 1 hour
- Juice of 2 lemons
- 4 drops of ruddy nourishment coloring (discretionary)
- 4 cloves garlic, minced
- 1-inch piece of new ginger, minced
- Two tsps. garam masala
- Two tsps. ground cumin

- Half tsp. cayenne pepper
- Legitimate salt
- 4 little lemons, additionally lemon wedges for decorate

Enlightening

1. Begin a 500°F-hot fire. Put a 6-inch-deep high-fired ceramic bloom pot with a 5- to 6-inch base upside down within the foot of the cooker on the off chance that employing a Enormous Green Egg, wood pellet smoker barbecue, or another kettleshaped barbecue. Put 3 inches of charcoal around the pot; mesquite charcoal is favored since it burns greatly hot.
2. Chicken ought to have its skin evacuated, rinsed, and dried. Make many cuts within the winged creature that are 12 inches profound. To form the breasts the same measure as the thighs, cut them in half.
3. In a enormous bowl, blend all the fixings for the marinade. Turn the chicken to coat it after including it for at slightest 4 hours or in a perfect world overnight, cover and chill.
4. In a strainer or colander, expel the chicken from the marinade and let it deplete for an hour.
5. To hold the chicken in put, stick 3 to 4 pieces of chicken approximately 2 inches from the best of the stick. To stick all of the chicken, rehash. The blasting coals ought to be somewhat dispersed separated employing a fire poker. Keep the chicken absent from the wood pellet smoker grill's sidewalls and uncover it to the brilliant warm by embeddings the pointed closes of the sticks into the deplete gap of the pot that has been turned upside down. To guarantee that the chicken is cooked equally, turn the sticks after 10 minutes of secured cooking. Cook the chicken beneath cover for 15 minutes, or until it is completely done. The sticks ought to be taken out of the cooker and cleared out to stand for 5 minutes.
6. Lemon wedges are suggested.

10. Plank-roasted pacific salmon

Prep time: 2hrs30mins | Serve: 8 | Calories: 233kcal

Fixings
Remedy

- Two tbsps. legitimate salt
- ¼ container sugar
- Two tsps. coriander seeds
- Two tsps. fennel seeds
- 15 dark peppercorns
- 3 narrows takes off
- Two glasses of dry white wine
- ⅓ container clipped new dill
- 8 4-ounce or 2 1-pound salmon filets, skin on and stick bones evacuated
- Olive oil, for brushing

Enlightening

1. Two 12 x 7 x 5/8-inch oak boards ought to be submerged in water for two hours.
2. In a nonreactive pot, combine the salt, sugar, coriander, fennel, peppercorns, inlet clears out, and wine to create the remedy. Cook for 2 minutes after bringing to a bubble and after that bringing down the warm to a stew. Include the dill after taking the pot off the warm and let it cool completely. Utilize right absent or store within the ice chest for up to a week.
3. Put the salmon filets in a preparing dish that can oblige them all in one layer. Pour the cooled remedy over the angle, flip it once or twice, and let it stand for 15 to 30 minutes. Deplete the angle after expelling it from the remedy. Any dill or zest that sticks to the salmon is worthy. Apply a lean layer of olive oil to the angle.
4. Plan a wood pellet flame broil fire at medium warm (400°F). To put

out flare-ups, keep a splash bottle of water at the prepared. At that point, cover the flame broil after setting the dampened boards on it. Warm for approximately 3 minutes, or until the boards begin to smoke and crackle to some degree.

5. Put the salmon skin side down on the assigned side of the sheets after turning them over. For approximately 6 minutes, barbecue the salmon with the cover on until it's fair cooked through and somewhat straightforward within the center.
6. Exchange the salmon off the board to a heatproof plate or to a plate or plates that have been warmed. Whether hot or cool, serve.

11. Fennel-rubbed halibut with fava bean ragout

Prep time: 1hr30mins | Serve: 6 | Calories: 364.6kcal

Fixings

- One-fourth glass of ground fennel seeds
- One-third glass of olive oil
- Six halibut filets, cleaned
- Half tbsp. legitimate salt
- One-fourth teaspoon of naturally ground white pepper

Ragout

- One container broth
- Legitimate salt and white pepper
- Half tsp. saffron strings
- One pound of chanterelle mushrooms
- One glass of dry white wine
- Four tbsps. unsalted butter
- One pound of infant carrots
- Four little youthful leeks
- Five sprigs thyme

- One pound fava beans
- Half glass parsley clears out
- Two tbsps. minced shallots

Informational

1. Construct a 450°F medium-hot fire in a wood pellet barbecue. Make a glue with the fennel seeds and olive oil. Include the pepper and salt. Apply the blend to each filet, at that point take off it at room temperature.
2. White wine and stock ought to be brought to a moo bubble in a little nonreactive skillet to form the ragout. Saffron strings ought to be included after evacuating the skillet from the warm.
3. In a sizable sauté skillet set over medium warm on a wood pellet smokergrill, liquefy Two tbsps of the butter. Include the shallots and sauté for three to five minutes, or until delicate, some time recently including the leeks and mushrooms. Include the sprigs of thyme. Mix to rub off the browned bits from the pan's foot some time recently including the saffron juice. Cook over moo warm for 5 to 7 minutes, or until the fava beans and carrots are delicate, after mixing within the remaining Two tbsps. Of butter. Include the parsley after evacuating the thyme. Utilize salt and pepper to taste to season. Keep warmed and set aside.
4. Include the halibut after lubing the barbecue lattices. Cook beneath cover for 8 to 10 minutes on one side or until the flesh is totally misty. The fragile halibut doesn't ought to be turned over and cooked on all sides when the cover is closed. Put the barbecued side up on a warming dish, cover with ragout, and serve.

Cleaning leeks

1. Leeks are like sand traps, but they allow carefully assembled soups a colossal profundity of flavor.

2. Partitioned the dull green clears out of the leeks and wash them in a dish of warm water to reveal any sand.
3. Then chop them up and provide them a great blend in a unused bowl of water.
4. Along with your fingers, evacuate the minced leeks, letting any dregs drop to the foot of the bowl.

Steaming Fava Beans

1. Attempt this time-saving procedure from Paula Wolfert rather than the difficult three-step prepare of shelling, whitening, and peeling fava beans.
2. Unshelled fava beans ought to be set in a steamer rack over bubbling water; cover and stew for 15 minutes oruntil shriveled. Once cold to the touch, expel from the steamer. Evacuate each fava bean's skin after evacuating the cases.

12. Barbecued shrimp with herb vinaigrette

Prep time: 1hr30mins | Serve: 6 | Calories: 377kcal

Fixings

Brine

- ⅓ container salt
- ⅓ container sugar
- 4 mugs water, at room temperature
- 1 pound extra-large shrimp (16 to 20 tally), shell on, scored down
- the back and deveined

Marinade

- 4 cloves garlic, minced Ground get-up-and-go of 1 lime
- Half tsp. ruddy pepper drops

- ¼ container dry white wine Juice of 2 limes
- ¼ glass olive oil
- 6 modest bunches of infant arugula Herb Vinaigrette

Informational

1. Break up the salt and sugar within the water to form the brine. Let the shrimp stand for 20 to 30 minutes after including it. Deplete.
2. Construct a 450°F medium-hot fire in a wood pellet barbecue. 30 minutes of water drench time for 6 wooden sticks.
3. In a huge bowl, combine all the fixings for the marinade. With the shrimp, hurl. 30 minutes of refrigeration covert.
4. Each stick ought to have 3 shrimp on it, each penetrated through both closes. 15 minutes ought to be given to stand at room temperature.
5. Barbecue them for 1-2 minutes per side, or until they are fair beginning to turn pink all over. Serve with the vinaigrette and a bed of infant arugula. Give the extra vinaigrette on the side for plunging.

13. Herb vinaigrette

Prep time: 20mins | Serve: 2 | Calories: 290kcal

Fixings

- 4 cloves garlic, whitened or poached
- 1 glass pressed new flat-leaf parsley
- ¼ glass new basil clears out
- ¼ glass new mint clears out
- One tsp. legitimate salt
- ¼ container naturally crushed lime juice
- Two tbsps. mirin (Japanese cooking wine)
- Three-fourth glass olive oil
- One tsp. nectar, or as required

Informational

1. In a nourishment processor or blender, combine all the fixings, with the exemption of nectar and olive oil.
2. Olive oil ought to be included slowly whereas the machine is working to deliver an emulsion.
3. As wanted, include nectar. Survey the flavor and flavoring.

14. Barbecued Panzanella with treasure tomatoes

Prep time: 40mins | Serve: 2 | Calories: 277kcal

Fixings

- 1 (1-pound) daydream of day-old provincial bread, such as Pugliese or ciabatta,
- 6 cloves broiled garlic
- Half tsp. Coarse ocean salt
- Two tbsps. extra-virgin olive oil, also more for brushing

Dressing

- ⅓ glass Champagne or white balsamic vinegar
- Half tsp. sweet pimentón (Spanish smoked paprika)
- Three-fourth glass extra-virgin olive oil
- Ocean salt
- 1 ruddy chime pepper, simmered, peeled, and torn into limit strips
- 4 green onions, finely chopped (counting half of the greens)
- 8 ounces haricots verts or infant Blue Lake green beans, whitened,
- depleted, and cut into julienne
- 8 ounces tomatoes in blended colors, cut into bite-sized pieces
- 3 lemon or English cucumbers, cut into little wedges
- ⅓ container dark oil-cured olives set
- Two tbsps. capers, flushed and depleted

- Legitimate Salt and dark pepper
- 1 dozen new basil takes off, torn into bite-sized pieces
- 4 ounces Parmesan cheese, cut into lean shavings

Enlightening

1. Whether employing a flame broil container or a wood pellet barbecue, plan a medium-hot (450°F) fire.
2. Cut the daydream of bread into one-inch pieces after trimming the heel closes. Make a glue with ocean salt and garlic. Two tbsps. The olive oil ought to be mixed in. Cuts of bread ought to be brushed with the garlic blend on one side.
3. In the event that utilizing, preheat a flame broil container over tall warm. Toast the bread, dry side down, for three minutes or until it starts to faintly brown. Oil the barbecue lattices or flame broil container. Rehash on the other side of the bread after flipping it over. Take the nourishment off the warm and permit it to cool to some degree. Put the bread in a huge bowl after it has been torn into bite-sized pieces.
4. In a little bowl, blend together the vinegar and pimentón to deliver the dressing. At that point, add the oil steadily to make an emulsion. Salt to taste, at that point stop.
5. In a bowl, blend the capers, ruddy pepper, green onions, beans, tomatoes, cucumbers, and olives. Dress basically and season with salt andpepper to taste. Include to the bread, mix, and let stand for 30 minutes. In the event that more dressing is required to cover the bread, include it. At that point, toss within the basil clears out once more. Serve with Parmesan cheese on a plate or in partitioned servings.

15. Salade niçoise with spring vegetables

Prep time: 30mins | Serve: 2 | Calories: 459kcal

Fixings
Dressing

- Two tbsps. minced shallots
- Two cloves of barbecued garlic
- One-fourth glass Champagne vinegar
- One glass of olive oil
- Two tsps. thyme takes off
- One-fourth container minced tarragon
- Half tsp. anchovy glue
- One and a half pounds of unpeeled potatoes
- Half-pound infant carrots
- Legitimate Salt and dark pepper
- Two tsps. Dijon mustard
- One and a half pounds of fish steaks
- Half glass of dark olives
- Salt and dark pepper
- One half quart of little tomatoes
- Two tbsps. parsley takes off
- Eight mugs of youthful lettuce
- One-fourth container capers
- Three hard-cooked eggs

Enlightening

1. Whether employing a flame broil container or a wood pellet flame broil, light a medium-hot (450°F) fire.
2. In a little bowl, include the shallots, anchovy vinegar, mustard and garlic glue, and whisk to mix. Oil ought to be whisked in slowly until the blend shapes an emulsion. Include salt and pepper to taste and

blend within the thyme and tarragon. Put aside.

3. For three to four minutes, or until crisp-tender, put the beans in bubbling salted water and cook for a whereas. Exchanging them to a bowl of ice water right absent will halt the cooking. When totally cooled, expel, at that point deplete, pat dry, and set absent. Utilize the same method to plan the carrots. The potatoes ought to be included to salted bubbling water, stewed revealed for fifteen to twenty minutes, at that point depleted into a colander. Whereas the potatoes are still warm, cut them in half and blend with a small dressing to coat. Set separated for cooling.
4. In the event that utilized, warm a flame broil container over tall warm some time recently bringing down it to mediumhigh.
5. Either oil the flame broil container or the flame broil lattices. Olive oil ought to be utilized to softly season the fish steaks on both sides with salt and pepper.
6. For medium-rare, cook revealed for approximately eight minutes by turning sides. After taking it off the warm, rest it for three minutes. Cut into pieces that are at slightest 3 inches in length.
7. Include almost Two tbsps. Of the dressing, Two tbsps. Of the lettuce, pepper and salt to a expansive bowl. Include the tomatoes to a little bowl with One tbsp. of the dressing and a small ocean salt. Fair some time recently serving, hurl the beans with a small dressing.
8. On a dish, partitioned off the potatoes, tomatoes, beans, fish, olives, lettuce and egg wedges. Serve after including the parsley. Include capers to the fish and sprinkle dressing over each serving.

16. Spanish-style potato serving of mixed greens with saffron-aioli dressing

Prep time: 30mins | Serve: 6 | Calories: 346kcal

Fixings

- 8 unpeeled ruddy potatoes Olive oil, for brushing
- Two tbsps. chopped new oregano clears out
- Two tbsps. new thyme clears out
- Coarse ocean salt, for sprinkling
- 1 to One and a half glasses Saffron-Aioli Dressing
- One tbsp. chopped new flat-leaf parsley
- One tbsp. finely chopped green onion

Informational

1. In a wood pellet flame broil, plan a medium warm fire. Employing a sharp cut, cut the potatoes into 1-inch-thick chunks. After drying, utilize olive oil and brush. Salt and herbs ought to be sprinkled equally over both sides.
2. Cook the potato cuts on the barbecue for approximately 8 minutes on each side or until they are brilliant and fresh.
3. Include ocean salt and exchange to a chopping board. Cut the pieces into 12-inch pieces after stacking them. Whereas the serving of mixed greens is still warm, dress it.
4. Include the parsley and green onion as embellish.

17. Saffron-aioli dressing

Prep time: 20mins | Serve: 2 | Calories: 326kcal

Fixings

- Little squeeze (around 20 strands) of saffron strings
- 1½ tablespoons warm water
- 2 huge egg yolks
- 1 expansive clove of garlic, minced
- ¼ teaspoon salt
- Three-fourth container extra-virgin olive oil
- Two tsps. crisply pressed lemon juice
- Naturally ground dark pepper

Enlightening

1. In a little bowl, douse the saffron strings in warm water for 20 minutes. In a huge bowl, blend the salt, garlic, and egg yolks employing a whisk.
2. Another alternative could be a blender. Up until about half of the oil has been included, exceptionally slowly include the olive oil in an awfully lean stream whereas whisking persistently.
3. The aioli will isolated in case the oil is included as well quickly. Pour the lemon juice into the dish with the saffron after including the saffron and its soaking water to capture any waiting saffron flavor. The aioli ought to be whisked with lemon juice.
4. Include many peppercorns for at slightest four hours or up to 48 hours, cover and chill.

18. Spit-roasted leg of sheep with tzatziki

Prep time: 2hrs30mins | Serve: 8 | Calories: 220kcal

Fixings

- One leg of sheep
- Half tsp. Chopped new thyme
- Two cloves of garlic, daintily cut, additionally one clove minced
- One-fourth glass chopped new flat-leaf parsley
- Two tbsps. chopped new mint

- Salt and dark pepper
- Half tsp. chopped new rosemary
- Four tbsps. extra-virgin olive oil
- Two tbsps. chopped new chives
- Tzatziki
- Half tsp. chopped new oregano

Enlightening

1. Get ready a medium-hot flame(425°F) in a wood pellet smoker-grill or a exceptionally hot fire (500°F) in a chimney.
2. The leg's outside ought to be on the work surface once you lay the lamb flat. Make numerous cuts within the sheep with the tip of a cut, and at that point tuck a cut of garlic into each one. Include a small pepper and salt for flavoring.
3. Combine the parsley, chives, mint, rosemary, thyme, oregano, chopped garlic, and three tablespoons of olive oil in a little bowl.
4. The lamb's uncovered side ought to be consistently secured with the herb blend. Sheep ought to be rolled and wrapped around the spit, at that point affixed with kitchen string or little metal turkey sticks. Salt and pepper the lamb's outside after brushing it with the remaining One tbsp. of olive oil.
5. Utilizing an electric or battery-powered gadget to turn the spit relentlessly, position the spit 6 to 8 inches from the fire and spit-roast the sheep for roughly an hour, or until an instant-read thermometer put into the thickest parcel of the lamb reads 58°C for medium-rare. If you lean toward, you'll cook the sheep within the wood pellet smoker-grill for 1, 12 to 2 hours, or until an instant-read thermometer put into the thickest parcel of the sheep peruses 58°C. Some time recently cutting, let the meat rest for at slightest 10 minutes. Serve nearby Tzatziki.

19. Mustard and lemon chicken

Prep time: 3hrs30mins | Serve: 8 | Calories: 370kcal

Fixings

Rub

- One tbsps. Hungarian paprika
- Two tbsps. crisply ground dark pepper
- Two tbsps. celery salt
- Two tbsps. sugar
- One tbsp. garlic powder
- One tbsp. dry mustard
- One tsp. cayenne pepper
- Get-up-and-go of 1 to 2 lemons, minced
- Two tbsps. unsalted butter
- One tbsp. Worcestershire sauce
- Two chickens
- One onion, cut into lean wedges
- One lemon, cut into lean wedges

Lemon wipe

- One and a half mugs of chicken stock
- Three-fourth container naturally crushed lemon juice
- Half onion
- Half glass unsalted butter
- One tbsp. Worcestershire sauce
- One tbsp. yellow mustard
- Half glass water

Enlightening

1. In a little bowl, combine all the rub fixings the night some time recently

you proposed to flame broil.
2. Liquefy the butter and include the Worcestershire sauce to a little pot.
3. Chickens ought to be stripped of their additional fat and giblets. The butter blend ought to be connected to both the interior and exterior of the hens, and it ought to be rubbed in as profoundly as conceivable without bursting the skin. After setting aside around a third of the rub, coat the winged creatures with the remaining blend and rub the skin completely on both sides.
4. Refrigerate the chickens after putting them in sizable self-sealing sacks.
5. In a wood-fired cooker, make a moo warm fire (200° to 220°F). The winged creatures ought to be taken out of the ice chest. After giving them another dry rub, put the onion and lemon wedges interior the body cavities. Donate the winged creatures almost 30 minutes to stand at room temperature.
6. In a pot, combine all the fixings and warm over moo warm to make the clean.
7. Place the chicken's breast down within the smoker. Cook for two hours, seasoning with a wipe as fundamental (or each 30 minutes). When the legs can move unreservedly, and an instant-read thermometer put on the thigh or breast peruses 180° to 185°F, turn the bird's breast side up and proceed to cook for an extra one and half hours.
8. Permit the feathered creatures to stand in a free tent made of aluminum thwart for five to ten minutes. Carve the chicken, at that point include the lemons and onions to the cavities some time recently serving.

20. Mushroom-rubbed plank-roasted steak

Prep time: 45-60min | Serve: 4 | Calories: 40kcal
Fixings

- Half tsp. legitimate salt

- ¼ teaspoon naturally ground pepper
- One tbsps. simmered mushroom powder
- 4 (8-ounce) meat tenderloin steaks,
- 1½ inches thick
- Smoked or flavored ocean salt for embellish, Disintegrated blue cheese for decorate

Informational

1. Four broiling sheets, each measuring 7 inches by 1 3/4 inches, ought to douse in water for an hour. In a wood-fired cooker, get ready a medium warm fire (375°F) for both coordinate and roundabout cooking. The board ought to be situated on a grind that's generally 8 inches over the warm source.
2. In a little bowl, blend the mushroom powder, salt, and pepper. Once the steaks are totally dry, knead them with the dry blend.
3. Deplete the sheets, at that point softly burn one side over coordinate fire (on a grind or over coals) to stamp.
4. Move the boards to backhanded warm after gently rubbing them with olive oil on the switch side. A cast-iron skillet ought to be warmed altogether. The steaks ought to be burned on both sides some time recently being set on the charred side of the sheets. Cover the cooker so that flavor-enhancing smoke covers the nourishment. For medium-rare, cook for 12 to 15 minutes.
5. Boards and all, expel steaks from fire and permit to rest for 5 minutes some time recently serving. The boards or plates may be utilized to serve the steaks.
6. Include smoked salt and a few blue cheese disintegrates as a decorate.

21. Wood-roasted antipasti platter

Prep time: 45-60min | Serve: 6 | Calories: 40kcal

Fixings

- 1 pound of substantial mushrooms (porcini, chanterelles, maitake, portobellos)
- Olive oil
- Ocean salt
- 1 pound each of 3 to 4 arranged vegetables, such as beets, infant
- Carrots, parsnips, ruddy chime peppers, eggplant, spring onions, radicchio,
- Asparagus, and/or Brussels grows
- 1 head garlic
- 6 shallots
- 3 to 4 sprigs of rosemary, thyme, or marjoram
- 1 modest bunch of quality brine-or oil-cured olives, blended or single assortment
- Serving wedges of one hard-aged cheese, such as Manchego or pecorino
- Cuts of one stellar cured meat, such as salami or prosciutto

Enlightening

1. In a wood smoker-grill or cooker, get ready a medium warm fire (350° to 375°F) or lower the temperature to 250°F to permit for moderate overnight simmering. Cut longwise, the mushrooms are put in a shallow simmering skillet with salt and olive oil.
2. Other veggies can be chopped into bite-sized pieces or, on the off chance that they are child vegetables, cleared out entirety. Put each assortment of vegetable in a partitioned little broiling skillet and hurl with salt and olive oil.
3. The vegetables ought to be heated until they are delicate and

caramelized.

4. Ruddy peppers ought to be specifically simmered on the ground or within the stove ashes for 10 minutes or until completely rankled.
5. After 15 minutes, put in a bowl, cover, and let rest some time recently peeling, seeding, and cutting into strips. The garlic head ought to be simmered until delicate.
6. Shallots ought to be cut in half longwise and after that combined with salt, olive oil, and herb sprigs until brilliant, caramelized, and delicate, cook in the oven. Just some time recently serving, rewarm the cheese and olives within the wood smoker flame broil. Serve on a platter with new olive oil, dried up bread, and your favored wine. Cheerful eating!

22. Mushroom-artichoke ragout

Prep time: 45-60min | Serve: 4 | Calories: 40kcal

Fixings

- 8 infant artichokes or huge artichoke hearts
- 1 pound asparagus, trimmed and peeled
- 1 pound new, substantial mushrooms, such as porcini
- 4 cloves garlic, cut
- Strips of lemon pizzazz Salt and dark pepper Olive oil, for sprinkling
- 2 long sprigs of thyme
- 1 inlet leaf
- One and a half mugs of dry white wine
- Juice of ½ lemon

Enlightening

1. In a wood smoker-grill or cooker, get ready a medium warm fire (350° to 375°F). Put a clay dough puncher at the hearth's edge and preheat it. Up until the youthful artichokes' pale green takes off, peel the external

clears out off. Cut off any parcels of the heart that came into contact with the external takes off and trim the stem. Evacuate any thorn choke some time recently cutting artichokes in half the long way.

2. Cuts of artichoke hearts ought to be 1/4 inch thick. Cut the asparagus lances into 2-inch-long sections on the inclining. Cut the cleaned and trimmed mushrooms longwise into 14-inch-thick pieces. Include the garlic, lemon pizzazz, salt, and pepper to a bowl with the vegetables, and after that include the olive oil. Include the thyme and cove leaf after layering the blend within the preheated clay dough puncher.

3. Put on the stove floor at that point covers with the white wine. About 30 minutes of broiling is required to create the veggies delicate and the mushrooms brilliant. Include the lemon juice after turning the warm off. To taste and season as fundamental.

23. Wood-roasted artichokes

Prep time: 45-60min | Serve: 4 | Calories: 40kcal

Fixings

- 2 artichokes
- Fine ocean salt
- Olive oil, for braising
- 2 lemons, cut into wedges or ¼-inch rounds

Informational

1. In a wood smoker flame broil, plan a tall fire (450°F) or permit the stove to cool after a more sultry bread is prepared. Move the ash heap to the oven's cleared out back. Take a number of of the artichokes' external clears out off.

2. Evacuate the chokes by cutting the artichokes in half. Sprinkle a small ocean salt on the uncovered range. Put the artichokes in a cast-iron skillet cut side down. Around half an inch of olive oil ought to be

included to the skillet some time recently including water to raise the fluid level to one inch.
3. In between the artichokes, put the lemon cuts. Almost 5 inches away from the flares, put the skillet within the broiler. Until delicate, cook for 12 to 15 minutes. Evacuate the dish from the broiler and set it on a wire rack to cool a small.

24. Best-ever brussels grows

Prep time: 45-60min | Serve: 4 | Calories: 40kcal

Fixings

- 1 pound Brussels grows
- 3 huge shallots, cut into ½-inch wedges
- ¼ container olive oil Legitimate salt
- 1½ tablespoons Dijon mustard
- Half glass of dry white wine
- Half tsp. crisply ground white pepper
- ¼ teaspoon dried savory (discretionary)

Informational

1. In a wood smoker-grill or cooker, get ready a medium-hot flame(400° to 425°F). Brussels grows ought to be cut in half lengthwise. Add salt to taste and hurl with the shallots within the olive oil. Select a medium cast-iron skillet or clay bread cook and oil it so that it'll fit the Brussels grows and shallots cozily in a single layer. Put the shallots and Brussels grows within the dish with the cut side confronting up and broil them within the oven or stove revealed. The dish can be put straightforwardly on the hearth when employing a wood smoker flame broil.
2. Combine the remaining fixings to make a sauce. Pour the sauce over the vegetables after 10 minutes.

3. Back within the cooker, carefully cover with aluminum thwart or a cover. Cook the Brussels grows for a assist 10 minutes, or until exceptionally delicate. For a couple of more minutes, or until browned, evacuate the top and broil.

25. Salt-roasted potatoes

Prep time: 45-60min | Serve: 6 | Calories: 40kcal

Fixings

- 5 pounds legitimate or coarse ocean salt
- 2 pounds little unpeeled ruddy or Yukon Gold potatoes
- 2 sprigs rosemary
- 1 narrows leaf

Enlightening

1. Plan a wood smoker-grill or cooker with a hot fire (500°F). One inch of salt ought to be utilized to line a 6-quart Dutch broiler, profound castiron Spyder, or clay casserole. Put the rosemary and inlet leaf inside the salt some time recently burying the potatoes. Cover the potatoes with the remaining salt.
2. Broil the potatoes for one hour, secured, or until they are delicate. Take off the pot's cover open whereas broiling for a smokier flavor, but make beyond any doubt the potatoes are well secured with at slightest 1 inch of salt. Angle out the potatoes, at that point pour the pot's substance into a bowl. Potatoes with salt buildup ought to be brushed off. Serve entirety or fork-crunched.

26. Simmered tomatoes provençal

Prep time: 60min | Serve: 8 | Calories: 40kcal

Fixings

- 8 huge, firm tomatoes
- Legitimate salt
- One and a half mugs coarse new bread pieces
- One tbsps. Chopped new flat-leaf parsley
- Two tbsps. new thyme takes off, additionally thyme sprigs for decorate
- ¼ glass ground Parmesan cheese
- 4 cloves garlic, whitened and minced
- Two tbsps. Capers depleted and washed. Crisply ground dark pepper
- ¼ glass olive oil

Enlightening

1. Set up a wood smoker-grill or flame broil with a medium-hot flame(400 to 425 degrees Fahrenheit). Evacuate the tomato tops and toss them absent. To carefully seed the tomatoes whereas keeping the shells intaglio, utilize a teaspoon or your finger. The interior of the tomatoes ought to be softly salted.
2. Put the tomatoes on paper towels with the cut side down to deplete for 15 minutes. In a little bowl, blend the cheese, minced garlic, capers, parsley, and Two tsps of thyme.
3. To taste, include salt and pepper. In a terra cotta dish or skillet enormous sufficient to incorporate all the tomatoes, warm the olive oil over medium warm. Put the tomatoes within the dish or skillet with the cut side confronting up and broil for 5 minutes.
4. Turn the tomatoes cut side up after taking them from the warm. Each tomato ought to have 2 to Two tbsps of the breadcrumb blend heaped on best. Sprinkle a small salt on beat after searing and splashing the topping. Prepare the topping for 30 minutes or until brilliant. Serve

with thyme as a decorate.

14

Conclusion

A wood pellet smoker flame broil is the leading choice for your following open air cooking contraption to utilize with a BBQ. Now that you've utilized the rest utilize the leading! No longer basic are huge grills and annually flame broil buys. You'll flame broil, cook, heat, smoke, and tenderly cook dinners over a wood pellet grill. Like propane barbecues, they require 10 to 15 minutes to warm up. Much appreciated to its roundabout warming framework, there are no flare-ups, and you never taste the strongly smoke odors once in a while made by charcoal or straight wood fires.

Agreeing to ordinary intelligence, smoke as it were enters proteins when the surface temperature of meat, poultry, and shellfish is underneath 140°F. It can stand up to temperatures as low as 140°F and offers good temperature control. Since a wood pellet smoker barbecue offers superior temperature control, you may be able to preserve the lower temperatures needed for the most excellent smoke arrangement.

This book has compiled a few truly delicious formulas to be made utilizing your wood pellet smoker flame broil. You may certainly appreciate them together with your adored ones at domestic.

15

Outdoor Gas Griddle

Book 2:

Outdoor Gas Griddle Cookbook

16

Presentation

Barbecuing is something we've all developed up seeing our guardians do since ready to keep in mind. We utilized to be astounded by seeing those colossal hot pooches swell up and part separated when we were adolescents. Keep in mind the smell of meat from those thick, succulent burgers, all that fat spilling over the shining ruddy ashes with a murmur, a burst of fire, and blue smoke wrapping around the sizzling edges? It's presently engaging to see your children or grandchildren's faces light up as they observe you flip burgers with tastefulness and dramatic skill. Barbecuing may be considered a normal slant. It's in our blood about from the minute we're born. The browning of sugars and proteins on meat and vegetables, which makes that dazzling coloring and extra flavor profile, is what truly makes barbecued dishes taste way better.

Genuine barbecuing comprises of cooking nourishment on an uncovered wire lattice with the warm either over or underneath the supper. Barbecuing is the term we utilize when the warm source is over, but it still falls inside our concept of grilling. Most individuals are ignorant that when veggies are barbecued, they hold more vitamins and minerals. Usually especially genuine of vegetables with moo water substance. Moreover, veggies hurled on the barbecue are for the most part new and in season, a step up from canned vegetables. This approach, whether secured in tin thwart or fair laid on best of the barbecue, is healthfully best than bubbling or singing your veggies. After you cook a bit of meat over an open flame, more thiamine and riboflavin are protected. These minerals are basic in a adjusted slim down and give a few wellbeing focal points. Cooking and eating exterior invigorates more development, which we all know could be a extraordinary way to include additional wellbeing benefits to your brilliant supper. This comprehensive direct to barbecuing incredible nourishments incorporates a part more data. On the off chance that you need to plan superb dinners and appreciate your dinner, you ought to certainly check it out.

17

Grilling: A Synopsis

Cooking your nourishment on a rack over any warm source, such as ceramic briquettes or charcoal fire warmed by the gas blazes, is called flame broiling. Coordinate warm right away burns the exterior of nourishment, giving wealthy, broiled, and sometimes delightfully burnt flavors as well as a beautiful hull. When nourishment is cooked over direct warm, it creates a hull and a smokier flavor.

Choosing the gear

Selecting between a gas and a charcoal flame broil could be a matter of individual inclination; they work so also, in case not indistinguishably. Select a barbecue with a huge cooking surface as well as a cover. A few individuals like gas flame broils since they are more helpful and give persistent warm, whereas others incline toward the handson strategy to construct a charcoal fire. Other valuable apparatuses are a charcoal chimney starter, long-handled tongs, a brush for seasoning, spatula, broiler gloves, a cleaning wire brush, expendable thwart container, and a meat thermometer.

Flame broiling utilizing coordinate warm

Cooking nourishment specifically over the warm source, regularly with the cover expelled, is known as coordinate flame broiling. This prepare cooks nourishment quickly with critical warm, comparative to broiling. Most vegetables, as well as lean cuts of meat that cook quick (burgers and other sorts of steaks and chops, for case), work best with this prepare. Bigger chunks of meat aren't prescribed since the tall warm might overcook them exterior some time recently they are done on the interior. Utilize coordinate warm on the off chance that the cooking time is less than 20-25 minutes.

Barbecuing utilizing roundabout warm

Use circuitous barbecuing for nourishment that has to cook longer (for illustration, pork bear or entirety chickens), in which a fire is set up on one or both sides of the nourishment, and hot discuss circulates it. Roundabout flame broiling requires the utilize of a secured flame broil to actuate warm convection. It's a gentler way of cooking than coordinate barbecuing, letting bigger pieces total cooking without unreasonably browning. Utilize backhanded warm in case the cooking time surpasses 20 to 25 minutes, indeed whereas huge angle filets can be cooked in fifteen minutes or less over coordinate fire. Since angle is so sensitive, direct grilling might overcook it and cause it to dry out. This can be due to the reality that coordinate flame broiling can cause skin oils to burn, coming about in a fishy odor which numerous individuals disdain. Angle will cook pleasantly and remain wet in case you utilize backhanded warm.

Keep your flame broil clean

Preheat the rack for 10-15 minutes on tall on all burners. This will burn any remaining buildup from the previous cookout, making cleanup simple. At that point, brush the barbecuing grates employing a barbecue brush with brass bristles. In the event that you are doing not have a brass-bristle cleaning brush, clean your grates with a folded heavy-duty aluminum thwart ball held between tongs. Clean the grates well to guarantee that the grates are smoothand clear of any nourishment buildup from later barbecuing. Each time you flame broil, brush the preheated flame broil racks.

Preheat the flame broil some time recently the begin of the barbecuing season Preheat the barbecue for an hour with all burners on tall or an indeed coating of preheated charcoal some time recently brushing the cooking grates at the begin of barbecuing season. This as it were should be done once to urge your grates prepared for the season.

Light up

For your gas barbecue, you simply got to touch off the burners as well as set them as well tall. Switch off one side of the barbecue when it's all preheated on the off chance that utilizing roundabout warm. A chimney starter is the foremost helpful way to light briquettes, charcoal, or protuberance hardwood on the off chance that you have got a charcoal barbecue. With 50 briquettes, a classic pot barbecue is most viable. Utilize a boring, an odorless gasoline starter or folded daily paper to begin the fire. Permit the charcoal to burn until it is totally secured in white-gray fiery debris, showing that it has come to the perfect cooking temperature. In case you're utilizing coordinate warm, similarly disseminate the briquettes around the charcoal grind. In case you're utilizing the roundabout cooking strategy, convey the briquettes equally on both sides of the grind and fill the space with an cheap expendable aluminum container. The nourishment is put on beat of a dribble pan, which collects dribbles and returns a few warm to the dish. Numerous cooks fill one side of the barbecue with charcoal and take off the other purge. Be that as it may, by setting briquettes on each side of the nourishment, a consistent warm is made that encompasses it.

Learn to control the warm

The warm on a charcoal flame broil is controlled utilizing discuss vents. Briquettes ought to not be put over the foot discuss vents to encourage wind current. Too, keep the top-of-the-grill vent at slightest mostly open. The flame broil will gotten to be more warmed on the off chance that the vents are cleared out open. Cover the vents midway in the event that you need medium warm.

Oil the nourishment

To attain telltale barbecue marks and to assist anticipate staying, coat the feast (not the barbecue rack) with oil or cooking splash at whatever point conceivable. On the off chance that you do not coat the nourishment some time recently barbecuing it, the normal juices will evaporate, leaving the nourishment dry as well as papery. This is often particularly genuine with vegetable cuts.

Foot line

See your open air flame broil as an expansion of your kitchen. Servings of mixed greens with dynamic flame broiled summer vegetables, effective entrées of angle, or flame broiled chicken and indeed a few flame broiled natural product sweets are possible. Best of all, once you've aced the essentials, anybody can gotten to be a gourmet griller. To assist you ended up a proficient griller, we have arranged this cookbook and accumulated a few delightful flame broiled angle, chicken, meat, sheep, and vegetable formulas which you'll get ready effortlessly with easy-to-follow informational.

18

Ideas for Grilled Fish

Now is the perfect time to choose from the many grilled fish recipes that have been compiled especially to make your outdoor grilling experience enjoyable.

1. Barbecued Angle Steaks

Arrangement and cooking time
1 hour 30 minutes
Servings
2 people
Dietary Truths
554 calories
Fixings

- 1 clove garlic, minced
- 1 teaspoon ground dark pepper
- 1 tablespoon new lemon juice
- 6 tbsp. olive oil
- 1 teaspoon dried basil
- 1 teaspoon salt
- 1 tablespoon chopped new parsley
- 2 (6 ounces) filets of halibut

Informational

1. Blend garlic, olive oil, basil, salt, pepper, lemon juice, as well as parsley in a stainless steel or glass bowl.
2. Pour the marinade over the halibut filets in a re-sealable plastic sack. Cover or seal the holder and chill for 60 minutes, blending once in a while.
3. Warm an open air barbecue to tall warm and brush the grind tenderly with oil. Put the grind 4 inches absent from the warm source.
4. Evacuate the halibut filets from the marinade and deplete any abundance fluid. Barbecue filets for 5 minutes on each side or until easily chipped with a fork.

2. Straightforward Prepared Flame broiled Angle

Planning and cooking time

9 minutes

Servings

4 people

Wholesome Realities

150 calories

Fixings

We have recorded underneath the fixings that you simply would require for cooking the sound and delicious supper:

- 16 ounces' angle filets (four 4-ounce filets, see notes)
- 1 teaspoon Ancient Cove flavoring
- 1/2 teaspoon paprika
- 4 teaspoons olive oil
- 1/2 teaspoon salt
- 1/2 teaspoon pepper
- Half lemon
- Chopped parsley for decorate, discretionary

Enlightening

1. Given underneath are the detailed instructions for cooking this delicious dinner. You would like to take after these informational within the given arrange.
2. To start, preheat your barbecue. Set the barbecue container, skillet, or sauté container over medium-high warm on the stove best to warm whereas planning the angle filets. When utilizing an indoor electric barbecue, take after the manufacturer's proposals for warming.
3. Brush the angle filets delicately with olive oil on one side.
4. Season with salt and pepper, as well as Ancient Cove and paprika.
5. Put the prepared side of the filets down on the flame broil.

6. Brush the moment side with olive oil & season with salt and pepper.
7. Cook the filets for 2 minutes on each side. Flip the filets over with a wide spatula and cook for another 2 minutes.
8. Put the cooked filets on a plate to cool. Sprinkle with lemon juice and embellish with chopped parsley (on the off chance that wanted).

3. Barbecued Lemon with Flame broiled Angle

Arrangement and cooking time
15 minutes
Servings
2 people
Dietary Realities
280 calories
Fixings

We have recorded underneath the fixings merely would require for cooking the solid and delicious feast:

- 1-pound firm white angle, such as walleye, halibut, or mahi-mahi
- 3 teaspoons Arrive O Lakes® Butter with Canola Oil, isolated
- 1/2 teaspoon garlic powder
- 1/2 teaspoon pepper
- 1 lemon, quartered
- Chopped new chives, as craved

Enlightening

1. Given underneath are the detailed instructions for cooking this delicious feast. You wish to take after these enlightening within the given arrange.
2. Preheat the barbecue container to medium-high.
3. One teaspoon of butter, as well as canola oil, is to be spread on one side of the filets. It ought to be sprinkled with 1/4 tsp garlic powder and 1/4

tsp pepper to taste. Put butter-side down in barbecue skillet. Spread 1 teaspoon of butter with canola oil on the angle, at that point season with the remaining pepper and garlic powder Cook for 5 minutes some time recently turning. Put the lemon cut-side down within the flame broil dish. Cook for another 5-7 minutes or until the salmon pieces effectively with a fork and the inner temperature comes to 165°F.
4. Pour remaining butter and canola oil over filets and permit it to dissolve. Serve with chives on best. Serve with lemon cuts that have been flame broiled.

4. Flame broiled Angle in Garlic Butter Sauce Formula

Arrangement and cooking time
40 minutes
Servings
6 people
Wholesome Realities
292 calories
Fixings
We have recorded underneath the fixings merely would require for cooking the sound and top notch supper:

- 500 gm angle filets
- 1/2 teaspoon rosemary
- dark pepper as required
- 175 gm salted butter
- 1/4 teaspoon lemon juice
- 2 tablespoons parsley
- Salt as required
- 9 cloves
- 1 teaspoon garlic
- 1/2 teaspoon sugar

Informational

1. Given underneath are the detailed instructions for cooking this delicious feast. You would like to take after these enlightening within the given arrange.
2. Put some olive oil in a dish and set it over medium warm. Put the angle filets within the hot oil after it has warmed up. Permit the filets to finish cooking some time recently flavoring with salt, 1/4 teaspoon sugar, dark pepper, and lemon juice. Flame broil it on all sides and after that exchange it to a platter once fresh filet.
3. Put a skillet over medium warm and include the cloves for the sauce. Gently cook them some time recently exchanging them to a processor jostle. Crush them together to induce a fine powdered blend. Include the butter to a partitioned skillet over medium warm, counting the chopped garlic. At that point, after the butter has liquefied, include the powdered cloves, salt, remaining sugar, and dark pepper powder and blend to combine. Combine all fixings in a huge blending bowl until they make a fragrant blend.
4. Evacuate the sauce from the warm and pour it over the angle filets that have been barbecued.
5. Embellish with parsley and rosemary, on the off chance that craved. To appreciate, serve your custom made Garlic Butter Flame broiled Angle hot.

5. Spicy Grilled Angle

Arrangement and cooking time
15 minutes
Servings
4 people
Wholesome Truths
347.4 calories
Fixings

IDEAS FOR GRILLED FISH

We have recorded underneath the fixings simply would require for cooking the sound and top notch feast:

- 24 ounces of catfish filets or other gentle angle
- 6 garlic cloves, finely chopped, approximately 1 Tbsp.
- 1/2 teaspoon of cayenne pepper
- Lemon wedge (discretionary)
- Chopped parsley (discretionary)
- 3 green onions, white and green parts (chopped)
- 1 teaspoon of onion powder
- 1/4 container of lemon juice
- 1/4 cup of vegetable oil
- 2 tablespoons of low sodium soy sauce
- 2 tablespoons finely chopped new ginger
- 1 teaspoon of paprika

Enlightening

1. Given underneath are the nitty gritty informational for cooking this top notch dinner. You would like to take after these enlightening within the given arrange.
2. Blend the soy sauce, lemon juice, vegetable oil, garlic, ginger, minced onion, green onions, paprika, and cayenne pepper.
3. Put the angle in a zip-top sack with the fluid blend and near the sack. Refrigerate for 1-2 hours after fixing and marinating.
4. Preheat the flame broilto medium-high and delicately oil the angle wicker container or barbecue grind. Cook the angle for four minutes on each side of the flame broil. As it were flip the angle once as well as brush with the reserved marinade.
5. When the color of the angle changes from translucent to dark, it is completely cooked (white).

6. Flame broiled Tilapia

Planning and cooking time
20 minutes
Servings
3 people
Dietary Actualities
221 calories
Fixings

We have recorded underneath the fixings merely would require for cooking the sound and top notch supper:

- 3 tbsp. extra-virgin olive oil, isolated
- Two tablespoons ruddy wine vinegar
- 1/4 little ruddy onion, daintily cut
- Two tablespoon new oregano takes off
- Legitimate salt
- Naturally ground dark pepper
- 3 (8-oz.) tilapia filets
- A half c. grape tomato

Enlightening

1. Given underneath are the detailed instructions for cooking this delicious supper. You wish to take after these informational within the given arrange.
2. Warm the barbecue to medium-high. Put two tablespoons olive oil + 2 tablespoons ruddy wine vinegar in a medium blending bowl and mix. Then season with dark pepper and salt after including the ruddy onion and oregano.
3. Within the another step, season tilapia with salt and dark pepper after brushing with the remaining olive oil. Put the filets as well as grape tomatoes on a barbecue that has been preheated. Cook grape tomatoes

for almost 4 minutes, or until delicate and rankled. Flame broil tilapia for 4 minutes per side, or until the edges are misty, as well as the tissue, effortlessly slides from the barbecue.
4. Exchange the angle to a serving platter. Hurl the barbecued tomatoes with the vinegar blend and pour it over the filets. Serve right absent.

7. Barbecued Branzino

Arrangement and cooking time
30 minutes
Servings
2 people
Dietary Truths
380 calories
Fixings

We have recorded underneath the fixings merely would require for cooking the solid and top notch feast:

- 1/2 teaspoon pepper
- 1/2 glass olive oil
- Split pepper
- 1 lemon
- A little modest bunch of herbs- rosemary, thyme, sage, or parsley
- 1 bunch of flat-leaf parsley, finely chopped
- 1/4 container of chopped protected lemons (skin and tissue)
- 2 garlic cloves, finely chopped
- 1 entire branzino- cleaned and gutted
- 1 tablespoon of olive oil
- 1 teaspoon of sea salt
- Discretionary chili chips

Enlightening

1. Given underneath are the point by point informational for cooking this top notch dinner. You would like to take after these informational within the given arrange.
2. Season the angle both interior and out with salt and pepper.
3. Cut a few lemons and stuff them into the fish's depth. Include new herbs like thyme, rosemary, sage, or parsley.
4. Make 2-3 openings into each side of the thicker conclusion of the angle employing a sharp cut. The flame broil will cook more equitably since the tail conclusion cooks quicker than the head conclusion.
5. Preheat the barbecue to 400 degrees Fahrenheit as well as oil the grates. Decrease the warm on one side on the off chance that craved.
6. Put the angle on a hot, oiled flame broil with the tail conclusion confronting down. Barbecue a oneand a half to two pound angle for approximately 5 minutes, secured, without moving it, or until flame broil marks show up.
7. To flip the flapjacks, utilize tongs and a lean metal spatula. Cover and cook for another 4-5 minutes or fresh with clear flame broil marks.
8. Make the tasty Protected Lemon Gremolata whereas the angle is broiling by combining all fixings in a blending bowl and blending well.
9. Serve with a verdant green serving of mixed greens and Ordinary Quinoa.

8. Barbecued Halibut

Planning and cooking time
25 minutes
Servings
4 people
Wholesome Realities
124 calories
Fixings
We have recorded underneath the fixings simply would require for

cooking the sound and delicious feast:

- 1 mango, diced
- 1 tbsp. crisply chopped cilantro
- Juice of 1 lime
- Legitimate salt
- 1 ruddy pepper, finely chopped
- 1/2 ruddy onion, diced
- 1 jalapeno, minced
- 4 (4-6-oz.) halibut steaks
- 2 tbsp. extra-virgin olive oil
- Legitimate salt
- Crisply ground dark pepper
- Naturally ground dark pepper

Informational

1. Given underneath are the detailed instructions for cooking this delicious feast. You would like to take after these informational within the given arrange.
2. Preheat the flame broil to medium-high as well as splash both sides of the halibut with oil some time recently flavoring with salt and pepper.
3. Barbecue for five minutes per side on the barbecue until halibut is cooked through.
4. In a medium blending bowl, combine all fixings as well as a season with salt and pepper.
5. Serve the salsa nearby the halibut.

9. Maple Coated Salmon Steaks

Arrangement and cooking time
26 minutes
Servings

THE FIRE BROIL AND FLAME BROIL BOOK OF SACROSANCT WRITINGS

4 persons
Wholesome Actualities
259 calories
Fixings

We have recorded underneath the fixings that you simply would require for cooking the solid and delicious dinner:

- 2 scallions, white and green parts daintily cut
- ¼ teaspoon ground cumin
- ½ teaspoon ground cumin
- ½ teaspoon legitimate salt
- ¼ teaspoon hot sauce
- 4 salmon steaks, each almost (6 ounces) and (1 inch) thick
- 1½ teaspoon
- 2 tablespoons chopped Italian parsley takes off
- 1 tablespoon new lime juice
- ¼ teaspoon naturally ground dark pepper
- 2 tablespoons maple syrup
- 2 tablespoons Dijon mustard
- 1 tablespoon extra-virgin olive oil
- 1 teaspoon new lime juice
- 2 ears corn, shucked
- Additional virgin olive oil
- 1 seeded poblano pepper, diced, almost (1 container)
- 1 container of diced grape tomatoes
- ½ teaspoon of naturally ground dark pepper

Enlightening

1. Given underneath are the nitty gritty informational for cooking this top notch dinner. You would like to take after these enlightening within the given arrange.
2. Preheat the barbecue to medium warm at 450°F- for coordinate

cooking.

3. Brush the corn with oil. With the cover closed, barbecue the corn straightforwardly over medium warm.
4. Put one tablespoon olive oil, lime juice, mustard, cumin, zesty sauce, salt, as well as pepper in a little blending bowl. Pour the blend over the corn and blend well. Whereas you're planning the salmon, keep it refrigerated.
5. Preheat the flame broil at medium-high heat-400° to 500°F- for coordinate cooking.
6. All of the coat components ought to be whisked together in a little bowl.
7. Season both sides of the salmon steaks with pepper and salt. Brush the salmon with the coat and put it on the barbecue over coordinate medium-high warm. Barbecue the salmon for eight to ten minutes, seasoning once or twice, with the top closed, until the steaks can be lifted off the hot grates without staying. Cook until an instant-read thermometer set within the thickest portion of the salmon appears 125° to 130°F, at that point flip the steaks and brush with the coat.
8. Serve the salmon steaks with the salsa whereas they're still warm.

10. Salmon with Flame broiled Lemons and Yogurt Sauce

Arrangement and cooking time
53 minutes
Servings
4 people
Nutritional Facts
510 calories
Fixings
We have recorded underneath the fixings that you simply would require for cooking the sound and top notch dinner:

- A quarter teaspoon of finely ground lemon pizzazz
- Dark pepper
- 1 huge lemon, cut (¼-inch) thick, seeds evacuated
- Legitimate salt
- A quarter teaspoon of Sriracha
- A quarter teaspoon legitimate salt
- 1 tablespoon extra-virgin olive oil
- One tablespoon of new lemon juice
- 1 little garlic clove, minced or pushed through a press
- 1 teaspoon soy sauce
- 1 teaspoon runny nectar
- A half teaspoon of Sriracha
- 4 salmon filets (with skin), each (6 to 8 ounces) and (1 to 1¼-inch) thick, pin-bones evacuated
- ¾ container whole-milk Greek-style yogurt
- 1 little garlic clove, minced or pushed through a press
- One tablespoon new lemon juice
- 2 teaspoons finely chopped new dill
- New dill sprigs, for decorate

Instructions

1. Given underneath are the nitty gritty informational for cooking this delicious dinner. You wish to take after these informational within the given arrange.
2. Whisk together the sauce fixings in a little bowl.
3. In a little bowl, blend together the marinade fixings.
4. Brush tissue sides generously with the marinade and season with pepper and salt. Permit it to rest for 15-30 minutes at room temperature some time recently serving.
5. Put the lemon cuts on a platter and brush with a few remaining marinade on both sides.
6. Preheat the flame broil to medium heat-350° to 450°F- for coordinate

cooking. Preheat the barbecuefor 10 minutes with a griddle or huge cast-iron skillet within the center.
7. Put the salmon directly on the warmed grill, flesh-side down to begin with, employing a metal spatula to equitably space the filets, so they are basic to turn. Near the top as well as burn the salmon filets over coordinate medium warm, secured, for around 3 minutes, or until they can be lifted off the grill without staying. Hurl the salmon filets within the sauce and turn them over. Near the top and cook until the meat is done to your enjoying, around three to five minutes more for medium-rare, based on thickness.

11. Simple Cedar Board Salmon Serving of mixed greens

Planning and cooking time
25 minutes
Servings
2 people
Dietary Realities
371 calories
Fixings
We have recorded underneath the fixings that you simply would require for cooking the sound and delicious supper:

- 1/2 container Celery, diced little
- 1/2 Barbecued Lemon, juiced
- 1/2-2/3 container Avocado Mayo (or favored mayo)
- 1/2 Ruddy Onion, diced little
- 1/4 container Capers (discretionary)
- 2 Stalks New Dill, minced
- 2 Salmon Filets
- 2 tsp. Olive Oil

- Salt & Pepper
- 1-2 tsp. Flavoring Salt or Ancient Narrows

Enlightening

1. Given underneath are the detailed instructions for cooking this top notch supper. You wish to take after these enlightening within the given arrange.
2. Preheat the barbecue to medium and plan it for roundabout flame broiling. Within the following step, fifteen minutes some time recently barbecuing, douse the cedar boards in water.
3. Put the salmon filets on the sheets, skin side down. Season liberally with salt and pepper after brushing the tops with fair a small olive oil. On backhanded warm, flame broil the salmon and lemon half till the inside temperature achieves 145 degrees Fahrenheit (almost 10-15 minutes).
4. Expel it from the fire and set it aside to cool.
5. Drop the salmon with a fork, taking off the skin on.
6. Season with salt, along side flame broiled lemon juice, as well as mayonnaise.
7. Serve and appreciate.

12. Garlic Butter Salmon

Planning and cooking time
25 minutes
Servings
4 people
Dietary Realities
464 calories
Fixings
We have recorded underneath the fixings that you just would require for cooking the sound and delicious supper:

- One tablespoon minced garlic approximately 2 cloves
- A half lemon juiced (approximately 1 tablespoon)
- 1 tablespoon finely minced new rosemary
- One teaspoon coarse ocean salt
- A half teaspoon of pepper
- Four salmon filets 6 ounces each

Enlightening

1. Given underneath are the nitty gritty enlightening for cooking this top notch supper. You wish to take after these informational within the given arrange.
2. Preheat the barbecue and liberally oil a barbecue container.
3. Blend the rosemary, garlic, lemon juice, salt, and pepper in a little bowl.
4. Utilize all of the garlic glue to coat each piece of salmon.
5. Expel the angle from the fridge and splash it four times.
6. Shower the foot of each piece of salmon and flip it over, so the skin side is up on the barbecue dish.
7. Cover and cook for 4-5 minutes some time recently flipping each salmon filet.
8. Expel the salmon from the barbecue when it is completely cooked and serve

19

Grilled Chicken Recipes

Presently you'll select from the different barbecued chicken formulas which have been particularly collected to assist you appreciate your open air flame broiling.

1. The Most excellent Flame broiled Chicken

Planning and cooking time

4 hours 18 minutes

Servings

4 persons

Wholesome Realities

413 calories

Fixings

We have recorded underneath the fixings simply would require for cooking the solid and delicious supper:

- 1-3/4 lbs. boneless, skinless chicken breasts
- 1/2 teaspoon dried oregano
- 1-1/4 teaspoon salt
- 6 tablespoons additional virgin olive oil
- 4 expansive garlic cloves, minced
- 1 teaspoon dried thyme
- 1/2 teaspoon naturally ground dark pepper
- One and a half teaspoons lemon get-up-and-go, from one lemon

Informational

1. Given underneath are the point by point informational for cooking this delicious feast. You would like to take after these enlightening within the given arrange.
2. Put the chicken breasts in a one-gallon zip-lock sack one at a time and pound to an even one and a half-inch thickness with a meat hammer.
3. In a 1-gallon zip-lock sack, combine all of the fixings with the exemption of the chicken.
4. Put the chicken breasts within the pack as well as knead the marinade equitably into the meat.
5. Put the pack in a bowl within the fridge and seal it. Permit at slightest

4 hours or overnight for the chicken to marinade.
6. Warm the flame broil to tall and coat the grates with oil. Cook the chicken breasts on the flame broil for 2 to 3 minutes per side, secured. Do not overcook the nourishment. Put the chicken on a serving plate and serve.

2. The Finest Delicious Barbecued Chicken

Arrangement and cooking time
40 minutes
Servings
6 people
Dietary Actualities
286 calories
Fixings

We have recorded underneath the fixings merely would require for cooking the sound and top notch feast:

- 2 to 3 pounds' boneless chicken breast or thighs, utilize skinless or skin-on chicken
- 1/2 teaspoon new ground pepper
- New herbs and lemon wedges, discretionary, for serving
- 1 tablespoon maple syrup or nectar
- 1 tablespoon Dijon mustard
- 1/2 teaspoon fine ocean salt
- Pizzazz of 1 lemon, peeled or finely ground
- 3 cloves garlic, pulverized with the side of a expansive cut or minced
- 1/4 container new lemon juice, from 1 to 2 lemons
- 2 tablespoons avocado oil or olive oil
- 1/4 teaspoon to 1/2 teaspoon ruddy pepper pieces, depending on how hot you like things

Instructions

GRILLED CHICKEN RECIPES

1. Given underneath are the point by point instructions for cooking this top notch feast. You would like to take after these informational within the given arrange.
2. Combine the lemon juice, oil, maple syrup or nectar, mustard, salt, ruddy pepper pieces, and dark pepper in a mixing bowl until the salt is totally broken down. Combine the garlic as well as lemon pizzazz in a blending bowl. Cover and store within the fridge. It can be used inside a day.
3. Pound the breasts as well as put them in a huge zip-lock pack, at that point pound them to an rise to thickness employing a meat hammer or rolling stick.
4. To marinate the chicken, combine the marinade and chicken in a food-safe sack or holder and marinate for at slightest 20 minutes within the fridge.
5. Evacuate the chicken from the fridge and warm the flame broil. Clean the grates, at that point preheat the barbecue with one side on tall (for coordinate cooking) and the other on moo (for backhanded cooking) (for backhanded cooking).
6. Brush the grates with a high-heat oil brush.
7. Evacuate the chicken from the marinade as well as shake off any garlic or lemon pizzazz that will have stuck to it. Put the chicken straightforwardly on the grill's most smoking side. Permit the chicken to cook for 3 to 5 minutes with the top open until the underside has flame broil marks.
8. Cautiously choose up each piece of chicken and put it over the cooler side of the flame broil, flame broil marks confronting up.
9. Near the top of the barbecue and cook for 5 to 10 minutes, or till an instant-read thermometer registers 165 degrees Fahrenheit.
10. Permit the cooked chicken to rest for 5 to 10 minutes on a platter freely secured with thwart some time recently cutting into thick cuts. All of the fluids from the cutting board and plate ought to be spared and poured over the cut chicken. Lemon wedges, as well as new herbs, ought to be scattered over the best.

3. Filipino BarbecuedChicken

Preparation and cooking time
1 hour 30 minutes
Servings
8 people
Wholesome Truths
393 calories
Fixings
We have recorded underneath the fixings that would be required by you for cooking the solid and top notch supper:

- 3 glasses water
- 2 tablespoons sugar
- 5 inlet takes off
- Two 3 1/2-pound chickens, cut into 8 pieces each
- Canola oil for brushing
- 1 tablespoon pulverized ruddy pepper
- 1 tablespoon dark peppercorns
- 5 entire star anise cases
- 1 container coconut vinegar or apple cider vinegar
- 1/2 container new lemon juice
- 1/2 container tamari or soy sauce
- 1/4 container Asian angle sauce
- 10 garlic cloves, pulverized
- Legitimate salt
- Naturally ground dark pepper

Informational

1. Given underneath are the point by point informational for cooking this delicious feast. You would like to take after these enlightening within the given order.

GRILLED CHICKEN RECIPES

2. Combine all of the fixings, but the oil, salt, and pepper, in a huge, durable re-sealable plastic pack. Seal the sack, press out the discuss, and shake to appropriately disseminate the chicken & adobo marinade. Refrigerate for at slightest one night.
3. Expel the chicken from the marinade and set it aside. Permit the chicken to rest at room temperature for thirty minutes after tapping it dry.
4. Meanwhile , preheat the flame broil. Season the chicken with salt and dark pepper after brushing it with oil. Flame broil over direct warm, sometimes turning, for almost 30 minutes, or until moderately charred, as well as an instant-read thermometer embedded within the thickest areas registers 165°. Some time recently serving, move the chicken to a dish and set aside for 10 minutes to rest.

4. Kentucky Flame broiled Chicken

Planning and cooking time
45 minutes
Servings
10 people
Wholesome Realities
284 calories
Fixings
We have recorded underneath the fixings that would be required by you for cooking the sound and top notch dinner:

- 1 container of cider vinegar
- 1/2 glass canola oil
- 5 teaspoons of Worcestershire sauce
- 4 teaspoons of hot pepper sauce
- 2 teaspoons of salt
- 10 (10 ounces each) chicken breast parts (bone-in)

Enlightening

1. Given underneath are the nitty gritty enlightening for cooking this top notch dinner. You would like to take after these enlightening within the given arrange.
2. Combine the fixings in a bowl or shallow dish. In a partitioned bowl, pour 1 container of the marinade; include the chicken and hurl to coat. Refrigerate for at slightest four hours after covering.
3. The remaining marinade ought to be secured and refrigerated for treating.
4. Remove the chicken from the marinade and dispose of it. Employing a dribble skillet, plan the barbecue for circuitous warm.
5. Put chicken breasts on an oiled rack, bone side down. Cook for almost 20 minutes on each side, secured, over circuitous medium warm till a thermometer peruses 170°. Amid this time, you ought to keep once in a while seasoning with the remaining marinade.

5. Barbecued Chicken Breast with Avocado Salsa

Planning and cooking time
1 hour 20 minutes
Servings
4 people
Dietary Realities
451 calories
Fixings
We have recorded underneath the fixings that would be required by you for cooking the solid and delicious supper:

- 1 1/2 pounds' boneless skinless chicken breasts or 4 chicken breasts
- ½ tsp smoked paprika
- 1 little ruddy onion diced
- 1 jalapeno seeded and chopped

- 1/4 container cilantro finely chopped
- Legitimate salt and dark pepper to taste
- 2 little ready but firm avocados or 1 expansive, diced
- 1 huge tomato chopped
- 2-3 garlic cloves minced
- 2 tbsp. olive oil
- ¼ container cilantro finely chopped
- 1 lime juice, and pizzazz
- 1/2 tsp ground cumin
- 1 lime juiced
- Legitimate salt and dark pepper to taste

Instructions

1. Given underneath are the detailed instructions for cooking this delicious dinner. You wish to take after these informational within the given arrange.
2. Combine all the marinade fixings in a huge mixing bowl and mix well to blend.
3. Blend within the chicken until it is well coated on all sides. Permit it to marinade within the fridge for up to 1 hour.
4. In the mean time, cut all of the vegetables into little pieces for the salsa. At that point mix them all together in a medium blending bowl. Keep it secured and chilled till prepared to serve.
5. Preheat an exterior barbecue or a huge barbecue dish over medium-high warm. Cook for 6 to 8 minutes per side, or until the chicken is completely done.
6. Let the chicken rest for 5 minutes after cooking some time recently cutting it. Serve the chicken with avocado salsa on the side.

6. Lexington Fashion Barbecued Chicken Formula

Arrangement and cooking time
2 hours 55 minutes
Servings
8-10 people
Wholesome Actualities
318 calories
Fixings
We have recorded underneath the fixings that would be required by you for cooking the solid and delicious supper:

- 1 glass of cider vinegar
- 1/4 container of solidly pressed dull brown sugar
- 4 teaspoons salt
- 1/4 container of vegetable oil
- 3 tablespoons of dried pulverized ruddy pepper
- 2 (3-pound) cut-up entire chickens
- 2 teaspoons of pepper

Enlightening

1. Given underneath are the point by point informational for cooking this delicious supper. You would like to take after these informational within the given arrange.
2. Hurl together the fixings fair until combined.
3. Seal a enormous zip-top plastic cooler sack with half of the vinegar blend and half of the chicken.
4. Put the remaining vinegar blend as well as chicken in a modern zip-top plastic cooler sack and rehash the method. Chill the chicken for at slightest two hours or up to 8 hours, turning it in presently and after that.
5. Expel the chicken from the marinade and dispose of the marinade.

6. Barbecue the chicken for 35 to 40 minutes, or until done, secured with the barbecue cover over mediumhigh warm (350° to 400° F). Refrigerate for at slightest 1 to 2 hours the marinade, turning once in a while. The chicken ought to be flame broiled for four to five minutes on each side or, until done, secured with a barbecue top over medium-high warm (350° to 400° F).

7. Barbecued Chicken Breasts with Lemon and Thyme

Planning and cooking time
55 minutes
Servings
4 people
Dietary Actualities
261 calories
Fixings
We have recorded underneath the fixings that would be required by you for cooking the sound and top notch feast:

- One and a half tablespoons lemon juice
- 1/4 teaspoon dried thyme
- A half teaspoon dried red-pepper drops
- 1 clove garlic, minced
- 1/4 container olive oil
- 1/4 teaspoon salt
- A quarter teaspoon fresh-ground dark pepper
- Four bone-in chicken breasts (approximately 2 1/4 pounds in all)

Instructions

1. Given underneath are the detailed instructions for cooking this delicious dinner. You would like. to take after these enlightening within the given arrange.

2. Light the pellet flame broil utilizing wood pellets. Combine the lemon juice, garlic, thyme, red-pepper pieces, oil, salt, as well as dark pepper in a shallow dish. Combine the fixings and coat the chicken.
3. Flame broil the chicken breasts for 8 to 10 minutes over medium-high warm. Cook for another 10 minutes, or when the chicken is fair done.

8. Barbecued Chicken Shawarma

Planning and cooking time
30 minutes
Servings
6 people
Wholesome Realities
314 calories
Fixings

We have recorded underneath the fixings that would be required by you for cooking the solid and top notch feast:

- 8 garlic cloves, minced
- 1 teaspoon ground dark pepper
- 2 teaspoon allspice
- 2 teaspoons legitimate salt
- 6 tablespoons olive oil
- 1/4 teaspoon cayenne pepper
- 2 teaspoon turmeric
- 1 teaspoon ground ginger
- 2 lbs. to 2 ¼ lb. chicken thighs (boneless and skinless, or skin on- see notes)
- 2 tablespoons ground cumin
- 2 tablespoons ground coriander

Enlightening

1. Given underneath are the point by point enlightening for cooking this delicious supper. You wish to take after these informational within the given arrange.
2. Combine all marinade fixings in a bowl and blend to combine or pulse to deliver a glue in a nourishment processor.
3. Marinade the chicken on all sides and set aside for twenty minutes-or up to 24-48 hours refrigerated. You'll be able on the other hand cut the chicken into 1-inch pieces and make sticks.
4. Barbecue, the chicken on a preheated wood pellet barbecue over medium-high warm for around 8 minutes on each side or until both sides have great flame broil marks. Exchange the chicken to a cooler parcel of the barbecue or wrap up cooking it in a 350 F stove for approximately 10 minutes, or until completely done.
5. Chicken shawarma can be served with Israeli serving of mixed greens, rice, and vegetables, as well as pita bread and tzatziki.

9. Bratwurst and Chicken Kabobs

Planning and cooking time
50 minutes
Servings
12 kabobs
Wholesome Truths
433 calories
<u>Fixings</u>
We have recorded underneath the fixings that would be required by you for cooking the sound and top notch supper:

- 1 teaspoon salt
- A half teaspoon of pepper
- 1/2 container olive oil, separated
- 1 can (15 ounces) peach parts in light syrup, depleted, and cut into 1/2-in. 3d shapes

THE FIRE BROIL AND FLAME BROIL BOOK OF SACROSANCT WRITINGS

- 2 each medium green pepper, sweet ruddy pepper, and yellow pepper
- 1 huge onion
- 3 tablespoons brown sugar bourbon flavoring
- 2/3 glass minced onion
- 1 bump (12 ounces) mango chutney
- 6 boneless skinless chicken breasts (6 ounces each)
- 1/4 container balsamic vinegar
- 1/4 container cider vinegar
- 2 tablespoons pepper jam
- Two tablespoons stone-ground mustard
- 1 bundle (14 ounces) completely cooked bratwurst joins

Informational

1. Given underneath are the point by point informational for cooking this delicious feast. You would like to take after these informational within the given arrange.
2. Combine the mustard, vinegar, pepper jam, salt, and pepper in a blending bowl. Whisk in onethird container olive oil in a moderate, consistent way until well combined. Hurl within the peaches, onion, and chutney.
3. Chicken ought to be cut into 1-inch 3d shapes, and bratwursts ought to be cut into 1-inch cuts.
4. Peppers ought to be cut into huge squares, and onions ought to be cut into 3d shapes. Hurl with the remaining oil and brown sugar bourbon flavoring.
5. String meat and veggies then again on 12 metal or damp wooden sticks. Cover and cook sticks on an oiled barbecue rack over medium-high coordinate warm, routinely flipping, for 10-12 minutes, or till chicken is no pinker, as well as vegetables are cooked. On the off chance that wanted, include more brown sugar bourbon flavoring amid the flame broiling handle. Serve with chutney on the side.

10. Chicken Breasts with Romesco Sauce

Arrangement and cooking time

1 hour 57 minutes

Servings

6 people

Wholesome Truths

533 calories

Fixings

We have recorded underneath the fixings that would be required by you for cooking the solid and delicious feast:

- 1 teaspoon legitimate salt
- 2 tablespoons sherry vinegar
- 1 teaspoon of smoked paprika
- ¾ teaspoon of legitimate salt
- A quarter teaspoon of cayenne pepper
- ½ teaspoon of finely ground lemon get-up-and-go
- ½ teaspoon of dried oregano
- 4 boneless and skinless chicken breast parts
- A quarter teaspoon of crisply ground dark pepper
- 2 medium ruddy chime peppers
- 2 expansive garlic cloves
- ¼ glass almonds, toasted
- ¼ glass extra-virgin olive oil
- 2 tablespoons tomato glue
- ¼ container extra-virgin olive oil
- A quarter glass new lemon juice
- 3 garlic cloves, minced or pushed through a press
- 1 teaspoon sweet paprika
- Lemon wedges for serving

Informational

1. Given underneath are the nitty gritty enlighteningfor cooking this top notch supper. You wish to take after these enlightening within the given arrange.
2. The marinade fixings ought to be whisked together in a little bowl.
3. Tenderly score the chicken breasts on the smooth (skin) side on the corner to corner, making 3 or 4 equitably divided (1/4 inch) profound cuts. Put the chicken in a blending bowl, pour the marinade, and equally hurl the coat. Cover the chicken with plastic wrap as well as refrigerate for at slightest one hour and up to eight hours, turning it once in a while.
4. Preheat the barbecue at medium-high heat-400° to 500°F- for coordinate cooking.
5. Clean the cooking grates with a brush. Flame broil your chime peppers at coordinate medium-high warm with the top secured for around 20 minutes, flipping each five minutes until browned all over. Put the peppers in a bowl with plastic wrap over them and steam for 10 minutes to fifteen minutes. Evacuate the peppers from the bowl, peeling absent the burned skin and disposing of it, as well as the stems. Exchange the peppers to a nourishment processor after coarsely chopping them. Combine all of the extra sauce fixings in a nourishment processor and beat until smooth. Put in a blending bowl.
6. Preheat the flame broil to medium heat-350° to 450°F- for coordinate cooking.
7. Evacuate the chicken from the marinade and let any additional marinade drop back into the bowl to maintain a strategic distance from flare-ups. Evacuate the marinade and dispose of it. Put the chicken on the grind bars, smooth (skin) side down, over direct medium warm. Flame broil for 4 to 6 minutes on the primary side, with the cover closed, till the chicken breasts are completely grill-marked and effortlessly expelled from the grates. Flip the chicken and cook for another 4-6 minutes, unless an instant-read thermometer put within the thickest portion of the chicken peruses 165°F. Evacuate from the barbecue and set aside to rest for 3 to 5 minutes at room temperature.

Serve with lemon wedges and Romesco sauce.

11. California Flame broiled Chicken

Arrangement and cooking time

40 minutes

Servings

4 people

Wholesome Realities

585 calories

Fixings

We have recorded underneath the fixings that would be required by you for cooking the solid and top notch supper:

- 2 tsp. Italian flavoring
- 4 cuts avocado
- 4 cuts tomato
- 2 tbsp. of Naturally cut basil for embellish
- Crisply ground dark pepper
- 4 boneless and skinless chicken breasts
- Legitimate salt
- 4 cuts of mozzarella
- 3/4 c. balsamic vinegar
- 1 tsp. of garlic powder
- 2 tbsp. nectar
- 2 tbsp. of extra-virgin olive oil
- Balsamic coat for sprinkling

Informational

1. Given underneath are the point by point informational for cooking this delicious feast. You wish to take after these enlightening within the given arrange.

2. Season with salt and pepper, as well as whisk together balsamic vinegar, nectar, oil, and Italian flavoring in a little bowl. Pour over the chicken and let it aside for 20 minutes to marinate.
3. Preheat the flame broil to medium-high when you're prepared to cook. Flame broil chicken till charred as well as cooked through, approximately 8 minutes per side, on oiled barbecue grates.
4. Cover the flame broil for 2 minutes to dissolve the avocado, mozzarella, and tomato on best of the chicken.
5. Sprinkle with balsamic coat and embellish with basil.

12. Barbecued Butterflied Chicken with Lemongrass Sauce

Planning and cooking time
4 hours 55 minutes
Servings
4 people
Wholesome Realities
527 calories
Fixings

We have recorded underneath the fixings that would be required by you for cooking the solid and delicious feast:

- 2 garlic cloves, finely chopped
- 1 Tbsp. cumin seeds
- 1 3½–4-lb. entire chicken, spine evacuated
- 3 Tbsp. Vegetable oil
- ½ container vegetable oil
- ½ tsp. Aji-No-Moto Umami flavoring
- Legitimate salt
- 2 Tbsp. coriander seeds
- 6 scallions, meagerly cut
- 3 lemongrass stalks, foot third as it were, extreme external layers

- expelled, finely chopped
- 1 2" piece ginger, peeled, finely chopped
- Purple Sticky Rice

Enlightening

1. Given below are the nitty gritty enlightening for cooking this tasty dinner. You wish to take after these informational within the given arrange.
2. Combine ginger, scallions, lemongrass, and garlic in a medium blending bowl. Warm the oil over tall warm in a little pot until it is hot but not smoking, roughly 2 minutes.
3. Pour the scallion blend on best. Permit 5 minutes to rest, regularly mixing to dodge burning the aromatics. Season with salt and pepper.
4. In a little dry skillet at medium warm, toast coriander and cumin seeds, regularly shaking, until fragrant and somewhat darker in color, almost 3 minutes. Permit it cool some time recently exchanging to a flavor processor or mortar and pestle. Exchange the flavor blend to a little bowl after finely pounding.
5. Put the chickenon a cutting board, skin side up. Press commandingly on the breastbone with your palms to straighten the breast; you might listen a break. This implies you're doing everything accurately. Put the chicken on a huge rimmed heating sheet, skin side up. Season both sides liberally with salt. At that point sprinkle zest blend all over, being beyond any doubt to urge into each niche and pore. (There may be a few flavor blend cleared out over.) Underneath the breast, tuck the wings. Chill for at slightest three hours and up to 2 days, revealed.
6. Permit 1 hour for the chicken to come to room temperature some time recently barbecuing. Sprinkle a few oil on everything and pat it down.
7. Plan the wood pellet barbecue for indirect warm at a medium-high setting; leave one or two burners off for a gas flame broil. Put the chicken on the grind, skin side down, over roundabout warm.

8. Put a vent (in case the flame broil has one) over the chicken to drag warm up and over it. Let it remain for 15–20 minutes on the flame broil until tenderly browned the skin. Cook, secured, for another 20–25 minutes, or until the skin is dull brilliant brown as well as fresh and an instant-read thermometer put into the thickest portion of the breast registers 160° F. Some time recently carving, exchange the chicken to a cutting board and after that let it rest for at slightest 15 minutes. Serve with rice and lemongrass sauce.

20

Cookbooks for Grilled Meat

Appreciate by choosing from the different barbecued meat formulas which have been particularly collected to assist you appreciate your open air barbecuing.

1. Flame broiled Meat Steaks

Arrangement and cooking time
40 minutes

Servings
4 people

Dietary Realities
210 calories

Fixings

We have recorded underneath the fixings that would be required by you for cooking the solid and delicious feast:

- 4 meat steaks, around 3/4-inch-thick (porterhouse, rib eye, sirloin, or T-bone steaks) or almost 1-inch-thick (tenderloin steaks)
- One tsp salt
- One fourth teaspoon pepper

Informational

1. Given underneath are the nitty gritty enlightening for cooking this tasty feast. You would like to take after these informational within the given arrange.
2. Coordinate warm can be produced by utilizing coals or a gas flame broil. Warm the flame broil to medium warm, which takes around 40 minutes for charcoal and 10 minutes for gas.
3. With a sharp cut, cut the exterior edge of fat on the steaks (but tenderloin steaks) crosswise at one-inch interims. It's superior not to cut into the meat since the liquids will vanish and the meat will dry up.
4. Over medium warm, put the steak on the flame broil rack. Cover the flame broil and cook for 6-8 minutes for the rib eye, 10-12 minutes for the T-bone or porterhouse and 13-15 minutes for tenderloin and sirloin turning once midway through cooking, till an instant-read

meat thermometer embedded within the thickest part reads 145°F for medium-rare or 160°F for medium doneness, or until an instant-read meat thermometer embedded within the thickest portion peruses 145°F for medium doneness. Season to taste with salt as well as pepper.

2. Argentinean Barbecued Meat Platter (Parilla)

Arrangement and cooking time
35 minutes
Servings
6 people
Wholesome Realities
590 calories
Fixings
We have recorded underneath the fixings that would be required by you for cooking the solid and delicious feast:

- 1 tomato, seeded and cut into little dice
- ¼ tsp ground dark pepper
- ¼ tsp salt
- 1 pork chop (bone-in)
- 1 (225g) rib-eye steak
- 2 chorizo wieners
- ½ lb. (225 g) sweetbreads, splashed (see note) (discretionary)
- 6 little sheep chops
- 1 little ruddy onion, finely chopped
- ½ green chime pepper, seeded and cut into little dice
- 4 tsp (20 ml) white wine vinegar
- 1 tbsp. (15 ml) olive oil
- ¼ tsp ground cumin
- 1 blood wiener, approximately 4 oz. (115 g)

Enlightening

1. Given underneath are the nitty gritty enlightening for cooking this top notch feast. You would like to take after these enlightening within the given arrange.
2. Blend all of the fixings in a blending bowl. Permit marinating at room temperature whereas you wrap up the rest of the method.
3. Fill a little pot midway with water and include the sweetbreads. Bring to a bubble and season with salt. Diminish the warm to moo and cook for 5 minutes. Turn off the warm. Deplete carefully after running beneath cold water. Evacuate the film that covers the sweetbreads together with your hands. At that point set it aside.
4. Preheat the flame broil to tall, with half of the burners on tall as well as the other half on medium.
5. Oil the grind.
6. Cook the pork chops, sheep chops, and steaks on the flame broil for 3 to 5 minutes per side for uncommon, and the sweetbreads, chorizo, and blood wiener on the cooler side for 3 to 5 minutes per side for medium. Permit for 5 minutes of resting time. Keep warm. Cut the meat on a work surface as well as orchestrate it on a wooden board or serving dish.
7. Serve with Criolla salsa or chimichurri on the side.

3. Barbecued Steak and Vegetables

Planning and cooking time
25 minutes
Servings
4 people
Wholesome Realities
423 calories
Fixings
We have recorded underneath the fixings that would be required by you for cooking the sound and top notch supper:

- 2/3 container lemon juice (from 6 lemons)
- 1 medium yellow onion, daintily cut
- Salt and pepper
- 1 teaspoon dried thyme, separated
- 2 expansive ruddy chime peppers, cut into 1/2-inch strips
- 2 medium zucchini, daintily cut
- One skirt steak (almost 1 1/4 pounds)
- 3/4 container olive oil, furthermore more for the flame broil

Instructions

1. Given underneath are the point by point informational for cooking this top notch dinner. You wish to take after these informational within the given arrange.
2. Preheat a flame broil or flame broil skillet to a tall temperature. Blend lemon juice, 1/2 tsp thyme, chime peppers, zucchini, and onion in a expansive blending bowl or zip-top pack; season with salt and pepper as well as marinate for 15 minutes.
3. Season the steak with the remaining 1/2 teaspoon thyme, salt, and pepper. Clean the hot flame broil and gently oil it. For medium, cook the steak for 12 minutes, flipping once. Tent with thwart and exchange to a cutting board. Permit to rest for 10 minutes some time recently cutting daintily against the grain.
4. Brush the warmed barbecue with a small oil. Flame broil the vegetables in an break even with layer on the flame broil, saving the marinade, for 8 to 10 minutes, or until browned and delicate. In a marinade, whisk together the oil and mustard. Half of the vegetables and half of the dressing for Lively Pork Sandwiches ought to be secured and refrigerated. The rest of the vegetables and steak should be served with the extra dressing.

4. Flame broiled Balsamic Flank Steak for Wraps and Servings of mixed greens

Arrangement and cooking time

13 minutes

Servings

4 people

Wholesome Truths

345 calories

Fixings

We have recorded underneath the fixings that would be required by you for cooking the sound and delicious supper:

- 2 tsp minced garlic
- ¼ glass soy sauce
- ¼ glass Worcestershire sauce
- ¼ glass balsamic vinegar
- 1 lb. flank steak
- Two tsp ketchup
- ¼ container olive oil
- Salt and pepper to taste

Enlightening

1. Given underneath are the nitty gritty enlightening for cooking this delicious supper. You wish to take after these informational within the given arrange.
2. In a gallon-sized cooler sack, blend balsamic vinegar, garlic, ketchup, Worcestershire sauce, soy sauce, olive oil, salt, and pepper. Near the sack as well as shake it to blend the fixings.
3. Put the flank steak interior the pack after opening it. Refrigerate for at slightest four hours or up to overnight, flipping every so often.

4. When you're prepared to cook flank steak, preheat the GEORGE FORMAN® barbecue. Preheat the barbecue to 425 degrees Fahrenheit. Put the flank steak on the barbecue once it is warmed. Cook for 8 minutes, till a thermometer put into the thickest area peruses 135°F or higher. Keep in mind that 135°F is for medium-rare; the time will change depending on how well you need your flank steak.
5. Cut and serve on beat of a serving of mixed greens; cut and wrap together with your favorite vegetables or cut and put on a pizza with sautéed onions and peppers as well as provolone cheese.

5. Flame broiled Marinated Steak Kebabs

Arrangement and cooking time
45 minutes
Servings
6 people
Dietary Actualities
301 calories
Fixings
We have recorded underneath the fixings that would be required by you for cooking the solid and top notch dinner:

- 4 cloves garlic, minced
- 1 orange chime pepper, cut into chunks
- Green chime pepper, cut into chunks
- 2-1/2 tablespoons Worcestershire Sauce
- 2 tablespoons additional light olive oil
- 2 pounds' sirloin steaks, or ribeye steak, cut into bite-size 3d shapes
- 1 ruddy chime pepper, cut into chunks
- 2 tablespoons Dijon mustard
- 1 tablespoon steak flavoring
- 1/4 glass lemon juice, naturally pressed
- 1/4 glass tamari

- 1 huge ruddy onion, cut into cubes

Informational

1. Given underneath are the nitty gritty informational for cooking this top notch feast. You would like to take after these enlightening within the given arrange.
2. Blend the steak flavoring, garlic, mustard, Worcestershire sauce, tamari, lemon juice and olive oil in a huge blending bowl. To legitimately mix, whisk everything together.
3. Hurl the onions, peppers, and sirloin 3d shapes within the marinade to coat. Permit 15 to 20 minutes for the steak to marinade on the countertop.
4. In the interim, preheat your flame broil to medium-high (550-600°F). Interchange skewering the steak with the peppers and onion until the steak is totally pierced. Whereas the steak kebabs are resting, any leftover peppers and onions can be put to a hot flame broil skillet.
5. Put the sticks on the flame broil once it's hot, at that point decrease the temperature to medium (400°) & proceed to cook, once in a while pivoting, until the exterior has fabulous barbecue marks.
6. Evacuate from the broiler and let aside for approximately 5 minutes some time recently serving.

6. Sweet Tea Marinated Ribeyes

Planning and cooking time
8 hours 30 minutes
Servings
4 people
Dietary Realities
329 calories
Fixings
We have recorded underneath the fixings that would be required by you

for cooking the solid and delicious feast:

- 1 teaspoon dark pepper
- A quarter glass lime juice
- 1 teaspoon salt
- 2 teaspoons sugar
- 1 teaspoon dried minced garlic
- 1 lime daintily cut
- 3 sprigs of new rosemary
- 4 Ribeye Steaks
- 10 ounces' grape or cherry tomatoes divided
- 4 mugs Milo's Popular Sweet Tea
- A half tablespoon dried minced onion
- A half tablespoon dried minced garlic
- 1 tablespoon salt
- 10 ounces solidified corn cooked concurring to bundle enlightening
- 12 ounces disintegrated feta
- 15 ounces' dark beans depleted and flushed
- A quarter container new cilantro chopped

Enlightening

1. Given underneath are the point by point enlightening for cooking this delicious feast. You would like to take after these enlightening within the given arrange.
2. Whisk the onion, salt, tea, garlic, and pepper in a expansive blending bowl. Embed the lime cuts as well as rosemary sprigs in a huge ziplock sack.
3. Put the ribeyes within the back and seal them appropriately.
4. Refrigerate the sack for 2-8 hours.
5. Evacuate the limes, fluid, and rosemary from the ice chest when prepared to cook.
6. Preheat the flame broil to 400 degrees Fahrenheit.

7. Season each steak with pepper and salt on both sides.
8. Cook for 8-10 minutes per side or until the inner temperature is 140-160 degrees Fahrenheit.
9. Serve with Confetti Corn Serving of mixed greens on beat.
10. Combine the feta, dark bean, tomatoes, corn, and cilantro in a expansive blending bowl. Whisk together the salt, lime juice, sugar, and garlic in a isolated little bowl.
11. The sauce blend is poured over the serving of mixed greens, and coat it totally with a wooden spoon.

7. Porterhouse with Summer Au Poivre Sauce

Arrangement and cooking time
3 hours 30 minutes
Servings
2-4 people
Wholesome Realities
266 calories
Fixings
We have recorded underneath the fixings that would be required by you for cooking the sound and delicious feast:

- ½ container (stuffed) mint takes off
- Legitimate salt
- 12 lb. porterhouse steak (around 2" thick)
- ½ container extra-virgin olive oil
- Vegetable oil (for the flame broil)
- 2 Tbsp. depleted cured green peppercorns
- ½ container (pressed) basil takes off

Informational

1. Given underneath are the nitty gritty informational for cooking this

top notch dinner. You would like to take after these enlightening within the given arrange.
2. Get ready a flame broil with tall circuitous warm.
3. Season the steak with salt and pepper. Barbecue until deeply browned on all sides at coordinate warm.
4. You have got to keep tenderloin (the littler side) absent from the foremost seriously warm. Keep in mind to keep turning steak each miniature or so to control flare-ups as well as guarantee indeed browning.
5. Cook the steak over indirect heat, turning each one to two minutes and moving closer or more distant absent from the warm as required to attain indeed color, for 10–12 minutes, or unless an instant-read thermometer set into the thickest portion of the steak registers 120° for mediumrare.
6. Permit 15–30 minutes to rest on a wire rack set on a rimmed preparing sheet.
7. Cut the meat absent from each side of the bone and cut crosswise on a cutting board a while later. Serve with the sauce and the peppercorns that were spared.

8. Hasselback Brief Rib Bulgogi

Planning and cooking time
3 hours 30 minutes
Servings
4 people
Wholesome Realities
482 calories
Fixings
We have recorded underneath the fixings that would be required by you for cooking the sound and delicious dinner:

- One tsp. sugar

- One tbsp. toasted sesame oil
- 1½ lb. 1"–1½"-thick boneless meat brief ribs, trimmed
- Vegetable oil (for the barbecue)
- Legitimate salt
- One tsp. toasted sesame oil
- 1 tsp. toasted sesame seeds
- 6 scallions
- 2 tsp. toasted sesame oil
- 2 tsp. unseasoned rice vinegar
- One tsp. toasted sesame seeds
- One 1" piece ginger, peeled, finely ground
- 2 garlic cloves, finely ground
- One scallion, exceptionally finely chopped
- ¼ container white miso
- One tsp. gochujang (Korean hot pepper glue) or hot chili sauce (such as Sriracha)
- ¼ glass soy sauce
- 2 Tbsp. unseasoned rice vinegar
- 2 Tbsp. light or dull brown sugar
- One tbsp. gochugaru

Enlightening

1. Given underneath are the point by point informational for cooking this delicious supper. You would like to take after these enlightening within the given arrange.
2. Combine the sugar, miso, scallion, gochujang, oil, sesame seeds, and one teaspoon of water in a little bowl.
3. Scallions ought to be trimmed and cutin half longwise. Hurl the scallions with the vinegar, oil, and sesame seeds in a medium blending bowl.
4. Combine the vinegar, ginger, gochugaru, garlic, soy sauce, brown sugar, and sesame oil in a medium blending bowl.

5. Chop brief ribs no more than midway through the meat with a sharp cut. Turn the scallion over and cut the other side. Hurl the meat with the marinade within the bowl, working the marinade into the slices within the meat. Cover bowl with a huge plate and set aside for at slightest 2 hours or up to 1 day at room temperature.
6. Prepare a flame broil for medium-high warm with vegetable oil on the grind. Evacuate the brief ribs from the marinade and season them gently with salt. Turn each 1–2 minutes, and if necessary, move to a cooler portion of the barbecue.
7. Transfer the brief ribs to a cutting board and set them aside for at slightest five minutes some time recently cutting over the slashes—or, to be genuine, fair tearing them separated.
8. Season the scallion serving of mixed greens with salt and dark pepper.

9. Flame broiled Steak Tacos

Planning and cooking time
2hours 10 minutes
Servings
4 people
Dietary Truths
473 calories
Fixings
We have recorded underneath the fixings that would be required by you for cooking the sound and delicious feast:

- 1/2 medium tomato, seeded and chopped
- One teaspoon fish flavoring
- One meat ribeye steak (1 pound), trimmed
- 8 flour tortillas (6 inches)
- 3 tablespoons of cut ready olives
- 2 tablespoons of canned entire part corn
- 2 tablespoons of chopped sweet ruddy pepper

- 2 tablespoons of lime juice
- 4 teaspoons of minced new cilantro
- 1/4 container of mayonnaise
- 2 teaspoons of Sriracha chili sauce
- 1/8 teaspoon sesame oil
- One medium ready avocado, peeled and finely chopped
- 1 teaspoon legitimate salt
- One teaspoon finely chopped onion
- One garlic clove, minced
- 1/4 teaspoon ground cumin
- 2 teaspoons pepper
- 2 teaspoons olive oil
- One teaspoon legitimate salt

Informational

1. Given underneath are the nitty gritty informational for cooking this top notch supper. You wish to take after these enlightening within the given arrange.
2. Blend the aioli fixings in a little bowl. Blend the salsa fixings in a partitioned bowl.
3. Refrigerate until prepared to serve.
4. Rub both sides of the steak with a blend of pepper, oil, salt, and fish flavoring.
5. Cover and cook over medium warm until the meat is done to your enjoying; for medium-rare, a thermometer must read 135°F. Permit for a 5-minute rest period.
6. Meanwhile , warm tortillas on the flame broil for forty-five seconds on each side Put daintily cut steak on tortillas. Serve with aioli, salsa, and your favorite garnishes.

10. Brisket

Planning and cooking time

7 hours

Servings

6 people

Wholesome Truths

579 calories

Fixings

We have recorded underneath the fixings that would be required by you for cooking the solid and delicious feast:

- ¼ container paprika
- 2 tablespoons dark pepper
- 2 tablespoons legitimate salt
- 5-pound Brisket
- ¼ container brown sugar

Informational

1. Given underneath are the point by point enlightening for cooking this top notch supper. You would like to take after these enlightening within the given arrange.
2. Evacuate huge chunks of fat as well as the fat cap from the brisket.
3. Select the rub you need to utilize.
4. Apply a overwhelming rub of the flavors to all sides of the brisket. It ought to at that point be refrigerated for a few hours or overnight after wrapping in plastic wrap. Expel 1 hour some time recently cooking from the fridge and set aside to rest at room temperature.
5. Set up the barbecue whereas the brisket is resting. A consistent temperature of 225°-250°F is perfect.
6. At that point cook on the backhanded side.
7. Cook until the internal temperature reaches 200°-205° F.

8. Wrap in thwart and one or two of towels after expelling them from the flame broil.
9. Permit it to rest for one to two hours some time recently serving by cutting daintily over the grain.

11. Santa Maria Broil Meat

Planning and cooking time
2 hours 30 minutes
Servings
6 people
Wholesome Actualities
495 calories
Fixings
We have recorded underneath the fixings that would be required by you for cooking the sound and top notch feast:

- 1 tablespoon garlic powder
- 1 meat tri-tip broil
- 2 mugs of drenched hickory wood chunks or chips
- 2 tablespoons of canola oil
- 1 tablespoon white pepper
- 1 tablespoon of celery salt
- 1 tablespoon ground cumin
- 4 tablespoons paprika
- 3 tablespoons brown sugar
- 2 tablespoons chili powder
- 1 tablespoon of dried oregano
- 1 tablespoon of pepper
- 2 teaspoons of cayenne pepper
- 1 teaspoon ground mustard

Enlightening

1. Given underneath are the point by point informational for cooking this top notch feast. You wish to take after these enlightening within the given arrange.
2. Combine the fixings and rub over the cook as wanted. Wrap in plastic wrap and put in the fridge overnight.
3. 1 hour some time recently barbecuing, expel the broil from the fridge. Employing a dribble dish, get ready the flame broil for roundabout warm.
4. Unwrap the cook and brush it with oil some time recently putting it over the dribble skillet. Cover and barbecue over medium-low roundabout warm for one to one and a half hour, or until meat comes to wanted doneness (a thermometer ought to examined 135 F for medium-rare).

12. California Burger Wraps

Arrangement and cooking time
45 minutes
Servings
8 people
Dietary Truths
391.1 calories
Fixings

We have recorded underneath the fixings that would be required by you for cooking the sound and top notch feast:

- 8 Bibb lettuce clears out
- 1/2 medium ready avocado, peeled and cut into 8 cuts
- 1/4 container chopped ruddy onion
- 1/3 glass disintegrated feta cheese
- 1-pound of incline ground meat (90% incline)
- 1/2 teaspoon of salt
- 1/4 teaspoon of pepper

- 2 tablespoons Marvel Whip Light

Informational

1. Given underneath are the nitty gritty enlightening for cooking this top notch dinner. You wish to take after these informational within the given arrange.
2. Combine meat, salt, and pepper in a huge blending bowl, blending delicately but completely. Frame eight 1/2-inch-thick patties.
3. At that point the burgers are to be flame broiled for three to four minutes on each side at medium warm or broil 3-4 inches from warm till a thermometer peruses 160°F. In lettuce clears out, put burgers.
4. Spread feta as well as Wonder Whip on beat of burgers.

21

Recipes for Grilled Lamb

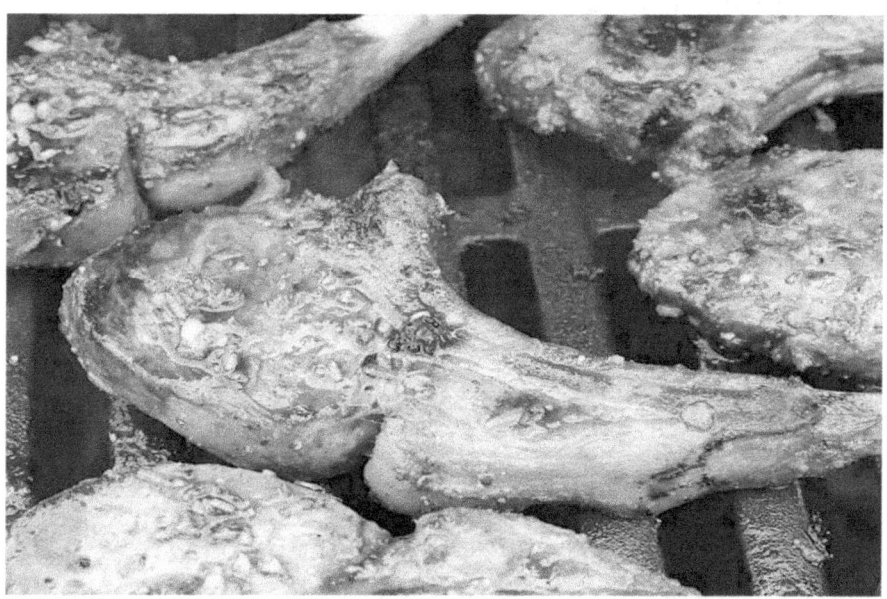

Appreciate your barbecuing by choosing from the particularly collected barbecued sheep formulas.

1. Racks of Sheep with Roasted-Shallot Vinaigrette

Planning and cooking time
49 minutes

Servings
4 people

Wholesome Realities
1398 calories

Fixings

We have recorded underneath the fixings that would be required by you for cooking the solid and delicious feast:

- 1 teaspoon Dijon mustard
- 2 tablespoons finely chopped new thyme takes off
- ½ teaspoon of legitimate salt
- ½ teaspoon of naturally ground dark pepper
- 1 teaspoon finely chopped new thyme takes off
- ½ teaspoon legitimate salt
- 1 expansive shallot, around 1 ounce, unpeeled
- ¼ glass extra-virgin olive oil, partitioned
- 1 tablespoon balsamic vinegar
- 2 sheep racks, each 1 to 1½ pounds, frenched
- Extra-virgin olive oil

Enlightening

1. Given underneath are the point by point enlightening for cooking this top notch supper. You wish to take after these enlightening within the given arrange.
2. Preheat the flame broil to medium heat- 350° to 450°F- for coordinate cooking.
3. Brush a little sum of olive oil all over the shallot.
4. Alter the flame broil to medium heat- 350° to 450°F- for backhanded

RECIPES FOR GRILLED LAMB

cooking.

5. Brush the sheep with oil as well as a season with thyme, salt, and pepper equitably. To keep the bones from burning, cover them freely with aluminum thwart. Burn the sheep over coordinate warm, bone side down to begin with, for two to four minutes, turning once, until softly browned. Put the sheep at backhanded medium warm, cover, and cook until done to your enjoying, around 15 minutes for medium-rare. Expel the chops from the flame broil and set them aside to rest for three to five minutes some time recently cutting them into person chops. With the vinaigrette, serve warm.

2. Flame broiled Sheep Chops

Planning and cooking time
23 minutes
Servings
4 people
Wholesome Actualities
239 calories
Fixings

We have recorded underneath the fixings that would be required by you for cooking the solid and delicious dinner:

- 1 container olive oil
- 3/4 glass lemon juice
- 1 tablespoon chopped mint
- 1 tablespoon chopped Italian parsley
- 10-12 cloves garlic
- 1 teaspoon salt
- 1/4 teaspoon new ground dark pepper
- 16 sheep chops
- 2 tablespoons avocado oil
- 2 tablespoons Greek Crack flavoring

- 1/4 teaspoon dry oregano

Enlightening

1. Given underneath are the nitty gritty informational for cooking this delicious dinner. You would like to take after these informational within the given arrange.
2. Permit the sheep chops to marinate for 30 minutes in a baggie with one-fourth to one-third container of the mint sauce.
3. Expel the crude sheep from the marinade, as well as dispose of the remaining sauce.
4. Warm the pellet flame broil to 450°F and season your sheep chops with Greek Crack flavoring some time recently setting them on the barbecue.
5. Cook for three to four minutes per side on each side, at that point set aside to rest.

3. Rosemary Sheep Chops

Planning and cooking time
32 minutes
Servings
4 people
Dietary Truths
157 calories
Fixings
We have recorded underneath the fixings that would be required by you for cooking the solid and delicious feast:

- 1 tablespoon chopped new rosemary clears out
- Extra-virgin olive oil
- 2 pounds' modern potatoes, each around 1½ inches in breadth, quartered

- 2 teaspoons chopped new thyme clears out
- 3 garlic cloves
- 1 teaspoon of legitimate salt
- ¾ teaspoon naturally ground dark pepper
- 8 sheep loin chops, each around 4 ounces and 1¼ inches thick, trimmed of abundance fat

Informational

1. Given below are the point by point enlightening for cooking this tasty feast. You wish to take after these enlightening within the given arrange.
2. Garlic ought to be generally chopped. At that point salt ought to be sprinkled on best.
3. Preheat the flame broil to medium warm (350° to 450°F) for coordinate cooking.
4. Brush both sides of the sheep chops with oil. Nearly half of the flavoring blend ought to be connected to both sides of the chops.
5. In a medium blending bowl, put the cut potatoes. Sprinkle 2 tablespoons of oil on beat and sprinkle with the remaining parcel of the flavoring blend. Hurl the potatoes to equally coat them.
6. Barbecue the potatoes for fifteen to twenty minutes, turning each five minutes, over coordinate medium warm with the cover closed. Whereas you're flame broiling the sheep, evacuate it from the flame broil and keep it warm.
7. Barbecue the sheep chops at coordinate medium warm with the cover closed, turning once or twice until done to your enjoying, almost 8 minutes for medium-rare. Permit resting for three to five minutes after evacuating from the flame broil. With the potatoes, serve warm.

4. Child Sheep Chops

Planning and cooking time
45 minutes
Servings
4-6 people
Wholesome Realities
295 calories
<u>Fixings</u>

We have recorded underneath the fixings that would be required by you for cooking the sound and delicious dinner:

- 1 container new orange
- 1 tablespoon clover nectar
- 1 tablespoon matured sherry vinegar
- 1 teaspoon finely ground orange get-up-and-go
- 2 mugs of pureed canned plum tomatoes
- 1/2 glass ketchup
- 1 tablespoon of smoked paprika
- 1/2 teaspoon ground coriander
- 2 tablespoons of canola oil, furthermore more for brushing
- 3 chopped shallots
- 2 chopped cloves garlic
- 2 tablespoons of light brown sugar
- Crisply ground dark pepper and Legitimate salt
- 12 bone on infant sheep chops

<u>Enlightening</u>

1. Given underneath is the point by point enlightening for cooking this top notch supper. You would like to take after these informational within the given arrange.
2. For coordinate flame broiling, preheat the flame broil to tall. On both

sides, brush your sheep with canola oil as well as a season with pepper and salt.
3. Put the chops on the flame broil for 2 to 3 minutes on each side. Flame broil for another 2 to 3 minutes after flipping and brushing with a few of the sauce. Exchange to a serving platter and beat with the saved sauce.

5. Sheep Chops Barbecued in Rosemary Smoke

Planning and cooking time
1hour 17 minutes
Servings
4 people
Dietary Actualities
916 calories
Fixings
We have recorded underneath the fixings that would be required by you for cooking the sound and delicious feast:

- 8 garlic cloves, minced
- 8 huge rosemary sprigs, stems with takes off (doused in water at slightest 30 minutes)
- Rosemary sprig (for embellish)
- 2 teaspoons salt
- 1 teaspoon pepper
- 2 teaspoons olive oil (or more on the off chance that required)
- 12 sheep loin chops, trimmed of overabundance fat (at slightest 1 1/2 inches/4 cm thick)
- 1/4 glass chopped new rosemary leaf (or 2 Tb dried)

Enlightening

1. Given underneath are the nitty gritty informational for cooking this

delicious feast. You wish to take after these enlightening within the given arrange.

2. Plan the flame broil for high-heat coordinate cooking. Put the rosemary stems straightforwardly on the charcoal or gas burners. When the rosemary starts to smoke, put the chops over coordinate warm and cook, secured, for 3-6 minutes on each side, until done to your enjoying.
3. Embed a moment thermometer absent from the bone or cut into the chops close the bone to check for doneness. For medium-rare, take out the chops from the flame broil when the thermometer peruses 130 degrees Fahrenheit (54 degrees Celsius), and the meat is still pink close the bone.
4. Move the chops to a platter and set aside for 5 minutes, secured freely with aluminum thwart.

6. Make-Ahead Moment Pot Barbecued Ribs

Planning and cooking time
2 hours
Servings
4 people
Dietary Truths
761 calories
Fixings

We have recorded underneath the fixings that would be required by you for cooking the solid and top notch feast:

- 2 Tbsp. brown sugar
- 2 Tbsp. ruddy or white wine vinegar
- 2 garlic cloves, pulverized
- 1/2 container coarsely chopped parsley, dill, and mint takes off
- 1 Tbsp. legitimate salt
- 1/2 tsp. ground cinnamon

RECIPES FOR GRILLED LAMB

- 4 lb. St. Louis–style pork spareribs, cut into 3- or 4-rib segments
- 1/4 container dry white wine
- 1 Tbsp. dark peppercorns
- 4 tsp. cumin seeds
- 1 1/2 tsp. pulverized ruddy pepper pieces
- Vegetable oil (for the flame broil)

Enlightening

1. Given underneath are the point by point enlightening for cooking this delicious dinner. You would like to take after these informational within the given arrange.
2. Preheat the flame broil to medium-high. Clean and grease up the grind. Solidified fat ought to be spooned out of the cooking fluid, and the remaining fluid ought to be exchanged to a little pot. Bring the blend to a bubble with vinegar and garlic.
3. Cook is every so often whirling the skillet until the fluid has been decreased by half, almost 3 minutes. Strain into a glass measuring container through a fine-mesh strainer.
4. Rub a little sum of oil onto the ribs to delicately coat them. Flame broil the ribs for approximately 2 minutes or until they are gently browned. Turn the ribs over, brush the sauce on the uncovered side, and flame broil for another 2 minutes, or until the underside is softly browned.
5. Put the ribs on a cutting board and set them aside. Permit 5–10 minutes to cool some time recently cutting into person ribs. Within the conclusion, sprinkle the remaining sauce on best, at that point beat with herbs.

7. 3-Ingredient Barbecued Pineapple, Steak and Avocado Serving of mixed greens

Arrangement and cooking time

50 minutes

Servings

4-6 people

Wholesome Truths

626 calories

Fixings

We have recorded underneath the fixings that would be required by you for cooking the solid and delicious feast:

- One teaspoon crisply ground dark pepper, furthermore more
- 1 pineapple, peeled, cut into 1/2" rounds, center evacuated, isolated
- 2 pounds of Unused York strip steak
- One and a half tsp of legitimate salt, isolated, furthermore more
- 3 tablespoons olive oil, additionally more for the flame broil
- 2 avocados

Instructions

1. Given underneath are the detailed instructions for cooking this delicious dinner. You wish to take after these enlightening within the given arrange.
2. Begin by flavoring the steak with one tsp salt and one tsp pepper. Permit it to sit for at slightest 1 hour at room temperature.
3. In a blender, puree one pineapple circular, a half teaspoon salt, and 2 tablespoons water until smooth. Mix in 3 tbsp. Oil till smooth; set aside.
4. Warm a barbecue to medium-high or a flame broil container to medium-high; oil the barbecue grind or dish. 8–10 minutes for

medium-rare, flame broil steaks as well as remaining pineapple rounds, every so often turning, till the pineapple is softly charred as well as an instant-read thermometer embedded in the center of the steak registers 120°F.
5. Put the steak on a cutting board and set it aside. Permit sitting for at slightest fifteen minutes some time recently cutting meagerly. To keep the pineapple warm, put it on a platter and cover it with thwart.
6. Cut avocados in half crosswise around the pit, at that point utilize your hands to carefully peel off the skin. Cut each half into 1/2" rings crosswise.
7. Organize cut steak, avocado, and pineapple on a platter. Season with salt and pepper and sprinkle with pineapple dressing.

8. Flame broiled Herb Crusted Rack of Lamb

Planning and cooking time
30 minutes
Servings
3 people
Dietary Realities
386 calories
Fixings

We have recorded underneath the fixings that would be required by you for cooking the sound and delicious feast:

- One and a half-pound to two pounds' rack of sheep trimmed of abundance fat
- 2 teaspoons mint chopped
- A half teaspoon lemon pizzazz
- 1/2 teaspoon legitimate salt
- 1/4 teaspoon naturally ground dark pepper
- 3 huge cloves garlic minced
- 2 teaspoons rosemary chopped

- Two teaspoons oregano chopped
- 2 tablespoons olive oil

Enlightening

1. Given underneath are the point by point informational for cooking this top notch supper. You wish to take after these instructions within the given arrange.
2. To create the marinade, combine all fixings in a little bowl to form thick glue. Cover the sheep rack with the marinade. Refrigerate for eight hours or overnight, secured in plastic wrap.
3. Preheat the flame broil to 500°-525° F. At that point put the rack of sheep on the barbecue for 5 minutes to burn the meat.
4. Decrease the temperature to 425°F. Turn the sheep over and broil for another 13-15 minutes, or until the lamb's inner temperature registers 120° F for medium-rare. Exchange the sheep to a chopping board and cover with aluminum thwart to keep it warm. Permit the sheep to rest for another 5-10 minutes.
5. Make double-cut chops out of the sheep. Put the sheep on a dish as well as pour any meat juices over it. Serve with a sprinkling of new herbs on top.

9. Tandoori Sheep Ribs

Planning and cooking time
45 minutes
Servings
4-6 people
Dietary Truths
595 calories
Fixings
We have recorded underneath the fixings that would be required by you for cooking the sound and top notch dinner:

RECIPES FOR GRILLED LAMB

- 8 cloves garlic, peeled
- Legitimate salt and crisply ground dark pepper, to taste
- Juice of 1 lemon, additionally wedges for serving
- Liquefied unsalted butter for serving
- One (4"-piece) ginger, peeled and daintily cut
- A half-cup whole-milk Greek yogurt
- 1/4 glass malt vinegar
- 3 tsp. cayenne pepper
- 2 racks (2 lb.) sheep spareribs (frequently called Denver's ribs)
- One tbsp. cumin seeds
- 1 tbsp. garam masala
- 2 tsp. ground cardamom
- One and a half tsp. ruddy nourishment coloring
- One tsp. naturally ground nutmeg

Informational

1. Given underneath are the point by point enlightening for cooking this top notch feast. You wish to take after these enlightening within the given arrange.
2. In a broiling dish, put the ribs. In an 8-inch skillet, toast cumin seeds and garam masala till fragrant, around 30 seconds; set aside to cool. To create a fine powder, move to a flavor processor.
3. Set a charcoal barbecue to tall warm or a wood pellet barbecue to tall warm; bank coals or switch off one burner. Flame broil ribs for 45 minutes to 1 hour, flipping once, till somewhat charred and delicate.
4. In case the ribs start to burn on the exterior some time recently they are completely cooked, consider moving them to a cooler portion of the flame broil as well as a cook until delicate. Rest the ribs for 20 minutes some time recently cutting them into person ribs. Serve with liquefied butter and lemon wedges.

10. Barbecued Leg of Sheep (Boneless or Bone-in)

Planning and cooking time
3 hours 20 minutes
Servings
6 people
Dietary Actualities
339 calories
Fixings

We have recorded underneath the fixings that would be required by you for cooking the solid and delicious feast:

- Two and a half to three pounds' boneless leg of sheep (almost 3/4 lb. more in case bone-in) coarse salt (ocean or legitimate), to taste your choice of smoking wood chunks or chips (apple, cherry, maple, hickory, and oak will work well)
- Dark pepper, ground, to taste
- Dried oregano, to taste

Informational

1. Given underneath are the point by point informational for cooking this top notch supper. You would like to take after these enlightening within the given arrange.
2. Preheat your flame broil to 225–250 degrees Fahrenheit.
3. Season the sheep on all sides with the flavoring mix.
4. Put the fat side of the sheep on the grill/smoker rack. There would be a part of smoke. To keep the temperature between 225 and 250 degrees Fahrenheit, recharge the charcoal as well as smoke wood as required.
5. Flame broil until the leg of sheep comes to an inside temperature of 140-150 degrees Fahrenheit.
6. Put the sheep on a cutting board as well as set it aside for 10 minutes

to rest. To keep it warm, cover it freely with aluminum thwart.
7. Carve and serve right absent.

11. Barbecued Sheep Chops American Fashion

Planning and cooking time
1 hour 10 minutes
Servings
4 people
Wholesome Truths
287 calories
Fixings
We have recorded underneath the fixings that would be required by you for cooking the sound and top notch feast:

- One rack of sheep
- Legitimate salt
- 4 garlic cloves minced
- Three tbsp. new rosemary finely chopped
- A half tsp ground dark pepper

Enlightening

1. Given below are the nitty gritty informational for cooking this tasty dinner. You wish to take after these informational within the given arrange.
2. Preheat the wood pellet barbecue to 225 degrees Fahrenheit (107 degrees Celsius).
3. Put the sheep rack on the circuitous side of the flame broil grates. At that point cook for forty-five minutes, or until the inner temperature of the meat comes to 115-120 degrees Fahrenheit (46-49 degrees Celsius).
4. Exchange the sheep to a coordinate warm source. Burn each side of

the rack for two minutes.
5. Cut the rack into four fats, double-wide chops by cutting in between each moment bone. Make beyond any doubt they're all the same thickness, so they cook at the same time. Then1, 2 hours some time recently cooking, season the meat with salt and dry brine it within the fridge.
6. Permit the rack to cool for 10 minutes after evacuating it from the warm. Mix the flavoring blend and set aside.
7. Per serving, cut into two chops. Serve with a flavoring blend on beat.

12. Sheep Leg Broiled

Planning and cooking time
50 minutes
Servings
4 people
Wholesome Realities
392 calories
Fixings
We have recorded underneath the fixings that would be required by you for cooking the solid and top notch supper:

- One leg of sheep (bone-in) almost 6 1/2 pounds
- 6 garlic cloves
- A quarter container hot brown mustard
- 1/3 glass extra-virgin olive oil
- 2 tablespoons stuffed brown sugar
- 1/8 teaspoon cayenne pepper
- One teaspoon legitimate salt
- One teaspoon coarse ground dark pepper

Informational

1. Given underneath are the point by point informational for cooking this delicious feast. You wish to take after these instructions within the given order.
2. Preheat your barbecue to 225 degrees Fahrenheit.
3. Put the sheep on a preparing sheet and set it aside.
4. Combine the olive oil, garlic, mustard, brown sugar, cayenne pepper, salt, and pepper in a nourishment processor. Mix everything completely.
5. Employing a spatula, equally disperse the mixture over the leg of sheep.
6. Cook the sheep on a rack within the wood pellet flame broil for almost 12 hours or until it comes to an inside temperature of 110 degrees F.
7. Put the sheep on a flame broil that has been preheated to medium-high warm. Burn the sheep equitably on all sides till it comes to an inside temperature of 140°F. Expel the sheep from the flame broil and set it aside to rest for 10 minutes some time recently cutting.

13. Rosemary and Garlic smoked grill sheep loin

Arrangement and cooking time
1 hour
Servings
4 people
Wholesome Realities
662 calories
Fixings
We have recorded underneath the fixings that would be required by you for cooking the sound and top notch supper:

- One kilogram of boned, rolled sheep loin
- 4 divided clove garlic
- 2 tablespoon of new rosemary sprigs
- One teaspoon of ocean salt chips

- One tablespoon of olive oil

Informational

1. Given underneath are the nitty gritty informational for cooking this top notch feast. You would like to take after these enlightening within the given arrange.
2. With a sharp cut, puncture the sheep in 8 places as well as thrust the garlic and half of the rosemary into the cuts. Salt the sheep and rub it with the oil.
3. Meanwhile , splash two modest bunches of smoking wood chips for 2 hours in a huge bowl of water.
4. Cook the sheep for 3 minutes on a hot, oiled flame broil, revealed until it is browned all over.
5. Put depleted smoking chips within the smoker box another to the sheep on the barbecue. Cook the sheep in a secured grill over backhanded warm for one and a quarter-hour for medium or till done to your enjoying. Rest the meat for ten minutes some time recently carving, sprinkling it with the remaining rosemary and covering it freely with thwart.

22

Vegetable Recipes for Grilling

Go for more advantageous eating by choosing from the different barbecued vegetables formulas which have been particularly collected to assist you appreciate your open air barbecuing.

1. Barbecued Eggplant Serving of mixed greens with Freekeh and Yogurt Dressing

Arrangement and cooking time

50 minutes

Servings

4 people

Wholesome Realities

336 calories

Fixings

We have recorded underneath the fixings that would be required by you for cooking the sound and top notch feast:

- A quarter glass Italian parsley, chopped
- 2 tablespoons new chopped dill (or mint, or parsley)
- 1–2 garlic cloves finely minced
- 1/4 teaspoon salt, or to taste
- 3 scallions, cut
- 1 tablespoon lemon get-up-and-go
- 4 tablespoons olive oil
- 3–4 tablespoons lemon juice
- 1/2 teaspoon salt, more to taste
- 1 glass dry Freekeh
- 2 1/2 mugs water
- 1 huge eggplant, cut into 1/4 inch cuts
- A quarter glass mint, chopped
- 1/4 container dill, chopped
- 1/2 teaspoon pepper
- A half teaspoon Aleppo chili chips
- 1 glass plain thick Greek yogurt
- 1 tablespoon lemon juice

Enlightening

1. Given underneath are the nitty gritty informational for cooking this top notch feast. You wish to take after these informational within the given arrange.
2. Preheat the flame broil to medium-high temperature.
3. In a medium pot, combine freekeh and water, bring to a bubble, cover, and cook for 15-20 minutes, or till water is retained as well as freekeh is delicate.
4. Brush or splash the eggplant cuts with olive oil. You ought to at that point season it with salt and pepper. Flame broil for 3-4 minutes on both sides or till flame broil marks show up. At that point wrap in thwart to steam and wrap up cooking. Hurl the eggplant with a fork and cut it into bite-size pieces.
5. Combine the cooked freekeh, eggplant, scallions, lemon juice, salt, olive oil, herbs, lemon pizzazz, pepper, and flavors in a blending bowl. Hurl everything together. Taste and adjust the salt and lemon as required. It ought to have a tart flavor. Because it sits, the smoky flavor will develop.
6. In a small bowl, whisk together the yogurt sauce fixings. (On the off chance that you're making a vegetarian adaptation, you might got to include a small more lemon)
7. To serve, spread the yogurt dressing on a platter and beat with the serving of mixed greens. Serve with torn mint leaves as a decorate.
8. Spread the yogurt sauce on the container's foot for lunch, at that point spoon serving of mixed greens on beat (or partitioned).
9. Serving of mixed greens will keep within the ice chest for 3-4 days with a yogurt dressing on the side.

2. Mexican-Style Corn on the Cob

Planning and cooking time
35 minutes
Servings
3 people
Wholesome Truths
305 calories
Fixings
We have recorded underneath the fixings that would be required by you for cooking the sound and delicious supper:

- 1 tablespoon new lime juice
- ¼ teaspoon chipotle chili powder
- 3 tablespoons ground cotija or Parmigiano-Reggiano® cheese
- 3 tablespoons mayonnaise
- 2 tablespoons acrid cream
- ¾ teaspoon arranged chili powder

Enlightening

1. Given underneath are the point by point informational for cooking this top notch feast. You would like to take after these enlightening within the given arrange.
2. Preheat the barbecue to medium heat-350° to 450°F- for coordinate cooking.
3. Blend the spread fixings in a little bowl and blend well. Blend the topping fixings in a moment little bowl and mix well.
4. Clean the cooking grates with a brush. Barbecue the corn for 10 to 15 minutes, every so often turning, over coordinate medium warm with the top closed, till the parts are browned in spots as well as delicate. Expel the steaks from the flame broil.
5. Spread the spread equally over the corn, at that point beat with the

topping. Serve promptly.

3. Simmered Root Vegetables with Garlic and Rosemary

Arrangement and cooking time

40 minutes

Servings

4 people

Wholesome Actualities

78 calories

Fixings

We have recorded underneath the fixings that would be required by you for cooking the sound and top notch dinner:

- 1 medium sweet potato, around 12 ounces, peeled
- 1½ teaspoon legitimate salt
- ½ teaspoon crisply ground dark pepper
- 3 tablespoons extra-virgin olive oil
- 2 tablespoons minced new rosemary clears out
- 1½ pound celery root (bulbs as it were), trimmed, peeled with a cut
- 8 ounces' medium carrots, peeled
- 8 ounces' medium parsnips, peeled
- 2 teaspoons minced garlic

Informational

1. Given below are the point by point informational for cooking this tasty meal. You would like to take after these informational within the given arrange.
2. A enormous pot of water ought to be brought to a bubble. Cut parsnips, celery root, carrots, and sweet potato. Cook for 2 minutes in bubbling

water with celery, carrots, and parsnips. Include the sweet potato and cook for another 6 to 8 minutes, or when the vegetables are mostly cooked.
3. Deplete well and set aside to cool totally.
4. Preheat a punctured barbecue dish for around 10 minutes and plan your flame broil for coordinate cooking at medium heat.
5. Whisk the pepper, salt, oil, rosemary, and garlic in a expansive blending bowl. Turn the vegetables within the bowl to coat them.
6. The vegetables are to be spread in a single layer on the barbecue skillet and cooked, every so often turning, till softly charred and very delicate, around 10 minutes over coordinate medium warm with the cover closed.
7. It ought to be served warm.

4. Zesty Barbecued Broccoli

Planning and cooking time
30 minutes
Servings
6 people
Dietary Actualities
122 calories
Fixings

We have recorded underneath the fixings that would be required by you for cooking the sound and top notch dinner:

- 1 tbsp. low-sodium soy sauce
- 1/4 tsp. pulverized ruddy pepper pieces, additionally more for serving
- 1/4 c. naturally ground Parmesan
- Lemon wedges, for serving
- 3 tbsp. ketchup
- 1 tbsp. nectar
- 3 cloves garlic, minced

- 2 lb. broccoli
- 1/4 c. extra-virgin olive oil
- 2 tbsp. Worcestershire sauce
- 1/2 tsp. legitimate salt, additionally more for sprinkling
- Crisply ground dark pepper

Enlightening

1. Given underneath are the nitty gritty informational for cooking this top notch supper. You would like to take after these enlightening within the given arrange.
2. Preheat the flame broil to medium. Trim the stringy foot half of the broccoli stem, at that point cut the broccoli head into quarters to form little trees.
3. Whisk together the oil, Worcestershire sauce, ketchup, soy sauce, nectar, and garlic in a large blending bowl. Utilize pepper, salt, and ruddy pepper drops to taste. Hurl within the broccoli as well as hurl to combine. Permit for a 10-minute rest period.
4. Put the broccoli on the barbecue and season softly with salt. 8 to 10 minutes on the barbecue, flipping each two minutes as well as treating with any remaining sauce until broccoli is knife-tender and somewhat charred.
5. Serve with lemon wedges and sprinkle more ruddy pepper chips on beat.

5. Flame broiled Carrots

Planning and cooking time
25 minutes
Servings
6 people
Dietary Actualities
106 calories

Fixings

We have recorded underneath the fixings that would be required by you for cooking the sound and top notch dinner:

- 2 tsp. nectar
- Legitimate salt and pepper
- 2 tbsp. pistachios, toasted and finely chopped
- 1 tsp. harissa glue
- 1/4 c. plain 2% Greek yogurt
- 2 bunches of lean carrots with tops, scoured and trimmed
- 1 tbsp. olive oil
- 2 tbsp. tahini
- 2 tbsp. new lemon juice

Enlightening

1. Given underneath are the point by point informational for cooking this top notch dinner. You wish to take after these informational within the given arrange.
2. Preheat the flame broil to moo. In the event that essential, cut any huge carrots in half longwise to guarantee that all carrots are the same width. Whisk the nectar, oil, and harissa in a huge blending bowl. Hurl in the carrots to coat.
3. Put carrots on flame broil and cook, secured, for 10 to 12 minutes, until charred and delicate, rolling or turning carrots midway through. Put on a serving platter.
4. In the mean time, combine lemon juice, yogurt, tahini, and 1/4 teaspoon salt and pepper in a blending bowl. Sprinkle in two tablespoons of warm water continuously, including more in the event that the blend gets to be as well thick. Sprinklethe dressing over the carrots and beat with pistachios.

6. Barbecued Pattypans

Arrangement and cooking time

15 minutes

Servings

2 people

Dietary Realities

54 calories

Fixings

We have recorded underneath the fixings that would be required by you for cooking the solid and top notch feast:

- 2 teaspoons hoisin sauce
- 1/4 teaspoon salt
- 1/8 teaspoon ground ginger
- 1 teaspoon rice vinegar
- 1/2 teaspoon sesame oil
- 6 glasses patty dish squash (almost 1-1/2 pounds)
- 1/4 glass apricot spreadable natural product

Informational

1. Given underneath are the nitty gritty informational for cooking this top notch supper. You would like to take after these informational within the given arrange.
2. Place the squash in a barbecue bushel that has been showered with cooking shower. Each side ought to be barbecued for four minutes, secured, over medium warm until delicate.
3. In the mean time, blend the remaining ingredients in a little bowl. Exchange the squash to a serving bowl and hurl tenderly with the sauce.

7. Barbecued Potato Serving of mixed greens with Chiles and Basil

Arrangement and cooking time

3 hours 30 minutes

Servings

4 people

Dietary Truths

279 calories

Fixings

We have recorded underneath the fixings that would be required by you for cooking the sound and delicious supper:

- 3 tbsp. angle sauce
- 3 garlic cloves
- 2 mugs basil takes off
- 2 tbsp. toasted sesame seeds
- 1 tbsp. nectar
- 1/4 glass furthermore 3 Tbsp. extra-virgin olive oil, also more for sprinkling
- 2 lb. child Yukon Gold potatoes
- 1/2 container legitimate salt, also more
- 2/3 glass unseasoned rice vinegar
- 2 ruddy Fresno chilies, daintily cut
- 1 huge ruddy onion

Enlightening

1. Given underneath are the nitty gritty enlightening for cooking this delicious feast. You wish to take after these informational within the given arrange.
2. In a huge pot, cover potatoes with three quarts of water. Embed half container salt. Over medium-high warm, bring to a stew.

3. Preheat the flame broil to medium-high warm. Combine the nectar, vinegar, angle sauce, and three tablespoons of oil in a little bowl. Include the chilies and blend well. Set aside the dressing after flavoring it with salt.
4. Cut the onion in half through the root. Another, cut each half into 5 wedges, keeping the root in put.
5. In a expansive blending bowl, finely grind the garlic. 14 container oil, whisked in. Hurl the onion wedges into the blending bowl. As you add the potatoes to the bowl, delicately crush them together with your hands and hurl delicately to coat them in garlic oil. Another season it is with salt and pepper.
6. Cook it for 12–15 minutes on the grill, occasionally turning, until potatoes and onion wedges are charred all over.
7. Hurl the potatoes within the dressing to coat them. Combine basil as well as sesame seeds in a bowl.
8. In a serving bowl, put the potato serving of mixed greens. Sprinkle a few oil on best.

8. Barbecued Artichokes

Planning and cooking time
43 minutes
Servings
8 people
Dietary Actualities
312 calories
Fixings
We have recorded underneath the fixings that would be required by you for cooking the solid and top notch dinner:

- 1 tablespoon Legitimate salt
- 2 cloves garlic, minced
- Salt & pepper, to taste

- 3 garlic cloves, crushed
- 2 lemon parts
- 3-4 artichokes
- 2-3 quarts of water
- 1/2 glass olive oil

Instructions

1. Given underneath are the point by point enlightening for cooking this delicious supper. You would like to take after these enlightening within the given arrange.
2. Trim the tops and stems off the artichokes some time recently cooking. Expel the fluffy choke from the center of each artichoke by cutting it in half and expelling it with a spoon. To dodge discoloration, rapidly rub with lemon wedges.
3. Fill a expansive pot mid way with water and set it over medium-high warm to bring to a bubble.
4. Crush the lemon parts to begin with, at that point include the garlic cloves, salt, and lemon parts to the water.
5. Bubble for 15-20 minutes, or until the artichokes are mellowed as well as reasonably delicate.
6. Take the artichoke parts out of the water and put them on a preparing sheet to dry.
7. In the interim, in a blending bowl, blend olive oil as well as minced garlic. Season each artichoke with salt and pepper after brushing it with garlic as well as olive oil on all sides.
8. Warm the flame broil to medium-high. Put the artichokes cut-side up on the flame broil. Barbecue it for three to four minutes, at that point turn and barbecue for another 3-4 minutes, cut-side down, until delicate and charred. Serve with a plunging sauce of your choice.

9. Flame broiled Veggie Pizza

Planning and cooking time

40 minutes

Servings

4 people

Wholesome Truths

274 calories

Fixings

We have recorded underneath the fixings that would be required by you for cooking the solid and delicious dinner:

- 1 little sweet ruddy pepper, cut
- 1 can (8 ounces) pizza sauce
- 2 little tomatoes, chopped
- 2 glasses destroyed part-skim mozzarella cheese
- 1 little onion, cut
- 1 tablespoon white wine vinegar
- 1 tablespoon water
- 4 teaspoons olive oil, separated
- 8 little new mushrooms, split
- 1 little zucchini, cut into 1/4-inch cuts
- 1 little sweet yellow pepper, cut
- 2 teaspoons minced new basil or 1/2 teaspoon dried basil
- 1/4 teaspoon salt
- A quarter teaspoon of pepper
- 1 prebaked 12-inch lean entirety wheat pizza outside

Enlightening

1. Given underneath are the nitty gritty enlightening for cooking this delicious feast. You wish to take after these informational within the given arrange.

2. Blend the onion, peppers, three tsp oil, mushrooms, zucchini, vinegar, water, and seasonings in a expansive blending bowl. Put in a barbecue wok or a barbecue wicker container. Cover and cook for 8-10 minutes, or until delicate, over medium warm, blending once.
3. Make beyond any doubt the flame broil is set to roundabout warm. Brush the remaining oil onto the outside and beat with pizza sauce. Flame broiled vegetables, tomatoes, and cheese go on beat. Cover and barbecue for 10-12 minutes over backhanded medium warm, or till edges are marginally browned as well as cheese is softened. To guarantee an equitably browned outside, pivot the pizza midway through cooking.

10. Portobello Burgers

Arrangement and cooking time
25 minutes
Servings
4 people
Dietary Realities
467 calories
Fixings
We have recorded underneath the fixings that would be required by you for cooking the solid and top notch feast:

- 2 Garlic Cloves minced
- Portobello mushroom
- 4 cheeseburger buns
- 1/4 container balsamic vinegar
- 1 Tablespoon soy sauce
- 1 Tablespoon Olive oil
- 1 Tablespoon Liquefied Butter
- One Tablespoon nectar
- Salt and pepper

Enlightening

1. Given below are the nitty gritty informational for cooking this tasty meal. You would like to take after these informational within the given arrange.
2. Whisk the soy sauce, garlic, olive oil, butter, nectar, salt, and pepper in a little bowl.
3. Expel the stems from the Portobello mushrooms delicately to get ready them. Rub the gills out with a spoon. In a nine-by thirteen-inch skillet, put the mushrooms. Douse for ten minutes within the marinade.
4. Warm the barbecue to a medium-high setting. Put the mushrooms on the flame broiled barbecue for 5 minutes on each side. Expel the burger from the flame broil and put it on a bun along with your favorite fixings.

11. Simple Barbecued Squash

Arrangement and cooking time
20 minutes
Servings
4 people
Dietary Actualities
178 calories
Fixings
We have recorded underneath the fixings that would be required by you for cooking the solid and top notch feast:

- Three tablespoons olive oil
- 2 garlic cloves, minced
- 1/4 teaspoon salt
- A quarter teaspoon of pepper
- 1 little butternut squash, peeled and cut longwise into 1/2-inch cuts

Informational

1. Given underneath are the nitty gritty enlightening for cooking this top notch feast. You wish to take after these informational within the given arrange.
2. Blend the oil, garlic, salt, and pepper in a little bowl. Brush the squash cuts with the oil.
3. Cover and flame broil squash for 4-5 minutes on each side over medium warm until delicate.

12. Brown Sugar Flame broiled Peaches

Planning and cooking time
16 minutes
Servings
8 people
Wholesome Truths
78 calories
Fixings

We have recorded underneath the fixings that would be required by you for cooking the sound and top notch supper:

- 2 tablespoons brown sugar
- ¼ teaspoon legitimate salt
- ⅛ teaspoon ground nutmeg
- ½ teaspoon cinnamon
- 2 huge peaches or 4 little
- 2 tablespoons unsalted butter liquefied
- ¼ teaspoon ground ginger

Informational

1. Given below are the nitty gritty enlightening for cooking this tasty

meal. You would like to take after these informational within the given arrange.
2. Blend ginger, brown sugar, cinnamon, and nutmeg in a little bowl. Then set it aside.
3. Expel the pit from the peaches and quarter them. Cut little peaches in half to create parts.
4. Brush the cut sides of the peaches with butter.
5. Preheat the flame broil (or barbecue container) to medium-high warm. Make beyond any doubt the flame broil grates are clean and oiled with vegetable oil.
6. Put the peaches cut side down on the hot flame broil and cook till the barbecue marks show up around 2 minutes. Barbecue for two minutes on the other cut side of the peach.
7. Turn the peaches over as well as sprinkle the brown sugar-spice blend on best. To assist dissolve the sugar, sprinkle the softened butter on best.
8. Cook for 2 minutes, or until the sugar has turned into a coat as well as the peaches are delicate.
9. More brown sugar topping can be included in case craved.
10. Exchange the peaches to a serving dish and serve with a scoop of ice cream or a serving of mixed greens.

13. Warm Artichoke Plunge

Planning and cooking time
29 minutes
Servings
6 people
Wholesome Realities
54.5 calories
Fixings
We have recorded underneath the fixings that would be required by you for cooking the sound and delicious feast:

- 1 glass destroyed mozzarella cheese
- Unsalted butter
- ⅓ container finely ground Parmigiano-Reggiano® cheese
- Flame broiled baguette cuts or fresh flatbread
- 1 can (4 ounces) chopped mellow green chili peppers, depleted
- ¼ glass acrid cream
- 2 teaspoons minced garlic
- 1 can (14 ounces) entire artichoke hearts pressed in water, depleted, and tapped dry
- ¾ container mayonnaise
- 6 ounces cream cheese, mollified
- 1 teaspoon mustard powder
- ¼ teaspoon hot pepper sauce
- A quarter teaspoon naturally ground dark pepper

Informational

1. Given underneath are the point by point enlightening for cooking this delicious supper. You would like to take after these informational within the given arrange.
2. Splash the wood chips for a least of thirty minutes in water.
3. Preheat the barbecue to medium-high heat-400° to 450°F- for roundabout cooking.
4. Deplete as well as include the wood chips to the gas grill's smoker box, as coordinated by the producer, and near the cover. When smoke begins to seem, flame broil the artichoke hearts at coordinate warm for 3 to 5 minutes, turning once until warmed through. Expel the steaks from the barbecue as well as chop coarsely.
5. Mayonnaise, mozzarella, chilies, hot sauce, cream cheese, mustard powder, acrid cream, garlic, and pepper ought to all be mixed. Smash the cream cheese against the bowl's interior with a wooden spoon to form a glue, at that point mix the blend until smooth. Include the artichoke hearts and mix well.

6. Utilizing butter, gently coat the interior of an eight-inch cast-iron skillet. Put the artichoke blend within the arranged skillet and sprinkle with Parmigiano-Reggiano® cheese equally. Cook for 20 to 25 minutes over backhanded medium-high warm with the top closed, till browned as well as bubbling on the surface. Serve with flame broiled baguette cuts as well as fresh flatbread after cooling for 10 minutes.

14. Flame broiled Vegetable Platter

Arrangement and cooking time
30 minutes
Servings
4 people
Wholesome Realities
144 calories
Fixings
We have recorded underneath the fixings that would be required by you for cooking the sound and delicious dinner:

- 1 teaspoon dried oregano
- 1 expansive sweet ruddy pepper, cut into 1-inch strips
- 1 medium yellow summer squash, cut into 1/2-inch cuts
- 1 medium ruddy onion, cut into wedges
- 1/2 teaspoon garlic powder
- 1/8 teaspoon pepper
- Sprint salt
- 1-pound new asparagus, trimmed
- 1/4 glass olive oil
- 2 tablespoons nectar
- 4 teaspoons balsamic vinegar
- 3 little carrots, cut in half the long way

Enlightening

1. Given underneath are the nitty gritty enlightening for cooking this delicious supper. You would like to take afterthese enlightening within the given arrange.
2. Whisk together the fixings in a little bowl. In a expansive blending bowl, combine 3 tablespoons marinade. Hurl within the vegetables and hurl to coat. Cover and take off to marinate at room temperature for 1 1/2 hours.
3. Put vegetables on a flame broiling framework and set them on the flame broil rack. Cover and flame broil vegetables over medium warm for 8-12 minutes, once in a while turning, until crisp-tender.
4. On a huge serving plate, orchestrate the vegetables. Sprinkle the remaining marinade over the beat.

15. Corn with Lemon-Pepper Butter

Planning and cooking time
35 minutes
Servings
3 people
Dietary Actualities
280 calories
Fixings
We have recorded underneath the fixings that would be required by you for cooking the sound and top notch dinner:

- Eight medium ears of sweet corn
- 1 glass butter, relaxed
- Two tablespoons lemon-pepper flavoring

Enlightening

1. Given underneath are the nitty gritty informational for cooking this top notch supper. You wish to take after these enlightening within

the given arrange.
2. Evacuate silk by carefully peeling back corn husks inside one inch of the bottoms. Supplant the husks on the corn and secure with kitchen string. Fill a stockpot halfway with cold water.
3. Splash for 20 minutes and after that deplete.
4. In the interim, combine butter as well as lemon pepper in a little bowl. Cover and barbecue corn for 20-25 minutes, or until delicate, over medium warm, turning as often as possible.
5. Evacuate the string as well as peel back the husks. Corn ought to be served with the butter blend.

16. Baba Ghanoush

Planning and cooking time
4 hours 5 minutes
Servings
6 people
Dietary Realities
248 calories
Fixings

We have recorded underneath the fixings that would be required by you for cooking the solid and top notch dinner:

- ½ lemon, juiced, or more to taste
- ½ squeeze cayenne pepper, or to taste
- ½ leaf new mint, minced
- 1 tablespoon chopped new Italian parsley
- 1 tablespoon and 1 teaspoon and ½ teaspoon tahini, or more to taste
- 1 tablespoon and 1 teaspoon and ½ teaspoon extra-virgin olive oil
- 2 huge Italian eggplants
- 1 clove smashed garlic
- 1 teaspoon legitimate salt, or to taste
- 1 tablespoon plain Greek yogurt

Instructions

1. Given underneath are the detailed instructions for cooking this top notch feast. You would like to take after these informational within the given arrange.
2. Warm an open air barbecue to medium-high warm and brush the grind gently with oil. The eggplant's skin is to be pricked with the tip of a cut a few times.
3. Put eggplants on the flame broil straightforwardly. Whereas the skin chars, turn it as often as possible with tongs. Cook for 25 to 30 minutes, or until the eggplants have collapsed and ended up exceptionally delicate. Permit cooling in a bowl, secured firmly with aluminum thwart, for around 15 minutes.
4. Part the eggplants in half and rub the substance into a colander set over a bowl once they've cooled sufficient to handle. Deplete for five to ten minutes.
5. Put the eggplant in a blending bowl. Squash within the smashed garlic as well as salt until the blend is rich but still has a few surface, roughly 5 minutes. Combine the olive oil, lemon juice, tahini, and cayenne pepper in a blending bowl. Include the yogurt and blend well.
6. Cover bowl with plastic wrap as well as chill for 3 to 4 hours, or until totally chilled.
7. At that point season with salt and pepper to taste. Include the mint and parsley and blend well.

23

Conclusion

Barbecuing has wellbeing benefits compared to dinners cooked within the broiler or on the stove. Nourishment that's barbecued does not incorporate any extra fat. When you're barbecuing, the fats trickle from the grates. Think of burgers that are cooked in a broiling skillet. Indeed once you exchange the meat to your dish, the fat amasses on the skillet. You'd be astounded to memorize that the minerals and vitamins are held when vegetables are flame broiled. This can be particularly genuine for veggies that have moo water substance. Flame broiled vegetables are moreover regularly hurled and prepared new. Cooking veggies in any barbecued way, whether wrapped in tin thwart or flame broiled uncovered, offers more wholesome benefits.

Moreover, barbecuing meat jam more supplements like thiamine and riboflavin. These supplements are fundamental for great wellbeing. Moreover, flame broiling does not require the utilize of butter. All of the fluids from the meats and vegetables stream out, making everything taste way better. This too involves expending less calories. Flame broiling takes you and your visitors outside. Whereas flame broiling, most families lock in other exercises. Barbecuing energizes everybody to spend more time outside. Open air physical activities, in expansion to your dinners, are a solid expansion to your way of life. In the event that you select lean meats for your flame broiling needs, you'll remain more advantageous.

Moreover, all of your barbecued nourishments must incorporate veggies. On your barbecue, you will cook onions, peppers, sweet corn, and zucchini. Vegetable kebabs can too be cooked utilizing the barbecue. To include more flavor and nourishment, embellish it with mellow vinaigrette. Begin cooking your more beneficial and more delicious nourishments outside.

www.ingramcontent.com/pod-product-compliance
Lightning Source LLC
LaVergne TN
LVHW011927070526
838202LV00054B/4517